Social Advantages in the Age of Globalization

Social Advantages in the Age of Globalization

Dr. Babita Agarwal

ABD PUBLISHERS
Jaipur ■ New Delhi

ABD PUBLISHERS

Regd. Off. "Bony Residency", Gate No. 2
Opp. Tilak Public School, Vishweswariya Nagar,
Gopalpura Road, Jaipur - 302018, India
Ph: 0141 - 2761280, Telefax: 2761381
Email: abdpublishersjpr@gmail.com

Delhi Office: 102, 1st Floor, Satyam House,
4327/3, Ansari Road, Darya Ganj,
New Delhi - 110002, India
Ph: 011-45652440

visit us: www.oxfordbookcompany.com

Published in India, 2024

ISBN : 9788183762229

Price : ₹ 1800/-

Typeset by Shivangi Computer, Jaipur

Printed and bound in India by Thomson Press Ltd.,
New Delhi

॥ श्री गणेशाय नमः ॥

वक्रतुण्ड महाकाव्य सूर्यकोटि समप्रभः।
निर्विघ्नं कुरुमे देव सर्वकार्येषु सर्वदा ॥

From the Desk of Editor . . .

Globalization is a great movement of people, goods, trade and investment. In turn it increases capital and ideas due to increased economic integration. It is like moving towards living in a world without border. There has always been a sharing of goods, services, knowledge and culture among the various countries, but in recent years due to reduction of barriers the speed of exchange is much faster. Globalization provides opportunities and challenges. Weak domestics policies, institutions and infrastructure and trade barriers restrict the ability of a country to take advantages of the changes in the advanced countries of the world. Each country makes decisions and policies to maximize the benefits presented by globalization.

The following description presents the advantages of globalisation:

1. The countries that have engaged well with the international economy have grown faster than those countries that have kept themselves with their own economies.
2. The countries which have registered faster economic growth due to globalization, living slandered have improved and poverty has reduced. More people can avail cheaper goods due to cheaper imports of goods.

3. The improved economic gains of globalization have increased the availability of clean water and health care devices, which in turn have increased the age of survival. We can now expect to live for at least sixty years.
4. The foreign direct investment has increased due to reduction in barriers, which has enhanced the growth in several countries.
5. Globalization has contributed in improving environment awareness. It has encouraged the use of more efficient technologies and imports of renewed sources of energy in place of domestic natural resources.
6. Due to globalization of economy World Trade Organisation (WTO) and World Bank manage the settlement of government-to-government disputes. This has helped in resolving international economic and political tensions and conflicts.
7. Globalization which has provided better technology has reduced the cost of production and prices.
8. Globalization has contributed to develop the liberal democracies in the world.
9. International migration that has been widely possible due to globalization has improved the democracy and cultural identities have safeguarded the human rights.
10. The global countries have voluntarily adopted their international production facilities in developing countries. It has made a significant contribution in respect of international labour standards in the developing countries.
11. Production of goods becomes cheaper because production takes places in other countries.
12. International travel and tourism increased because people around the world are more connected to each other.

In reference to these advantages we can say that globalization provides opportunities and challenges, great profit and great market for goods, which lead to greater wealth for investing in development and reducing poverty. In age of globalization country makes decisions and policies to maximize the benefits and minimize the problems.

This book is a collection of various papers on social advantages in Indian context and underlines various related core issues. We are sure that this book shall help those who have interest in this subject.

We are thankful to various learned writers/paper contributors who made possible to publish this book. We are also thankful to the ABD publisher, Jaipur for publishing this book.

2009 **Dr. Babita Agarwal**

List of Contributors

Dr. Anoop Pant
Prof. APEEJE Institute of Management, Noida.

Dr. Anurob Roy
Sr. Faculty Member, Amity Business School, Amity University, Lucknow.

Dr. Anita Gupta
Reader in English Deptt., VMLGPG College, Ghaziabad.

Dr. Arun Bhadoria
Programme Coordinator, Amity School of Rural Culture Management (ASRAM), Amity University, Lucknow.

Dr. Babita Agrawal
HOD and Reader in Economics, AKPG College, Hapur and Additional Editor in UPUEA Economic Journal, Varanasi.

Dr. Jyotsana Shukla
Faculty Amity Institute of Behavioural and Allied Sciences, Amity University, Lucknow.

Manoj Sharma
Lecturer in Economics, Deptt. of Humanities, National Institute of Technology (NIT), Hamirpur, Himachal Pradesh.

Mamta Singh
Lecturer in Economics, IIC Management College, Noida.

Pooja Singh
Research Scholar in Economics, University of Allahabad.

Preetee Arpita
Christ College, Bangalore, Karnataka.

Dr. R.K. Kaundal
Sr. Lecturer in Economics,
Govt. PG College,
Dharamshala.

Mohd. Rais Khan
Research Scholar, NET-JRF
Med / Mod. History Deptt.,
University of Allahabad.

Shalini Singh
Lecturer, SS Khanna Girls
Degree College, Allahabad.

Shilpi Tiwari
Research Scholar in
Economics, University of
Allahabad.

Shaily Tiwari
Research Scholar in Zoology,
University of Allahabad.

Shalini Tiwari
Research Scholar in Economics,
University of Allahabad.

Sonika Singh
Lecturer in Economics
Lord Krishna College of
Engineering, Ghaziabad.

Tushar Singh
Lecturer in Economics, Amity
Institute of Behavioural and
Allied Sciences,
Amity University, Lucknow.

Contents

Chapter 1

Impact of Globalization in India

— Anoop Pant

Globalization has become an expression of common usage. Whiie to some, it represents a brave new world with no barriers, for some others, it spells doom and destruction. It is, therefore, necessary to have a clear understanding of what globalization means and what it stands for, if we have to deal with a phenomenon that is willy-nilly gathering momentum.

"The Era of Globalization" is fast becoming the preferred term for describing the current times. Just as the Depression, the Cold War Era, the Space Age, and the Roaring 20s are used to describe particular periods of history; Globalization describes the political, economic, and cultural atmosphere of today.

While some people think of globalization as primarily a synonym for global business, it is much more than that. The same forces that allow businesses to operate as if national borders did not exist also allow social activists, labour organizers, journalists, academics, international terrorists and many others to work on a global stage.

Gains from Globalization

The gains from globalization can be analyzed in the context of the three types of channels of economic globalization.

Trade in Goods and Services

According to the standard theory, international trade leads to allocation of resources that is consistent with comparative advantage. This results in specialization, which enhances productivity. It is accepted that international trade, in general, is beneficial and that restrictive trade practices impede growth. That is the reason why many of the emerging economies, which originally depended on a growth model of import substitution, have moved over to a policy of outward orientation. However, in relation to trade in goods and services, there is one major concern. Emerging economies will reap the benefits of international trade only if they reach the full potential of their resource availability. This will probably require time. That is why international trade agreements make exceptions by allowing longer time to developing economies in terms of reduction in tariff and non-tariff barriers. "Special and differentiated treatment", as it is very often called, has become an accepted principle.

Movement of Capital

Capital flows across countries have played an important role in enhancing the production base. This was very much true in 19th and 20th centuries. Capital mobility enables the total savings of the world to be distributed among countries which have the highest investment potential. Under these circumstances, one country's growth is not constrained by its own domestic savings. The inflow of foreign capital has played a significant role in the development in the recent period of the East Asian countries. The current account deficit of some of these countries had exceeded 5 per cent of the GDP in most of the period when growth was rapid. Capital flows can take either the form of foreign direct investment or portfolio investment. For developing countries the preferred alternative is foreign direct investment. Portfolio investment does not directly lead to expansion of productive capacity. It may do so, however, at one step removed. Portfolio investment can be volatile particularly in times of loss of confidence. That is why countries want to put restrictions on portfolio investment. However, in an open system such restrictions cannot work easily.

Financial Flows

The rapid development of the capital market has been one of the important features of the current process of globalization. While the growth in capital and foreign exchange markets have facilitated the transfer of resources across borders, the gross turnover in foreign exchange markets has been extremely large. It is estimated that the gross turnover is around $ 1.5 trillion per day worldwide (Frankel, 2000). This is of the order of hundred times greater than the volume of trade in goods and services. Currency trade has become an end in itself. The expansion in foreign exchange markets and capital markets is a necessary pre-requisite for international transfer of capital. However, the volatility in the foreign exchange market and the ease with which funds can be withdrawn from countries have created often times panic situations. The most recent example of this was the East Asian crisis. Contagion of financial crises is a worrying phenomenon. When one country faces a crisis, it affects others. It is not as if financial crises are solely caused by foreign exchange traders. What the financial markets tend to do is to exaggerate weaknesses. Herd instinct is not uncommon in financial markets. When an economy becomes more open to capital and financial flows, there is even greater compulsion to ensure that factors relating to macroeconomic stability are not ignored. This is a lesson all developing countries have to learn from East Asian crisis. As one commentator aptly said "The trigger was sentiment, but vulnerability was due to fundamentals".

Concerns and Fears

On the impact of globalization, there are two major concerns. These may be described as even fears. Under each major concern there are many related anxieties. The first major concern is that globalization leads to a more iniquitous distribution of income among countries and within countries. The second fear is that globalization leads to loss of national sovereignty and those countries are finding it increasingly difficult to follow independent domestic policies. These two issues have to be addressed both theoretically and empirically.

The argument that globalization leads to inequality is based on the premise that since globalization emphasizes efficiency, gains will accrue to countries which are favourably endowed with natural and human resources. Advanced countries have had a head start over the other countries by at least three centuries. The technological base of these countries is not only wide but highly sophisticated. While trade benefits all countries, greater gains accrue to the industrially advanced countries. This is the reason why even in the present trade agreements, a case has been built up for special and differential treatment in relation to developing countries. By and large, this treatment provides for longer transition periods in relation to adjustment. However, there are two changes with respect to international trade which may work to the advantage of the developing countries. First, for a variety of reasons, the industrially advanced countries are vacating certain areas of production. These can be filled in by developing countries. A good example of this is what the East Asian countries did in the 1970s and 1980s. Second, international trade is no longer determined by the distribution of natural resources. With the advent of information technology, the role of human resources has emerged as more important. Specialized human skills will become the determining factor in the coming decades. Productive activities are becoming "knowledge intensive" rather than "resource intensive". While there is a divide between developing and the advanced countries even in this area—some people call it the digital divide—it is a gap, which can be bridged. A globalized economy with increased specialization can lead to improved productivity and faster growth. What will be required is a balancing mechanism to ensure that the handicaps of the developing countries are overcome.

Apart from the possible iniquitous distribution of income among countries, it has also been argued that globalization leads to widening income gaps within the countries as well. This can happen both in the developed and developing economies. The argument is the same as was advanced in relation to iniquitous distribution among countries. Globalization may benefit even within a country those who have the skills and the technology. The higher growth rate achieved by an economy can be at the expense of declining incomes of people who may be rendered redundant. In this context, it has to be noted that while globalization may accelerate the process of technology substitution in developing economies, these countries even without globalization will face the problem associated with moving from lower to higher technology. If the growth rate of the economy accelerates sufficiently, then part of the resources can be diverted by the state to modernize and re-equip people who may be affected by the process of technology upgradation.

The second concern relates to the loss of autonomy in the pursuit of economic policies. In a highly integrated world economy, it is true that one country cannot pursue policies, which are not in consonance with the worldwide trends. Capital and technology are fluid and they will move where the benefits are greater. As the nations come together whether it be in the political, social or economic arena, some sacrifice of sovereignty is inevitable. The constraints of a globalized economic system on the pursuit of domestic policies have to be recognized. However, it need not result in the abdication of domestic objectives.

Another fear associated with globalization is insecurity and volatility. When countries are inter-related strongly, a small spark can start a large conflagration. Panic and fear spread fast. The downside to globalization essentially emphasizes the need to create countervailing forces in the form of institutions and policies at the international level. Global governance cannot be pushed to the periphery, as integration gathers speed.

Empirical evidence on the impact of globalization on inequality is not very clear. The share in aggregate world exports and in world output of the developing countries has been increasing. In aggregate world exports, the share of developing countries increased from 20.6 per cent in 1988-90 to 29.9 per cent in 2000. Similarly the share in aggregate world output of developing countries has increased from 17.9 per cent in 1988-90 to 40.4 per cent in 2000. The growth rate of the developing countries both in terms of GDP and per capita GDP has been higher than those of the industrial countries. These growth rates have been in fact higher in the 1990s than in the 1980s. All these data do not indicate that the developing countries as a group have suffered in the process of globalization. In fact, there have been substantial gains. But within developing countries, Africa has not done well and some of the South Asian countries have done better only in the 1990s. While the growth rate in per capita income of the developing countries in the 1990s is nearly two times higher than that of industrialized countries, in absolute terms the gap in per capita income has widened. As for income distribution within the countries, it is difficult to judge whether globalization is the primary factor responsible for any deterioration in the distribution of income. We have had considerable controversies in our country on what happened to the poverty ratio in the second half of 1990s. Most analysts even for India would agree that the poverty ratio has declined in the 1990s. Differences may exist as to what rate at which this has fallen. Nevertheless, whether it is in India or any other country, it is very difficult to trace the changes in the distribution of income within the countries directly to globalization.

India's Stance

What should be India's attitude in this environment of growing globalization? At the outset it must be mentioned that opting out of globalization is not a viable choice. There are at present 149 members in the World Trade Organization (WTO). Some 25 countries are waiting to join the WTO. China has recently been admitted as a member. What is needed is to evolve an appropriate framework to wrest maximum benefits out of international trade and investment.

This framework should include (1) making explicit the list of demands that India would like to make on the multilateral trade system, and (2) steps that India should take to realize the full potential from globalization.

Demands on the Trading System

Without being exhaustive, the demands of the developing countries on the multilateral trading system should include: (1) establishing symmetry as between the movement of capital and natural persons, (2) declining environmental standards and labour related considerations from trade negotiations, (3) zero tariffs in industrialized countries on labour intensive exports of developing countries, (4) adequate protection to genetic or biological material and traditional knowledge of developing countries, (5) prohibition of unilateral trade action and extra territorial application of national laws and regulations, and (6) effective restraint on industrialized countries in initiating anti-dumping and countervailing action against exports from developing countries.

The purpose of the new trading system must be to ensure "free and fair" trade among countries. The emphasis so far has been on "free" rather than "fair" trade. It is in this context that the rich industrially advanced countries have an obligation. They have often indulged in "double speak". While requiring developing countries to dismantle barriers and join the mainstream of international trade, they have been raising significant tariff and non-tariff barriers on trade from developing countries. Very often, this has been the consequence of heavy lobbying in the advanced countries to protect "labour". Although average tariffs in the United States, Canada, European Union and Japan—the so called Quad countries—range from only 4.3 per cent in Japan to 8.3 per cent in Canada, their tariff and trade barriers remain much higher on many products exported by developing countries. Major agricultural food products such as meat, sugar and dairy products attract tariff rates exceeding 100 per cent. Fruits and vegetables such as bananas are hit with a 180 per cent tariff by the European Union, once they exceed quotas. The tariffs collected by the US on $2 billion worth of imports from Bangladesh are higher than those imposed on imports worth $30 billion from France. In fact, these trade barriers impose a serious burden on the developing countries. It is important that if the rich countries want a trading system that is truly fair, they should come forward to reduce the trade barriers and subsidies that prevent the products of developing countries from reaching their markets. Otherwise the pleas of these countries for a competitive system will sound hollow.

To some extent, conflicts among countries on trade matters are endemic. Until recently, agriculture was a major bone of contention between US and EU countries. Frictions are also bound to arise among developing countries as well. When import tariffs on edible oil were increased in India, the most severe protest came from Malaysia, which was a major exporter of palm oil. Entrepreneurs in India complain of cheaper imports from China. In the export of rice, a major competitor of India is Thailand. If development is accepted as the major objective of trade as the Doha declaration proclaimed, it should be possible to work out a trading arrangement that is beneficial to all countries.

There have been protracted negotiations at WTO in reforming the trade system. Admittedly, the tariff and non-tariff barriers are coming down. However, there are apprehensions that the concerns of developing countries are not being addressed adequately. Looked at from this angle, the recent Hong Kong Ministerial is a modest success. Despite reservations, we must acknowledge that it is a step forward. Domestic support to agriculture by developed countries constitutes a major stumbling block to third world trade expansion. However, India's stand in relation to agriculture has been "defensive". We are not a major player in the world agricultural market. The impact of what has been accepted in relation to Non-Agricultural Market Access and services will vary from country to country. Despite some contrary opinion, the gain to India from services can be significant. However, the Hong Kong Ministerial is only a broad statement of intentions. Much will depend upon how these ideas are translated into concrete actions.

Actions by India

The second set of measures that should form part of the action plan must relate to strengthening India's position in international trade. India has much strength, which several developing countries lack. In that sense, India is different and is in a stronger position to gain from international trade and investment. India's rise to the top of the IT industry in the world is a reflection of the abundance of skilled manpower in our country. It is, therefore, in India's interest to ensure that there is a greater freedom of movement of skilled manpower. At the same time, we should attempt to take all efforts to ensure that we continue to remain a frontline country in the area of skilled manpower. India can attract greater foreign investment, if we can accelerate our growth with stability. Stability, in this context, means reasonable balance on the fiscal and external accounts. We must maintain a competitive environment domestically so that we can take full advantage of wider market access. We must make good use of the extended time given to developing countries to dismantle trade barriers. Wherever legislations are required to protect sectors like agriculture, they need to be enacted quickly. In fact, we had taken a long time to pass the Protection of Plant Varieties and Farmers' Rights Act. We must also be active in ensuring that our firms make effective use of the new patent rights. South Korea has been able to file in recent years as many as 5,000 patent applications in the United States whereas in 1986, the country filed only 162. China has also been very active in this area. We need a truly active agency in India to encourage Indian firms to file patent applications. In effect, we must build the complementary institutions necessary for maximizing the benefits from international trade and investment.

Changes in the foreign trade and foreign investment policies have altered the environment in which Indian industries have to operate. The path of transition is, no doubt, difficult. A greater integration of the Indian economy with the rest of the world is unavoidable. It is important that Indian industry be forward looking and get organized to compete with the rest of the world at levels of tariff comparable to those of other developing countries. Obviously, the Indian Government should be alert to ensure that Indian industries are not the victims of unfair trade practices. The safeguards available in the WTO agreement must be fully utilized to protect the interests of Indian industries.

Indian industry has a right to demand that the macro-economic policy environment should be conducive to rapid economic growth. The configuration of policy decisions in the recent period has been attempting to do that. It is, however, time for Indian industrial units to recognize that the challenges of the new century demand greater action at the enterprise level. They have to learn to swim in the tempestuous waters of competition and away from the protected waters of the swimming pools. India is no longer a country producing goods and services for the domestic market alone. Indian firms are becoming and have to become global players. At the minimum, they must be able to meet global competition. The search for identifying new competitive advantages must begin earnestly. India's ascendancy in Information Technology (IT) is only partly by design. However, it must be said to the credit of policy makers that once the potential in this area was discovered, the policy environment became strongly industry friendly.

Over a wide spectrum of activities, India's advantage, actual and that which can be realized in a short span of time must be drawn up of course, in a number of cases, it will require building plants on a global scale. But, this need not necessarily be so in all cases. In fact the advent of IT Is modifying the industrial structure. The revolution in telecommunications and IT is simultaneously creating a huge single market economy, while making the parts smaller and more powerful. What we need today is a road map for the Indian industry. It must delineate the path different industries must take to achieve productivity and efficiency levels comparable to the best in the world.

Globalization, in a fundamental sense, is not a new phenomenon. Its roots extend farther and deeper than the visible part of the plant. It is as old as history, starting with the great migrations of people across the great landmasses. Only recent developments in computer and communication technologies have accelerated the process of integration, with geographic distances becoming less of a factor. Is this "end of geography" a boon or a bane? Borders have become porous and the sky is open. With modern technologies, which do not recognize geography, it is not possible to hold back ideas either in the political, economic or cultural spheres. Each country must prepare itself to meet the new challenges so that it is not being bypassed by this huge wave of technological and institutional changes.

Nothing is an unmixed blessing. Globalization in its present form though spurred by far reaching technological changes is not a pure technological phenomenon. It has many dimensions including ideological. To deal with this phenomenon, we must understand the gains and losses, the benefits as well as dangers. To be forewarned, as the saying goes, is to be forearmed. But we should not throw the baby with bath water. We should also resist the temptation to blame globalization for all our failures. Most often, as the poet said, the fault is in us.

Risks of an open economy are well known. We must not, nevertheless, miss the opportunities that the global system can offer. As an eminent critic put it, the world cannot marginalize India. But India, if it chooses, can marginalize itself. We must guard ourselves against this danger. More than many other developing countries, India is in a position to wrest significant gains from globalization. However, we must voice our concerns and in cooperation with other developing countries modify the international trading arrangements to take care of the special needs of such countries. At the same time, we must identify and strengthen our comparative advantages. It is this two-fold approach, which will enable us to meet the challenges of globalization, which may be the defining characteristic of the new millennium.

The key to India's growth lies in improving productivity and efficiency. This has to permeate all walks of our life. Contrary to the general impression, the natural resources of our country are not large. India accounts for 16.7 per cent of world's population whereas it has only 2.0 per cent of world's land area. While China's population is 30 per cent higher than that of India's, it has a land area, which is three times that of India. In fact, from the point of view of long-range sustainability, the need for greater efficiency in the management of natural resources like land, water and minerals has become urgent. In a capital-scarce economy like ours, efficient utilization of our capacity becomes even more critical. For all of these things to happen, we need well-trained and highly skilled people. In the world of today, competition in any field is competition in knowledge. That is why we need to build institutions of excellence. I am, therefore, happy that the Ahmedabad Management Association, besides other functions, is also focusing on excellence in education. Increased productivity flowing from improved skills is the real answer to globalization.

So we need to work towards our own, alternative definition of globalization in opposition to the definition, which is being forced upon us by international capitalist institutions, and to work out strategies for reaching our goal. This can only be done through discussion and debate among those who share this vision throughout the world. The sooner this process begins, the sooner we will be able to find a third alternative to the domination of global capitalism on one side, and reactionary fascistic national capitals on the other.

References

Globalization and Poverty: Centre for International Economics, Australia.

Globalization Trend and Issues: T.K. Velayudham,

Globalisation and India Lecture: Prof. Sagar Jain, University of N. Carolina.

Repositioning India in the Globalized World Lecture: V.N. Rai.

Globalization of Indian Economy: Era Sezhiyan.

Globalization and India's Business Prospectives Lecture: Ravi Kastia.

Globalization and Liberalization Prospects of New World Order: Dr.A.K. Ojha.

Third Concept: *An International Journal of Ideas*, Aug. 2002, Anoop Pant.

Globalization and India: John Wojcik, *People's Weekly World Newspaper*.

Impact of Globalization on Development (ed.) Meenu Agrawal. New Delhi, Deep and Deep, 2008.

Impact of Globalization on Indian Culture: V Sundaram, IAS, Retd.

2 Chapter

Ecotourism as a Tool for Social Development in the Era of Globalization

— Shalini Singh

Travel and tourism has emerged as one of the worlds most centralized and competitive industries, and hardly any other economic sector illustrates so clearly the global reach of transnational corporation and in this era of globalization and liberalization of tourism will bring wealth, progress, social, achievements and improved environmental standards to developing countries need to be seriously questioned. Recently ecotourism has emerged as development tool, which aims to protect the natural environment and cultural diversity and it offers various advantage in this globalized world.

Ecotourism is entirely a new approach in tourism. It essentially means ecological tourism; where ecological has both environmental and social connotations. Born in its current form in late 1980s, ecotourism came of in age in 2002, where the United Nations celebrated the "International Year of Ecotourism". The term *ecotourism* was coined by Hector Ceballos-Lascuràin in 1983, and was initially used to describe nature-based travel to relatively undisturbed areas with an emphasis on education. The concept has, however, developed to a scientifically based approach to the planning, management and development of sustainable tourism products and activities. Ecotourism is currently the fastest growing sector of global tourism industry. Most estimates indicate that the demand for ecotourism is growing at an annual rate of 10 to 30 per cent.

The Concept of Ecotourism

Ecotourism in simple words means management of tourism and conservation of nature in a way as to maintain a fine balance between the requirement of tourism and ecology on one hand and the need of local communities for job, on the other. Ecotourism is a sub-component of the field of sustainable tourism (UNEP, 2002). It is purpose travel to natural areas for understanding the cultural and natural history of environment, while producing and providing economic opportunities to local inhabitants. To make ecotourism clear some definitions are given below.

One of the most widely embraced definitions of Ecotourism is one developed by Ceballos-Lascurain in 1983, which focuses on the importance of natural areas, cognitve and affective, and behaviour:

> "Travelling to relatively undisturbed or uncontaminated natural areas with the specific objective of studying, admiring, and enjoying the scenery and its wild plants and animals, as well as any existing cultural manifestations (both past and present) found in these areas."

> According to World Conservation Union,

> "Environmentally responsible travel and visitation to relatively undisturbed natural areas, in order to enjoy and appreciate nature that promotes conservation, has low negative visitor impact, and provides for beneficially active socio-economic involvement of local population" (Bernardo Duha Buchsbaum, 2004).

The International Ecotourism Society (2004) defines ecotourism as "Responsible travel to natural areas that conserves the environment and sustains the well-being of local people."

Features of Ecotourism

1. All nature based forms of tourism in which the main motivation of the tourist in which the main motivation of the tourist is the observation and preservation of nature as well as the traditional cultures prevailing in natural areas.
2. It contains educational and interpretation features.
3. It minimizes negative impacts upon the natural and socio-cultural environment.
4. It supports the protection of natural areas by
   (a) Generating economic benefits for host communities
   (b) Providing alternatives employment and income opportunities for local people
   (c) Increasing awareness towards the conservation of natural and cultural assets both among locals and tourists
   (d) Involves responsible action on the part of tourists and the tourism industry.

Ecotourism is often perceived as an excellent tool for promoting social development as its main aim is to benefit the local people.

Ecotourism and Social Development

Ecotourism promotes sustainable development by establishing a durable productive base that allows local inhabitants and ecotourism service providers to enjoy rising standards of living. An ecotourism incorporates the social dimensions of productive organization and environmental conservation.

Today's market place is becoming greener and more environmentally sensitive than ever, with 85 per cent of the industrialized world does citizen believe that the environment is the number one public issue. This attitude has evidently had an effect on the rise in popularity of ecotourism. Ecotourism has emerged as one of the most important sectors of the international tourism industry. It is a responsible travel to natural areas that safeguards the integrity of the ecosystem and produces economic benefit for local communities. The earnings from ecotourism industry results in socio-economic status of the host community. This earning is spent on the improvement of schools and other community facilities. With the socio-economic impact on the local people there is also an exposure to the popular media like, radio, television newspaper and magazines and hence the people become more enlightened. In addition to being a source of income and employment ecotourism is frequently a source of amenities for the resident population of the tourist destination. Because of visitor traffic residents, may enjoy a higher standard of public transport, shopping and entertainment facilities than they would be able to support otherwise. The following points discussed below shows the benefits of ecotourism.

1. Employment Opportunities for the People

Ecotourism industry is highly labour-intensive service industry and hence is a valuable source of employment. It employs a large number of people and provides a large range of jobs that starts with highly unskilled to highly specialized positions. According to one estimate an investment of one million rupees creates 89 jobs in the hotel and restaurant sector, a key component of tourism industry as against 44.7 jobs in agriculture and 12.6 in manufacturing industry.

2. Growth in GDP

GDP is considered to be the pulse of a nation. Tourism is now considered to be one of the major components of it. GDP of many countries have reached new heights with the opening of their doors to tourists on exploring new tourist destination. The GDP growth and the percentage increase is shown in the form of graph below.

3. Infrastructure and Rural Development

Ecotourism is one of the best courses to initiate and generate infrastructure development and improvement. This development is the primary component for the beginning of ecotourism in any region.

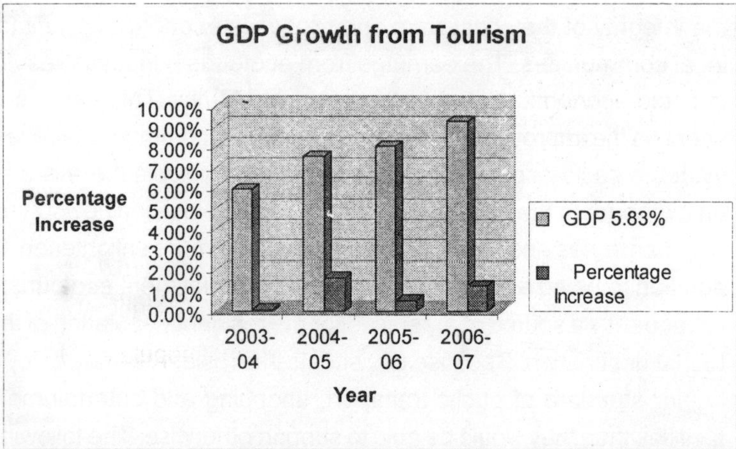

Source: (C.S.O).

The construction and provision of roads, railway lines, airport, electricity and gas supplies, sanitation, water supply and a number of other things are undertaken to attract and facilitate tourists from outside. Taking the help this external economy variety of industries may be established, which may not be directly linked with tourism. Thus, the expenditure by the tourists directly or indirectly is a stimulating force to give birth to a number of economic activities.

4. Increase in International Trade

Ecotourism is one of the most important trade items after oil. Unlike oil, it does not impose any burden on the country's economy. International trade in ecotourism has stimulated employment and investment. It has also made a positive contribution to balance of payment and national income of the country.

Besides economic gain tourism provides wide scope for promotion of human understanding. It helps in bringing about close understanding between the people of diverse nationalities, customs, religion and social background. Ecotourism has further acted as a vehicle for the realization of men's highest aspiration in the quest for knowledge, acceptance of the originality of culture, education, understanding and respect for the culture and heritage of different people.

5. Largest Foreign Exchange Earner

Ecotourism is the third largest and net earner of foreign exchange and contributes 6.0 % towards Gross Domestic Product. Global recognition is evident from the rising number of India-bound tourist. From just 17,000 international arrivals in 1951 the number has grown to 45 lacks in 2005. The year 2005 has been a highly successful year so far as tourism in India is concerned. For the third successive year, India witnessed a positive growth in foreign tourist arrivals reaching a level of 3.92 million against 3.46 million during last year. The growth rate of 13.2% during 2005 was achieved over and above a growth of about 26.8% witnessed, and that the expected growth the world over during 2005 is estimated to be about 5-6% only. With this growth, the share of India in world tourism, which was however between 0.38% to 0.39% for number of years, is expected to be around 0.49%, as shown in table below.

Year	World Tourist Arrivals	Tourist Arrival to India	Share of India in World Tourism
2000	685.5	2.65	0.39%
2001	683.8	2.54	0.37%
2002	702.8	2.38	0.34%
2003	690.9	2.73	0.39%
2004	766	3.46	0.45%
2005	808	3.92	0.49%

Source: (World Tourism Organization).

6. Exchange of Tradition and Culture

Ecotourism creates opportunities for the residents as well as the visitors to learn more about each other culture that may result in greater mutual understanding or atleast tolerance of different value system and tradition. Ecotourism has helped in conservation of its cultural heritage since ages. It is because of tourism that regular care of temples, archaeology, sculptures and carvings is done. In country like India, domestic tourism provides an opportunity to the people to achieve cross-culture understanding and thereby build a sense of national unity among diverse group of population Ecotourism creates an opportunity for the host to develop a sense of pride in their own culture, especially when they find tourist appreciating it. Tourism may also enable minority culture communities to maintain their distinct identity.

7. Conserves the Environment

Ecotourism is being promoted as a means of "giving nature value" and hence of achieving sustainable tourism. Environmental education and interpretation are the major components of ecotourism and can influence tourists, communities and industry behaviour and assist in the long-term sustainability of tourist activity in natural area. Ecotourism minimizes negative impacts upon the nature and increases awareness towards the conservation of natural assets of the country.

8. Support for Creation of Community Facility

Ecotourism aims to create economic opportunities for the local people it involves the local community in tourism activities, this not only benefit the environment but also improves the quality of tourist experience. As tourism supports the creation of community facilities and services that otherwise might have not been developed. It can bring higher standard of living to a destination. Benefits can include new sport recreational facilities restaurant and public spaces as well as an influx of better quality commodities and food. Tourism business depends extensively on each other as well as on other business, goverenment and residents of local community. Economic benefits and cost of tourism reach virtually every one in the region one way or other way.

Conclusion

If the government sees good future in ecotourism, it can be here said that it only favors a very small mostly non-autochthon group leading to neo-colonialism, xenophobia. Over the last three decades, there has been growing debate on the effect of ecotourism growth in developing countries. Developmental activities including promotion of ecotourism for socio-economic improvement have caused notice degradation of natural eco-system where adequate attention has not been given. Several organizations make tall claims of a natural experience and loosely use the word ecotourism to describe their package. How much of the money earned is ploughed back for local development? And there is hardly any resources being invested back. If so why are we risking our few remaining patches of natural resources at the hand of those who have no understanding of the term ecotourism? This creates a responsibility on the part of the government to formulate national, regional and local ecotourism policies and development strategies that are consistent with the overall objective of sustainable development. Educational programme addressed to children, and young people to enhance awareness about nature conservation should be done.

> "Recognizing the need to develop a tourism that meets economic expectations and the environmental requirements, and respect not only the social and physical structure of destinations, but also the local population."
>
> That is what ecotourism should be.

References

Satish, Nigam Chandra (2006), *Ecotourism and Sustainable Development*, Rajat Publications, pp. 1-4, 14-20.

WTO-UNEP Concept Paper-International Year of Ecotourism (2002). http://SC stsenvis.nic.in/qubec.html. http:/www.uneptie.org. www.world-tourism.org.

Buchsbaum, Duha Bernardo (2004). Ecotourism and Sustainable Development in Costa Rica. http:Scholar.lib.vt. edu/theses/available/etd.05052004-17190/ unrestricted Ecotourism Costa Rica.

Deccan Herald (2002). Can Ecotourism Save Tourism.http://www.doccentre.net/eldoc/g21

Fennel, A. David (2001). *Current Issues in Tourism*, Vol. 4, No.5, pp. 403-405, httpwww.commerce.otago.ac.nz/tourism/current-issues/home page.htm

Barkin, David (1996), Ecotourism as Tool for Sustainable Development.http://www.Planeta.com

Rajput, Diksha, Ecotourism for Sustainable Development www.tourism.com

Chapter 3

Health Insurance in India with Special Reference to Women Health in UP

— Mamta Singh

Abstract

Improvement in the health and nutritional status of the population has been one of the major thrust areas for the social development programmers of the country. This was to be achieved through improving the access do and utilization of health, family welfare and nutrition services with special focus on under-served and under-privileged segments of the population. The present study focuses on health insurance conditions after liberalization; the first section of this paper discusses health insurance on structure and quality of private provision. The second section discusses objective of study and women health problems of Uttar Pradesh. The third section of this paper discusses about importance of health and education and government provisions and the last section of the paper discusses the conclusion.

Section-1

Liberalization is a part of globalization. The insurance sector has shown the first indication of liberalization in April, 2000 with setting up of the IRDA as a statutory body for the regulation and development of the insurance sector. The Authority was established with the objective of protecting the interests of the holders of insurance policies, and to regulate, promote and ensure the orderly growth of the insurance industry and for the matters connected/ incidental thereto. The first few registration certificate to private players were issued in October 2000. The process of de-monopolization has opened wide vistas with the advent of the private players. As a result, the state owned insurers, on introspection, have begun reviewing their functioning and streamlining their operation so as to remain competitive in the emerging scenario. That the mandate has thrust upon the regulator the task of not only regulating the industry—both, the insurers and the intermediaries but also that of developing the market, in order to disperse the gains of insurance to every nook and corner of the country, only heightens the promotional role of the regulator. It is thus well accepted that while aiming at achieving global standards, the insurance industry cannot afford to lose sight of the geographical spread and the need to provide risk cover to the disadvantaged section of the society.

Health Insurance Scene in India

Health insurance can be defined in very narrow sense were individual or group purchases in advance health coverage by paying a fee called "Premium". But it can be also defined broadly by including all financing arrangements where consumer can avoid or reduce their expenditure at time to use of services. The health insurance existing in India covers a very wide spectrum of arrangement and hence the latter. Broader interpretation of health insurance is more appropriate.

Health insurance is very well established in many countries. But in India it is a new concept expect for the organized sector employees In India only about 2 per cent of total health expenditure is funded by public/social health insurance while 18% is funded by government budget. In many other low and middle income countries contributed of social health insurance is much higher.

After the enactment of the policy of the liberalization in the parliament, private companies were allowed to enter in the insurance industry and the share of the private sector is increasing in a rapid pace since then. One of the significant goals of the opening up of the Indian insurance industry was to improve the customer service and to extent the coverage of the insurance. But even after a long time of private sector operating in the industry, the significant goal of extended coverage in the health sector continues to be an exception rather than a rule. Since health insurance is of growing importance because of its potential, we focus our attention towards the health insurance industry. As of now very low percent population has some kind of health insurance to cover the unprecedented risks, and the goal set for the health sector of India—"Health for all through coverage for all" is still a distant one .

In India, the population can be broadly classified into two sections:

1. A huge vulnerable section of poor population.
2. The rich or the well segment.

Now we can say that hardest hit by lack of health coverage are the poor, who have much higher levels of mortality, malnutrition and fertility than the rich.

Now at the any point of time, individual health depends upon a range of factors. These obviously include endowment of health at birth, genetic aspect, parental health, as well lifestyle factors, consumptions of alcohol and frequency of exercise, quality of nutrition and access of good medical care when falls ill.

The passage of the Insurance Regulatory and Development Authority Bill in the Indian Parliament marked the last phase in the move towards the privatization of the insurance sector in India the relevant policy goals for this quality and with an equitable distributed burden of health care expending.

A primary study (Gupta, Indrani 2002, EPW) in Delhi shows that percentage of health expenditure in total expenditure is very revealing and more importantly, low income categories. The study shows, that 2.8 per cent (1999) of their total consumptions expenditure they spend on health, in contrast to due middle and high income households who spends 0.5-0.6 per cent (1999). So they are the class of people who spend the most on health expenditure and in an economy like India they are the one who basically determine the level of per capita health expenditure. And these are the percentage of population whom, it is very difficult to bring them under the umbrella of the health insurance. These are the people who are least willing to buy a health insurance unless they are covered by the employment. Now the very negligible per cent of total population is engaged in the organized sector employment that get coverage through employment and the percentage gradually diminishing.

Impact of Health Insurance on Structure and Quality of Private Provision

The experiences in liberalizing the private health insurance suggest that it has undesirable effects on the costs of health care. The costs of care generally go up. Given the present system of fee for service and current scenario of health infrastructure in private sector, the development of insurance will need improvements in quality and change in structure. The new investments to improve quality will result into high cost and therefore increase in prices of insurance products. There would be developments in the direction of exploring options of managed care, which would help in reducing the costs. The developments would be needed in the direction of strong information base and accreditation system for providers. The structure of the health sector will have to change from multiple-single doctor hospitals and clinics to larger hospitals and polyclinics, which provide services of multiple specialties and can operate at larger scale. This will allow them to provide high quality professional care at competitive prices. As one of the responses to these issues Third Party Administrators (TPA) are rapidly emerging in India. Here we can learn from the models, which have emerged elsewhere. But their applicability to Indian situation needs to be examined carefully. These aspects of the health sector will need detailed study.

We lack adequate information base to operate insurance schemes at large scale. The insurance mechanism prevalent in many developed countries has their history. Health reforms experiences in many countries are replete with the suggestion that the systems cannot be replicated easily. Self-regulation is an important in any market driven system. The regulation from outside does not work. Implementation of regulation in this sector is difficult. We significantly lack mechanisms and institutions, which would ensure self- regulation and continuing education of provides and various stakeholders. The accreditation systems are hard to implement without mechanisms to self-regulate. For example, it took 35 years in US to put the accreditation system effectively in place. For example, it has been difficult for many states in India to put nursing homes legislation in place. Given the deterioration on standards in medical education, lack of regulation by medical council and rising expectations of the community it is difficulty to ensure quality standards in Indian health care system. Given this situation health insurance systems will have to deal with this complex issue of quality of care in years to come.

Section-2

Objective

The present study discusses about the health insurance in India, the problems of women health, role of insurance, etc. The main objectives of the research paper to discuss are:

1. The basic problems of women health.
2. Role of health and education.
3. Impact of health insurance on structure and quality of private provision.
4. Role of government for providing help to the women.

Main Problems of Women Health

1. Nutritional Status of Women

In the national family health survey the indicator used in this section to assess the nutritional status of women is the body mass index or BMI which is the ratio of the weight of a person to the square of her height. A BMI below 18.5 kg/m indicates chronic energy deficiency (CED), caused by a highly deficient diet.

Table 1

Nutritional Status in Terms of BMI of Women in Uttar Pradesh

Categories	Mean BMI of Women (kg/m)	% Women with BMI<18.5
Rural	19.5	39.1
Urban	21.8	23.3
Regions		
Western	20.5	31.1
Central	19.8	40.1
Eastern	19.7	37.5
Bundelkhand	19.4	43.1

Source: NFHS-2, 1998-99, Uttar Pradesh Report.

As we can see in the table, women suffer from CED, more so in rural than in urban areas. The regional picture shows nutritional status to be highest in the western region, while in other three regions it is lower, ranging between 19-20 kg/m. the proportion of women with BMI below 18.5 also shows the same pattern with the lowest proportion in western region, followed by eastern region. In the central and bundelkhand regions the proportion is well above 40 per cent, indicating a very high prevalence of CED in these regions.

2. Anaemia

Anaemia is among most widespread deficiency diseases in India, predominantly among women and children. Anaemia has a detrimental effect on women's health and may lead to enhanced risk of maternal and perinatal mortality. According to the survey, over 49 % of women in (U.P) had some form of anaemia prevalence was higher in the age group 15-19 years (52.8%) and declined marginally with increasing age. Urban women had a slightly lower prevalence of anaemia than rural women. By social groups, anaemia prevalence was highest for STs (53%) followed by SCs (52%) and OBCs (51%). The upper castes showed lowest prevalence of anaemia with a proportion of 45.2 per cent.

Table-2

Proportion of Women with Anaemia across Region in Uttar Pradesh 1998-99

Regions	% Women with Any Kind of Anemia
Western	37.6
Central	54.0
Eastern	57.9
Bundelkhand	41.2

Source: NFHS-2, 1998-99, Uttar Pradesh.

The regional level data shows highest anaemia prevalence in the eastern region followed by the central region, Bundelkhand and lastly the western region. There was little difference in anaemia between pregnant (46%) and non-pregnant women (47.5%).

3. Reproductive Health Problems in Women

The proportion of women reporting any reproductive health problem was very high in Uttar Pradesh—41 per cent in urban and 37 per cent in rural areas. The highest proportion of women reporting any reproductive health problem belonged to western Uttar Pradesh (48%). The eastern region had 35 per cent women reproductive health problems, and the lowest figure of 23 per cent was recorded in central Uttar Pradesh.

Table 3

Proportion of Women Reporting any Reproductive Health Problem in Uttar Pradesh, 1998-99

Categories	% Women with Any Reproductive Health Problem
Rural	37.4
Urban	40.8
Regions	
Western	47.8
Central	23.2
Eastern	34.7
Bundelkhand	41.0

Source: NFHS-2, 1998-99, Uttar Pradesh.

4. Antenatal Care

The proportion of pregnant females that received antenatal care is quite low in Uttar Pradesh. Only 35% birth received antenatal checkups of which majority were carried out by doctors. In rural areas as many as 70% births did not receive any antenatal care, while in urban areas the figure was much lower at 34 per cent.

The highest proportion of birth without antenatal checkups was recorded in the Western region, followed by bundelkhand, eastern and Central Uttar Pradesh, all above 60 per cent. The former hill region of the unbifurcated state was the only region with more than 40 per cent births having received antenatal checkups followed by SCs, OBCs and STs. Antenatal care increased with increasing level of economic status of households, and also with increasing level of education of the female.

Section-3

Importance of Health and Education

According to Dreege & Sen (1995), education and health can be valuable to the freedom of a person at least in five distinct ways:

1. **Intrinsic Importance:** Being educated and healthy are valuable achievements in themselves, and the opportunity to have them can be of direct importance to a person's effective freedom.
2. **Instrumental Personal Roles:** A person's education and health can help him or her to do many things—'other' than just being educated and healthy – that also valuable. They can, for instance, be important for getting a job and more generally for making use of economic opportunities. The resulting expansion in incomes and economic means can, in turn, add to a person's freedom to achieve functioning that he or she values.
3. **Instrumental Social Roles:** Greater literacy and basic education can facilitate public discussion or social needs and encourage informed collective demands (e.g., for health care and social security); these in turn cap help expand the facilities that the public enjoys, and contribute to the better utilization of the available services.
4. **Instrumental Progress Roles:** The process of schooling can have benefits aside from formal education. For example, the incidence of child labour is intimately connected with non-schooling of children, and the expansion of schooling can reduce the distressing phenomenon of child labour so prevalent in India. Schooling also brings young people in touch with others and thereby broadens their horizons, and this can be particularly important for young girls.
5. **Empowerment and Distributed Roles:** Greater literacy and educational achievements of disadvantaged groups can increase their ability to resist oppression, to organize politically, and to get a fairer deal. The redistributive effects can be important not only between different social groups or households, but also within the family, since there is evidence that better education (particularly female education) contributes to the reduction of gender-based inequalities.

Government Provisions

Health is wealth, recognizing the importance of health in the process of country's socio economic development and improving the quality of life of its people, the government of India launched the national rural health mission in April 2005. The main purpose of the mission is to carry out necessary architectural correction in the basic health care delivery system. It is estimated that around 20% of the country's requirement of health care is met through public health care system and remaining through private health care systems. The mission seeks to provide effective health care to rural population throughout the country. The mission will operate over a period of seven years from 2005-2012.

A major highlight of the mission is the inclusion of Janani Suraksha Yojana (JSY). It is being proposed by way of modifying the existing National Maternity Benefit Scheme (NMBS). While NMBS is linked to provision of better diet for pregnant women from BPL families, JSY integrates the cash assistance with antenatal care during the pregnancy period, institution care during delivery and immediate post-partum period in a health centre by establishing a system of coordinated care by field level health worker. It would be a 100 per cent centrally sponsored scheme. Its vision is to reduce overall maternal mortality ratio and infant mortality rate and to increase institutional deliveries in BPL families.

The on-going Reproductive & Child Health Programme (RCH) is a component of Health Mission. The services under provided under RCH programme will be strengthened through:

1. Implementation of Janani Suraksha Yojana under which cash incentives are provided to pregnant women belonging to families. Below Poverty Line(BPL), if they deliver at a health centre/hospitals.
2. Appointment of accelerated social health activist (ASHA) for every village with a population up to1000.
3. Operationalizing 2000 community health centres as first

referral units (FRU) for providing Emergency Obstetric and Child Health Services.

4. Making 50 per cent primary health centres functional for providing 24-hour delivery services over the next five years.
5. Ensuring quality of services by implementing Indian Public Health Standards for primary health care facilities.

Tenth Plan Strategy to Improve Delivery Care

In view of massive differences between states /districts in the proportion of institutional deliveries and neonatal mortality rates, a differential strategy to achieve incremental improvement in maternal and neonatal care will be taken up during Tenth Plan.

In all districts efforts will be made to identify women with complication during pregnancy through antenatal check up and refer them to appropriate institution for safe delivery.

In districts with low institutional delivery, attempt will be made to:

1. Screen all women in the last four weeks of pregnancy and ensure that those with complications deliver in institution.
2 Train TBAs in clean delivery.
3. Train TBAs to recognize problems that arise during labour and refer those women to hospitals.
4. Ensure that referral are honoured.
5. Build up community support for transport of women with problems of functional FRUs.

In districts with high institutional delivery, efforts will be made to:

1. Improve the quality of services available.
2. Address problems and needs of the women in labour seeking institutional deliveries.
3. Aim at universal institutional deliveries by making institutions people friendly.
4. Perform medical audit for progressive improvement in quality of care.

Specific effort will be to strengthen FRUs/CHCs/district hospitals to provide emergency obstetric care for all referred cases. The attempt will be to:

1. Operationalize adequate number of FRUs/CHCs by posting specialist in obstetrics, gynaecology/paediatrics in institution where infrastructure is available.
2. Provide for funding specialists on contact part time basis, if necessary, so that care is available when needed.
3. Improve access to anaesthesists and banked blood.

Section-4

Conclusion

As the insurance industry has liberalized recently, health insurance is going to develop rapidly in future. The challenge is to see that it benefits the poor and the weak in terms of better coverage and health services at lower cost without the negative aspects of cost increase and over use of procedures and technology in provision of health care. The insurance market was opened up in order to serve the consumers in a better way as well as contribute positively to do the growth of economy.

But the insurance sector is characterized by the existence of uncertainty and asymmetry of information which make this market different from all other markets. Therefore things happen differently when compared to other markets. We have found out that the private health care expenditure is increasing alarmingly with the market share of the private health insurance. Now in a country like India where the dominant segment of the population is high risk, specially women and children, any policy changes should be taken keeping the welfare of this section in mind.

References

UP Development Report, Vol. 2, Planning Commission, Government of India, Social Development, Chapter-2.

Rao, V. Mohan (2005), Rural health Facilities, *Kurukshetra*, October (2005).

Bhatt, Ramesh, Malvankar, Dileep(2000), Health Insurance in India, Opportunities, Challenges and Concerns, Indian Institute of Management, Ahmedabad.

Joyti, K. Kamlan and B. Rajlaxmi, Reproductive Wealth Awareness among College-going Girls, *The Indian Journal of Social Work*, Vol. 66, Issues 4, October (2005).

Nag, Moni (1994), Beliefs and Practices about Food during Pregnancy Implications for Maternal Nutrition, *Economic and Political Weekly*, 29(37), September.

Ramanna, Mridula (2007), Maternal Health in Twentieth Century Bombay, *Economic and Political Weekly*, January 13, (2007).

Amrith, Suneel (2007), Political Culture and Health in India: A Historical Perspective, *Economic and Political Weekly*, January 13, (2007).

Devdasan (2006), Community Health Insurance Scheme, *Yojana*, April 2006.

Chenappa, D. (2004), Development of Insurance in India: A Study, *The Journal of Institute of Public Enterprise*, Vol. 27, 1 & 2 (2004).

4 *Chapter*

Gender Budgeting: A Concept in the Era of Globalization—A Case Study of Uttar Pradesh

— Shalini Tiwari

The situation of women is well summarized by James Gustave Speth, referring to gender disparities, "the most persistent of these (disparities) has been gender disparities, despite a relentless struggle to equalize opportunities between women and men. The unfinished agenda for change is still considerable". The question of gender equalities goes around the power of women in society. The lack of access to and control over resources, a coercive gender division of labour, devaluation of their and lack of control over their own labour, mobility as well as sexuality and fertility, their poor capabilities as measured by literacy and educational levels and status of health, etc., are the result of absence of power among women.

The Government of India done a lot of work in this direction like, from the Vth Five Year Plan (1974-78) onwards there has been a marked shift from welfare to development in the approach to women issues. After adopting the approach of globalization, leading to special policy formulation like,

1. National Commission for Women 1993.
2. India has also ratified various international conventions and human rights instruments committed to securing equal

rights of women, like the Convention on Elimination of All Forms of Discrimination Against Women (CEDAW) in 1993.

3. Reservation of seats in the local bodies of panchyats and municipalities for women, 1997.
4. National Policy for the Empowerment of Women, 2001.
5. Gender budgeting.

The theme line of this paper is gender budgeting and its implications on women development indicators. Concept of gender budgeting is new, while formulating budget to think of women development, through budgetary allocations, with a view to alleviating inequality between male and female and to bring them at par, is gender budgeting.

The concept of gender has emerged very forcefully in India after globalization, while the Eighth Five Year Plan (1992-97) highlighted for the first time a gender perspective and the need to ensure a definite flow of funds from the general development sectors to women. The Ninth Five Year Plan (1997-2002) adopted, "Women Component Plan" as one of the major strategies and directed both the central and state government to ensure "not less than 30% of the funds/ benefits are earmarked in all the women related sectors".

The National Policy for Empowerment of Women, 2001 envisaged introduction of a gender perspective in the budgeting process as an operational strategy. The Tenth Five Year Plan reinforced the commitment to gender budgeting to establish its gender differential impact and to translate gender commitments. It is perceived as a powerful tool not only for tracking allocation of resources for women but also covers implementation issues and outcomes. The union expenditure Budget 2005-06 has institutionalized gender budgeting in the budget document, wherein it has been indicated that the budget provision in the BE 2005-06, substantially meant for welfare of women and children is Rs. 14,378.68 crore. At present gender budget cells have been set up in 35 departments of the Government of India.

Gender based differences are built into the social and economic fabric of our society, so gender budgeting exercise is relevant in the development process. The intention behind this is to assess and highlight the biases inherent in the budget and to suggest the ways to change the outlook of government policies towards the promotion of equality between genders.

Methodology

The objective of the study is to analyze the expenditure on women development. Under the study it is very difficult to get disaggregated data of expenditure on women relating to education, health, employment and other women related issues. Therefore the budgetary expenditure on Department of Women and Child Development (DWCD) is the main source of expenditure on women development because, the DWCD deals with all kinds of women related issues and many programmes for upliftment of status were governing by this department like; Swavalamban, STEP, Swadhar, Swa-Shakti, Swayamsidha, etc.

The study area, which was selected, is the state of Uttar Pradesh, because, Uttar Pradesh had a highest populace state (about 16%) in India and the women development indicators were very low in this state. The gender budgeting is also start working in Uttar Pradesh. So the main idea of this study is to analyze that the gender budgeting concept does really works in Uttar Pradesh or does it able to improve the status of women in Uttar Pradesh. The data related to expenditure on women and child development in Uttar Pradesh and selected indicators of women development in Uttar Pradesh were analyzed to reach the conclusion.

The DWCD was set up in 1985 as a part of Ministry of Human Resource and Development to give the needed imputes to the holistic development of women and children. The DWCD in Uttar Pradesh established with the objective of specific attention to the integrated development of women and children and their social and economic problems.

The department's activities are aimed at raising the status of women at all levels and improving health and nutrition facilities for the children with special focus on the children belonging to lower income groups such as landless labourers. The department formulates plans, policies, programmes, etc., and guides, coordinates the efforts of both governmental and non-governmental organizations working in this field. The ultimate aim of all these programmes is to make women independent and self-reliant.

A Review of Expenditure on Women Development and Its Implications

The expenditure of DWCD in Uttar Pradesh was improved in last few years especially after the government of Uttar Pradesh adopted the concept of gender budgeting. Expenditure of DWCD in UP is given in Table 1 during the year 2000-2006.

Table 1
Expenditure of DWCD in Uttar Pradesh during 2000-2006

Year	Expenditure (in crores)
2000-01	2,55,127
2001-02	2,53,771
2003-04	1,18,787
2004-05	1,41,018
2005-06	2,87,091
2006-07	2,86,930

Source: Annual Plan of UP, 2006.

Table 1 shows that during 2000-01 the expenditure on DWCD is Rs. 2,55,127 crore and after that it's goes down till 2005-06, and reached the level of Rs. 1,41,018 crore. In the 2005-2006 it once again increased to the level of Rs. 2,87,091 crore and till 2006-07 it is Rs. 2,86,930 crore. Here, the expenditure on DWCD is fluctuated, this shows that the state government had may be not considered this matter as serious as it is.

In Uttar Pradesh the DWCD works on women employment, education, health services, etc., and for this purpose it required the proper amount of funds to avail all these facilities. There is another question which is more important, the implications of these expenditure on women development indicators. For this some selected indicators were chosen under the study like; female literacy rates, sex ratio, infant mortality rates (IMR), maternal mortality rates

(MMR), and institutional deliveries in Uttar Pradesh. Comparative study was also done to clarify the situation of Uttar Pradesh.

Table 2 shows the female literacy rates, sex ratio and female life expectancy in Uttar Pradesh during the year 1981-2001.When we saw the data related to female literacy, there is much deference between the years 1981-1991 to 1991-2001. The literacy level of females in Uttar Pradesh was increased from 8.57% points to 17.67% points, which is more than twice. This is possibly because; more efforts were done in this state during globalization era and also the DWCD was established in UP in the same period. Same thing occurred with sex ratio and female life expectancy trends in Uttar Pradesh. The sex ratio increased from 885 in 1981 to 898 in 2001. The female life expectancy was also increased from 56.9 in 1991 to 64.09 in 2001. But, one thing, which is disturbing, is the speed of

Table 2

Selected Indicators of Women Development in 1981-2001

Year	Female Literacy	Sex ratio	Female Life Expectancy
1981	16.74	885	-
1991	25.31	879	56.9
2001	42.98	898	64.09

Source: Census Report, 2001, GOI.

this kind of development, it is very slow as compare to other states and far behind as regard to other women development indicators like; IMR, MMR and institutional delivery. This trend was shown in Table 3.

The data in the Table 3 show that, the situation of Uttar Pradesh is far lower than the other selected states. When we saw the situation of Kerala in the year 2001, IMR was only 12, and MMR was 110, which is in good position and the percentage of institutional deliveries were very high, which is 97.8%. Therefore Kerala had a good score in Gender Development Index (GDI), which is 0.874 in 2001. Tamil Nadu had second place in the selected states in the

Table 3
Statewise Selected Indicators of Women Development in 2001

State	IMR	MMR	Institutional Delivery in %
U P	72	517	22.4
Punjab	45	178	48.7
Hariyana	61	162	35.1
Kerala	12	110	97.8
Tamilnadu	41	134	86.1
Andhra Pradesh	59	195	60.9

Source: Economic Survey, 2005-06, Planning Commission, GOI.

study because it has second place in the lowest IMR and MMR, which is 41 and 134 respectively, and the second largest percentage of institutional deliveries were happened in this state, which is 86.1%. Andhra Pradesh and Punjab goes up and down with all the above indicators, because Andhra Pradesh has a highest percentage of institutional deliveries then Punjab (60.9% and 48.7% respectively). On the other hand, Punjab has a lowest IMR and MMR as compare to Andhra Pradesh (45 vs. 59 and 178 vs. 195 respectively). After that Hariyana was in the second last position, here IMR was 61, MMR was 162 and the percentage of institutional deliveries were 48.7%. When we come to Uttar Pradesh there was very depressing situation in all the selected indicators, because all were the lowest among the selected states. The IMR of Uttar Pradesh was 72, MMR was 517 and the institutional deliveries were only 22.4%, which is alarming.

After analyzing the whole situation this is clear that, in the state of Uttar Pradesh women are very much in under lining situation and all the efforts which was govern by the government and non-government institution, did not reached the target persons, therefore the women in this state did not aware about the real situation of herself. The low level of literacy, which is shown in Table 2, is the main reason behind this and the reason lie in the socio-economic position of women in Uttar Pradesh.

Table 3 shows that in southern India women are more able to cope up the facilities for themselves as compare to northern India. The position of women in Uttar Pradesh is notably poor. Traditional societies in Uttar Pradesh is hierarchical and dominated by men, as evidenced by marriage system. Sons are the major source of economic security in old age. So there is need do adopt an effective gender development programmes and for this the gender budgeting is the first step in this direction.

In spite of a small increase in expenditure on DWCD in Uttar Pradesh, it feels that it is not enough. The basic aim of these efforts is to have an open communication with policy maker to make policies based on women need and preference.

Here one thing also wants to be suggested that, for effective implications of gender budgeting, there should be the close interaction between activists in the movements, policy makers and general people.

In the era of fast globalization our national objective of streamlining the women force in development process requires the social acceptance of multiple roles of women as homemakers, mothers and also the breadwinners. Marriage and motherhood, which contribute to the continuation of the society, should not be considered disabilities in the gainful participation of women in the economic process. The three aspects of gender budgeting is health and education of women, eradication of gender barriers in employment and full participation of women in democracy must be given maximum attention, which helps in transformation of millions of women of India in the mainstream of national development.

References

Report of Department of Women and Child Development, 2003.

Human Development Report, 2005.

Economic and Political Weekly, Oct 30- Nov. 5, 2004, Vol. XXXIX No. 44, Mumbai.

Economic Survey 2005-06, Planning Commission, GOI.

Annual Plan of Uttar Pradesh 2006, Government of Uttar Pradesh.

Census Report 2001.

Chapter 5

Impact of Globalization on the Agricultural Exports of India

— R.K. Kaundal and Manoj Sharma

Agriculture can make a significant contribution to the foreign exchange earnings through substitution of imports by domestic production and by expanding exports. It plays a crucial role in generating foreign exchange through increased agricultural exports. Primary products and agricultural commodities are the major sources of foreign exchange fro developing countries. Economic development is one of the main objectives of every society in the world and economic growth is fundamental to economic development. Agricultural sector has been the most crucial sector of Indian economy, which contributes about 25 per cent of Gross Domestic Product (GDP) and provides employment to around 2/3rd of the total population. Exports are a must for India's economic development. Agricultural exports have been the backbone of India's export efforts and they continue to be the beacon for the future export growth. Agricultural exports are sustainable and their potential to grow is very high (Dattatreyalu, 1994). Agricultural exports contribute around 10 per cent to India's total export earnings. Agricultural exports play a significant role in employment generation particularly in rural areas. The low import intensity of exports further enhances the significance of agricultural exports. Agricultural exports contribute to increase the income of the rural population, particularly the landless labourers, and the small and marginal farmers and improve the quality of the life of rural masses. Rural development and agricultural export are intertwined. If this is not achieved agricultural exports, despite earning foreign exchange, will lose all their significance (Dattatreyalu, *op. cit.*).

In addition to traditional commodities in the world market, India has great potential to export fresh and processed fruits and vegetables. The export growth depends not only on domestic production and distribution situation, but on many other factors such as world economic scenario, prices of Indian exports relative to world prices, exchange rates and inflation rate in the countries competing with India for world market and taxes and subsidies on exports. As per the agricultur at policy solution 1993, India has natural comparative advantage in its exports on account of lower import needs of inputs, low level of cost and existence of diverse agro-climate conditions. The major emphasis should be given for raising the production and exports of those commodities that have potential for export (Goyal, Pandey and Singh, 2000).

Diversified agriculture is equally India's strength. Diverse climate conditions and diverse soil conditions are contributing to diversified agriculture. The country has food crops, commercial crops, plantation crops, horticulture, floriculture, pisciculture, viticulture, aquaculture, sericulture, animal husbandry and dairying, forestry, and processed food products. Abundant sunshine, adequate river waters and skilled and talented labour are the other assets (Dattatreyalu, *op. cit.*).

Before the policy measures taken during 1990s by the Government of India, most of agricultural exports were subjected to controls of one kind or the other. The main factors behind the export control have been to maintain the domestic prices at reasonable levels as the export can affect domestic prices by reducing the domestic supply particularly of those commodities whose supply falls short of demand. The protection of agricultural exports has been resulted into high protection to some commodities such as oil seeds and sugar (domestic prices being higher than international prices). This created uncertainty for exporters and importers, discouraging them from investing in long-term marketing facilities and relationship (Pursell *et. al.,* 1993).

The importance of trade in agricultural products cannot be over-emphasized in the context of economic growth especially in less developed countries (LDCs). Many LDCs have a comparative advantage in the production of agricultural products. The export of these products can pay for the import of capital goods, technology and other manufactured products necessary for sustained growth in LDCs. In effect, the market for developed countries (DCs) will expand and the trade in agricultural products will be of mutual benefit to both DCs and LDCs. However, the mutuality of interest is not so obvious in real world mainly because of the poor bargaining power of LDCs in world market and tariff and non-tariff protection strategy followed by DCs (Pal, 1992).

Also as often argued, the exports of LDCs fluctuate more than the DCs. This is because of the fact that the exports of LDCs mainly comprise agricultural products having erratic supply (Ghatak and Ingersent, 1984). Agricultural exports can make a significant contribution to the foreign exchange earnings through substitution of imports by domestic production and by expanding exports. It plays a most crucial role in generating foreign exchange through increased agricultural exports. Primary products and agricultural commodities are the major source of foreign exchange for developing countries (Chand and Tewari, 1991).

In the light of these facts, the present study is an attempt to analyze the impact of globalization on the agricultural exports of India for the last sixteen years, i.e. (1991-92 to 2006-07). For the in-depth analysis of the problem the total period has been further divided into two categories, i.e., first generation reforms (1991-92 to 1998-99) and second generation reforms (1999-00 to 2006-07).

Examination of the above issue would throw light on the impact of globalisation on the agricultural exports of India. The agricultural exports included in the analysis include the items which constitute about 80 to 90 per cent of the total agricultural exports.

Data and Methodology

The present study is exclusively based upon the time series secondary data collected from different published sources of government agencies such as Economic Survey, Government of India, Ministry of Finance, New Delhi, Handbook of Statistics on Indian Economy, Reserve Bank of India, Mumbai. The values of exports are in US dollars to iron out the effect of changes in exchange rate. This study broadly covers the period from 1991-92 to 2006-07.

The compound growth rates were computed to examine the trends in agricultural exports by using the following type of function:

$$Y_i = a (b_i)^t$$

$$\text{Log } Y_i = \log a + t \log (b_i)$$

where,

Y_i = export value of ith item,

t = time variable.

Annual compound growth rate (r) is computed as:

$$r = [\text{Anti log } (b_i)\text{-}1]*100.$$

Measurement of Instability

The measurement of instability in time-series data requires an explicit assumption of what constitute the acceptable and unacceptable components. A systematic component which can be predicted does not constitute instability and hence it could be eliminated from the data. The remaining unacceptable component represents the instability. Two methods, viz., moving average and trend fitting have been used in the literature to capture the predictable component. As a measure of instability this analysis utilizes an exponential index (IXEXP). IXEXP are defined as the coefficient of "unexplained" variations observed from the estimated time trend. The equation of the exponential trend is written as:

$$X_{it} = a_i e^{bit} u_{it}$$

$$\text{Log}(X_{it}) = \log a_i + b_{it} + \log u_{it} \quad (t = 1,2, \text{———}, n)$$

where (X_{it}) is the value of principal exports, t represents time and u is the disturbance term, OLS is then used to estimate the equations. IXEXP measures deviations from constant growth rate trend line.

$$\frac{100}{\overline{X}}\left[\frac{\sum_{t=1}^{n}\left(X_{it} - \hat{a}e^{\hat{b}_{it}}\right)^2}{n-2}\right]^{\frac{1}{2}}$$

$\overline{X}$ being the mean of Xi.

Since we wish principally to consider export-earning variability, which comprises of quantum variability, price variability and their covariance, relative variability is more appropriately measured by the coefficient of variation (more appropriately to term it as coefficient of "unexplained" variations) than the standard error of the estimate. Because different export products have different mean levels of quantum and price, standard deviations are likely to be higher for the export products with absolute values of these variables. A comparison of standard deviations therefore would be of little value. Hence in our present study we make use of the relative variability.

Instability Index (I) is:

$$I = \frac{1}{\log \overline{x}} * \sqrt{\frac{\sum_{t=1}^{n} \log x^2{}_i - \frac{\left(\sum_{i=1}^{n} \log x_i\right)^2}{n} - \log \beta^2 \sum_{i=1}^{n} t_i{}^2}{n-2}} * 100$$

This instability index has two advantages. Firstly, this is scale independent and can be used for cross comparisons. Secondly, the bias entering the instability measure due to an element of growth gets minimized.

Analysis of Agricultural Exports of India

Composition of India's Exports

In India, the major exportable products are classified into five main groups, namely, primary products, manufactured products, petroleum products, others and total exports. The relative contribution of exports for each group at different point of time is presented in Table 1. It is found that the share of manufactured goods was highest in total exports followed by primary products and petroleum products. The composition remained almost the same but proportion of different items has changed over the years. For instance, the share of primary products was 23.1 per cent in 1991-92, which increased up to a maximum of 24.01 per cent in 1996-97 and then started declining over the years, it was accounted 15.47 per cent in 2006-07. In case of manufactured goods, the share was 73.6 per cent in 1991-92 with little fluctuations it reached to maximum 80.7 per cent in 1999-2000 and subsequently declined to 65.56 per cent in 2006-07. The share of petroleum products to total exports was 2.32 per cent in 1991-92, with declining trend it reached to 0.11 per cent in 1999-2000 and finally started increasing and reached to its highest level of 14.69 per cent in 2006-07. The share of other unclassified items to total exports was 0.95 per cent in 1991-92, which in the subsequent years have increased and stood at 4.28 per cent in 2006-07.

Share of Principal Agricultural Exports in Total Exports

Table 2 presents the share of agricultural and allied products in total exports. The share of agricultural and allied products in total Indian exports was 17.9 per cent in 1991-92, which reached a maximum of 20.5 per cent in 1996-97 and subsequently declined to 9.91 per cent in 2006-07. Among the principal agricultural and allied products the share of marine products was highest, i.e., 3.28 per cent in 1991-92, which touched the highest level of 4.27 per cent in 1994-95. After that it started declining over the years and finally settled at 1.38 per cent in 2006-07. The share of tea in India's total exports was 2.75 per cent in 1991-92 which subsequently declined to 0.88 per cent in 1996-97, its share improved and reached at 1.62 per cent in 1998-99 which in subsequent years declined and stood at it lowest level 0.34 per cent in 2006-07. Coffee is the commodity whose share in total exports was 0.75 per cent, which increased and stood at 1.24 per cent in 1998-99, subsequently declined and reached at 0.34 per cent (minimum ever) in 2006-07. The commodities whose share in total export either remained more or less stable or increased are sugar, rice, raw cotton and meat and meat preparations. Oil cakes, tobacco, cashew, spices, fruits and vegetables and miscellaneous processed foods are the commodities whose share in total exports remained more or less stable or declined.

Share of Principal Agricultural Exports to Total Agricultural Exports

Share of principal agricultural exports (commodity wise) in total agricultural exports is shown in Table 3. Among the various agricultural commodities the share of marine products was highest, i.e., 18.3 per cent in 1991-92. Thereafter, the share of fish and fish preparations in total agricultural exports increased to 26.7 per cent in 1994-95, but it declined sharply to 16.62 per cent in 1995-96. After that it showed increasing trend and reached at 23.33 per cent in 2000-01. Since 2001-02, it is continuously declining and is at its lowest level in 2006-07, i.e., 13.9 per cent. Tea ranked second in respect of its share in total agricultural exports, which was 15.3 per cent in 1991-92, it declined to a minimum level, i.e., 4.26 per cent in 1996-97. Thereafter it increased to 8.92 per cent in 1998-99, and then it followed a declining trend and reached at its lowest level of 3.45 per cent in 2006-07, could be attributed to the fact that Indian tea is facing a stiff competition from Sri Lanka and rise in the cost of production. The share of oil meals in total agricultural exports was 11.7 per cent in 1991-92, it reached to the highest level of 18.4 per cent in 1993-94. Thereafter, it declined to 6.74 per cent in 1999-00, which finally, with mixed trend, stood at 9.72 per cent in 2006-07.

The share of rice in total agricultural exports was 9.57 per cent in 1991-92, it increased to the highest level of 24.7 per cent in 1998-99 in total agricultural exports and then sharply declined to 10.74 per cent in 2000-01, which increased and stood at 18 per cent in 2002-03 and then finally settling at 12.4 per cent in 2006-07. The share of cashew in total agricultural exports was 8.56 per cent in 1991-92, which increased to 9.4 per cent in 1994-95, but declined to 5.29 per cent in 1996-97, and increased to the highest level of 10.1 per cent in 1999-2000, and then followed a declining trend to reach at its lowest level of 4.43 per cent in 2006-07. Rice, cotton raw including waste, spices, fruits and vegetables, processed fruits, juices, miscellaneous, sugar and molasses, meat and meat preparations, and other unclassified items are the commodities whose share have increased in 2006-07 and the share of tea, coffee, wheat, tobacco, cashew including cashew nut shell liquid, oil meals, and marine products has declined in 2006-07 as compared to 1991-92.

Share of Agricultural Exports of India in World Agricultural Exports

Share of India's agricultural exports in world agricultural exports is shown in Table 4. India's share of total exports in world exports remained very low, i.e., less then one per cent in-between 1991 to 2004. First time it has crossed one per cent in 2005, whereas share of agricultural exports in world agricultural exports (for principal commodities) was higher than the share of India in world's total exports. However, the exports of some of the commodities have increased while those of others have decreased over the period 1991 to 2005. For instance, among the various agricultural commodities, the share of tea in world export was the highest, i.e., about 18.6 per cent in 1991 but; it declined to 13.6 per cent in 1994. Thereafter, it increased sharply to 18.8 in 1999, and then it subsequently declined and reached at 9.6 per cent in 2005. The sharp decline in tea export particularly in early nineties could be because of decline in overall world exports of tea and a stiff competition India was facing from Sri

Lanka. Spices ranked second in respect of its share in world exports, which was 8.7 per cent in 1991, it increased to 11.4 per cent in 1998, then subsequently declined to 8.2 per cent in 2004. The share of rice in world exports was 7.6 per cent in 1991, which increased to 18.9 per cent in 1995 and then declined to 8.4 per cent in 2001. During 1991, the share of marine products was 1.5 per cent, which increased to 2.5 per cent in 1994, and it was 2.7 per cent in 2001. Coffee, tobacco, meat and meat preparations, fruits and vegetables, cereals and cereal preparations and oil seeds are the commodities whose share in world exports although is low, yet increasing over the years. These commodities have the potential to increase in future in world exports.

Exports and Economic Growth

The role of exports in growth process of less developed countries (LDCs) is usually attributed to three types of mechanisms. First, it is believed that LDCs growth largely depends on industrialization (World Bank, 1987). But, the level of domestic demand in most LDCs is low; hence, the importance of pursuing export-based trade strategies in order to have access to the world demand. Second, although it is acknowledged that export promotion policies are not fully satisfactory as regards microeconomic efficiency, yet they are nevertheless least damaging; in other words, they benefit total factors productivity more than any other policy (Balassa, 1978). Third, it is claimed that exports make growth easier also in the long run, since they lead to more savings, higher technological progress, better ratings in the international financial markets (and thus easier access to foreign loans) (Krueger, 1989).

It is argued that LDCs face a higher degree of instability in export earnings, which in turn, affects their efforts at economic development. India is among the developing countries, whose economic development programme is largely dependent on availability of foreign exchange. Therefore, instability in export earnings is expected to hamper the process of economic development (Sharan,

1984). Moreover, instability in export earnings adds to the uncertainties of planning and the crisis that arise often calls for drastic actions that adversely affect important development projects. Export instability is important because of its effects on the level of living, on internal economic stability, on the rate of economic growth and on the distribution of income and wealth. It is also important because of its effects on the internal and external policies of many countries (Coppock, 1962).

Measurement of Growth and Instability

In line with the established practice in this field, export instability is defined as the short-term variations in export earnings around the underlying trend. Export instability may be determined by the factors, which operate either through demand, or through supply, termed as (1) instability of demand, (2) instability of supply. From the exporting countries point of view it is clearly the former, which is of any importance.

Table 5 sets out the estimated annual compound growth rates and instability indexes of five principal groups for the period 1991-92 to 2006-07 and the sub-periods 1991-92 to 1998-99 and 1999-00 to 2006-07. The annual compound growth rate for primary products export was highest 17.97 per cent with least instability of 1.07 per cent during the second sub period. The manufactured products export was also highest during the second sub period with low instability, i.e., 16.59 per cent and 0.72 per cent respectively. During 1999-00 to 2006-07 for all the five groups, viz., primary products, manufactured products, petroleum products, others and total exports the growth rate was highest with a declining instability except for others where the instability has increased over the first period (1991-92 to 1998-99). The growth rate was higher for primary products than the manufactured products during the second sub period (1999-00 to 2006-07). The total exports too have increased at a higher rate, i.e., 19.47 per cent than the primary products and the manufactured products. Petroleum products have shown a higher growth (95.26

per cent) with higher instability whereas manufactured exports showed lower growth rate (16.59 per cent) with low instability. The annual compound growth rates for primary products and the manufactured products were less than total export growth. Petroleum products and others have higher growth and higher instability as compared to total exports. It also reveals that primary products growth rate was higher than the manufactured products exports. Instability for primary products, manufactured products and total exports have declined whereas for petroleum products and others have increased during 1999-00 to 2006-07 over 1991-92 to 1998-99. The instability in exports discourages investment in the production of the commodities, limits the economic horizon and destroys the sense of continuity, which is necessary for planning production (Chand and Tewari, 1991). The values of instability indices help the policy makers for formulating product-by-product export promotion and investment policies.

Growth and Instability of Principal Agricultural Exports of India

India is predominantly an agricultural economy. The liberalization policies adopted by it have paved the way for agricultural export promotion policies. Agricultural exports are sustainable and their potential to grow is very high. It is labour intensive and is the, most competitive sector of the Indian economy. Agricultural exports are presently contributing about 10 per cent to total exports (Table 2). Agricultural exports play a significant role in employment generation, particularly in the rural sector. India has natural comparative advantage in its exports on account of lower import needs of inputs, low level of cost and existence of diverse agro-climatic conditions (Goyal *et. al.*, 2000)

Despite the rapid growth of industrial production, India's dependence on agriculture sector is significant. There are several good reasons why agricultural exports should make a higher contribution to the total exports than the present level of 10 per cent; (1) the domestic resource cost of each rupee of foreign exchange earned is lower in agriculture sector than in manufacture sector (91 paise and 96 paise respectively) (Sengupta, 1986); (2) factor incomes generated at home per rupee of output exported (directly and through backward linkages) amount to 71 paise for agricultural compared with 59 paise for manufactured (Sengupta, *op. cit*); (3) basically, agricultural commodity exports require the least amount of cash assistance. Net foreign exchange earnings are positive in most of the agricultural products (Dattatreyulu, 1987); (4) world demand for some of the higher value agricultural products such as dairy products, fruits and vegetables and marine products has been increasing for the last few years; (5) India enjoys a fairly large potential for agricultural, horticultural and marine products due to the large geographical area with varied climates, temperatures and variety of soils accompanied by the largest coast line in the world.

The exports of LDCs fluctuate more than that of DCs. This is because of the fact that the export of LDCs mainly comprises agricultural products having erratic supply. The unstable export tends to destabilize the income of LDCs as long as export earnings constitute a significant proportion of national income, which in turn has serious political and economic implications (Pal, 1992).

Table 6 presents the detailed analysis of growth and instability of principal agricultural exports. The growth rate of tea, coffee, rice, cashew including cashew nut shell liquid, spices, processed fruits, juices, miscellaneous, marine products and others have shown a higher growth rate during 1991-92 to 1998-99 whereas for commodities wheat, cotton raw including waste, oil meals, fruits and vegetables, sugar and molasses and meat and meat preparations it was higher during 1999-00 to 2006-07. The instability was highest for the commodities like tea, coffee, rice, wheat, tobacco, oil meals, fruits and vegetables, processed fruits, juices, miscellaneous, marine products, sugar and molasses, meat and meat preparations and others during the first sub period. The instability has declined only for three commodities, viz., cotton raw including waste, cashew including cashew nut shell liquid and spices during the second sub period. The commodities like tea, coffee, rice, processed fruits, juices, miscellaneous, marine products and others have shown a higher growth and higher instability during the first sub period. Whereas the commodities, viz., wheat, tobacco, oil meals, fruits and vegetables, sugar and molasses and meat and meat preparations have shown higher growth and lower instability during the second sub-period and certainly the star performers for the future. Cashew including cashew nut shell liquid and spices are the commodities whose exports are declining and instability is increasing. These are certainly the commodities whose exports need a careful attention. The commodities with higher growth and declining instability are really the star performers of the future and should be encouraged to take the full benefit of the export sector.

Conclusions and Policy Implications

The recapitulation of the preceding discussion provides that the levels of India's exports of principal groups and principal agricultural products have shown variations in exports. The annual compound growth rates for primary products and the manufactured products were less than total export growth. Petroleum products and others have higher growth and higher instability as compared to total exports. It also reveals that primary products growth rate was higher than the manufactured products exports. Instability for primary products, manufactured products and total exports have declined whereas for petroleum products and others have increased during 1999-00 to 2006-07 over 1991-92 to 1998-99.

In terms of export earnings of principal agricultural exports, commodities with fairly decent growth rate and low instability include wheat, tobacco, oil meals, fruits and vegetables, sugar and molasses and meat and meat preparations. The commodities with high growth and high instability include cashew including cashew nut shell liquid and spices. The products with low growth and low instability are processed fruits, juices, miscellaneous and marine products and others. The prospect of future growth in the export of agricultural commodities lies in the commodities with high growth and low instability. It is further concluded that the position of agricultural exports have improved in the second generation reforms period over the first generation reforms period when the reforms were intensified.

Table 1
Composition of India's Exports 1991-92 to 2006-07.

(Value in million US$)

No.	Commodities	1991-92	%	1992-93	%	1993-94	%	1994-95	%	1995-96	%	1996-97	%	1997-98	%	1998-99	%
1	**Primary products**	**4132.2**	**23.1**	**3873.5**	**20.9**	**4915.7**	**22.1**	**5214.4**	**19.8**	**7256.9**	**22.8**	**8035.1**	**24**	**7687.3**	**21.9**	**6927.9**	**20.8**
	A. Agriculture and allied products	3202.5	17.9	3135.8	16.9	4027.5	18.1	4226.1	16.1	6081.9	19.1	6862.7	20.5	6626.3	18.9	6034.5	18.1
	B. ores and minerals	929.7	5.2	737.8	3.9	888.2	3.9	988.3	3.7	1174.9	3.6	1172.4	3.5	1061.1	3	893.4	2.6
II.	**Manufactured products**	**13148.4**	**73.6**	**14038.8**	**75.7**	**16656.7**	**74.9**	**20404.4**	**77.5**	**23747**	**74.6**	**24613.4**	**73.5**	**26546.6**	**75.8**	**25791.5**	**77.6**
	A. Leather and manufactures	1268.8	7.1	1277.5	6.8	1299.5	5.8	1610.6	6.1	1752.2	5.5	1605.8	4.7	1656.7	4.7	1660.7	4.9
	B. Chemical sand related products	1868.8	10.5	1786.1	9.6	2377.2	10.6	3066.8	11.6	3597	11.3	3912.8	11.6	4396.3	12.5	4009.2	12
	C. Engineering goods	2253.1	12.6	2480.8	13.3	3038.1	13.6	3508	13.3	4391	13.8	4962.7	14.8	5336.2	15.2	4463.9	13.4
	D. Textile and textile products	4693.1	26.3	5007.4	27	5472.3	24.6	7117.7	27	8031.6	25.2	8635.7	25.8	9050.4	25.8	8866.3	26.6
	E. Gems and jewellery	2738.2	15.3	3071.7	16.5	3995.8	17.9	4500.4	17.1	5274.8	16.5	4752.7	14.2	5345.5	15.2	5929.3	17.8
	F. Handicrafts (excluding handmade carpets)	241.5	1.35	275.9	1.4	318.5	1.4	386.3	1.47	433.9	1.3	475.7	1.4	525.4	1.5	633.1	1.9
	G Other manufactured products	84.9	0.48	139.3	0.7	155.3	0.6	214.5	0.8	266.5	0.8	267.9	0.8	235.6	0.6	228.9	0.6
III.	**Petroleum products**	**414.7**	**2.3**	**476.2**	**2.5**	**397.8**	**1.7**	**416.9**	**1.5**	**453.7**	**1.4**	**481.8**	**1.4**	**352.8**	**1**	**89.4**	**0.2**
IV.	**Others**	**170.1**	**0.5**	**148.6**	**0.8**	**268**	**1.2**	**294.9**	**1.1**	**337.3**	**1.1**	**339.4**	**1**	**419.8**	**1.1**	**410**	**1.2**
V.	**Total Exports**	**17865.4**	**100**	**18537.2**	**100**	**22238.3**	**100**	**26330.5**	**100**	**31794.9**	**100**	**33469.7**	**100**	**35006.4**	**100**	**33218.7**	**100**

(Value in million US$)

No.	Commodities	1999-00	%	2000-01	%	2001.-02	%	2002-03	%	2003-04	%	2004.-05	%	2005-06	%	2006-07P	%
1	**Primary products**	**6524.2**	**17.7**	**7126.2**	**15.9**	**7163.6**	**16.3**	**8706.1**	**16.5**	**9901.8**	**15.5**	**13553.3**	**16.2**	**16377.4**	**15.8**	**19547.8**	**15.4**
	A. Agriculture and allied products	5608	15.2	5973.2	13.4	59.102	13.4	6710	12.7	7533.1	11.8	8474.7	10.1	10213.8	9.9	12514.6	9.9
	B. ores and minerals	616.1	2.4	1153	2.5	1262.3	2.8	1996	3.7	2368.7	3.7	5078.6	6	6163.6	5.9	7033.1	5.5
II.	**Manufactured products**	**29714.4**	**80.7**	**34335.2**	**77**	**33369.7**	**76.1**	**40244.5**	**76.3**	**48492.1**	**75.9**	**60730.7**	**72.7**	**72562.8**	**70.3**	**82817.8**	**65.5**
	A. Leather and manufactures	1590.2	4.3	1944.4	4.3	1910.1	4.3	1848.3	3.5	2163	3.3	2421.6	2.8	2697.7	2.6	2933.1	2.3
	B. Chemical sand related products	4706.5	12.8	5885.9	13.2	6051.8	13.8	7455.3	14.1	9445.9	14.8	12443.7	14.9	14769.5	14.3	16727.1	13.2
	C. Engineering goods	5152.1	14	6818.6	15.3	6957.8	15.8	9033	17.1	12405.4	19.4	17348.3	20.7	21718.8	21	29079.1	23
	D. Textile and textile products	9822.1	26.7	11285	25.3	10206.5	23.2	11617	22	12791.5	20	13555.6	16.2	16402.1	15.9	17009.7	13.4
	E. Gems and jewellery	7502.3	20.4	7384	16.5	7306.3	16.6	9029.9	17.1	10573.3	16.5	13761.8	16.4	15529.1	15	15585.7	12.3
	F. Handicrafts (excluding handmade carpets)	668.6	1.8	661.5	1.4	549	1.2	785.3	1.4	499.7	0.7	377.4	0.4	462	0.4	371.7	0.2
	G Other manufactured products	272.6	0.7	355.8	0.7	388.3	0.8	475.6	0.9	613.3	0.9	822.3	0.9	983.7	0.9	1111.4	0.8
III.	**Petroleum products**	**38.9**	**0.1**	**1869.7**	**4.1**	**2119.1**	**4.8**	**2576.5**	**4.8**	**3568.4**	**5.5**	**6989.3**	**8.3**	**11639.6**	**11.2**	**18551.9**	**14.6**
IV.	**Others**	**544.9**	**1.4**	**1229.2**	**2.7**	**1174.3**	**2.6**	**1192.3**	**2.2**	**1880.3**	**2.9**	**2262.3**	**2.7**	**2510.7**	**2.4**	**5413.7**	**4.2**
V.	**Total Exports**	**36822.4**	**100**	**44560.3**	**100**	**43826.7**	**100**	**52719.4**	**100**	**63842.6**	**100**	**83535.9**	**100**	**103090.5**	**100**	**126331.1**	**100**

Source: Reserve Bank of India (Mumbai), *Handbook of Statistics on Indian Economy*, various issues.

Table 2
Share of Agricultural Exports in Total Exports

(value in million US $)

Commodity	1991-92	%	1992-93	%	1993-94	%	1994-95	%	1995-96	%	1996-97	%	1997-98	%	1998-99	%
Agriculture and Allied Products	**3202.5**	**17.9**	**3135.8**	**16.9**	**4027.5**	**18.11**	**4226.1**	**16.05**	**6081.9**	**19.13**	**6862.7**	**20.5**	**6626.2**	**18.9**	**6034.5**	**18.2**
1 Tea	491.5	2.75	337.2	1.82	337.7	1.519	310.7	1.18	350.1	1.101	292.1	0.873	504.9	1.44	538.4	1.62
2 Coffee	134.7	0.75	129.9	0.7	173.9	0.782	335.3	1.273	449.3	1.413	401.9	1.201	456.4	1.3	410.7	1.24
3 Rice	306.5	1.72	336.8	1.82	410.2	1.845	384	1.458	1365.7	4.295	893.6	2.67	907	2.59	1492.9	4.49
4 Wheat	51.5	0.29	3.5	0.02	0.1	4E-04	13.5	0.051	109.6	0.345	196.7	0.588	0.1	0	0.3	0
5 Cotton raw including waste	123.7	0.69	62.8	0.34	208.4	0.937	44.5	0.169	60.8	0.191	443.5	1.325	221.1	0.63	49.2	0.15
6 Tobacco	152.9	0.86	163.7	0.88	147	0.661	81.1	0.308	133.6	0.42	213.2	0.637	288	0.82	181.1	0.55
7 Cashew including cashew nut shell liquid	274	1.53	258.5	1.39	334.2	1.503	397.2	1.509	369.9	1.163	362.9	1.084	378.6	1.08	387.8	1.17
8 Spices	151	0.85	135.8	0.73	181.4	0.816	195	0.741	237.2	0.746	338.6	1.012	379.3	1.08	388	1.17
9 Oil meals	373.8	2.09	533.5	2.88	740.9	3.332	572.6	2.175	702.1	2.208	984.6	2.942	924.3	2.64	461.5	1.39
10 Fruits and vegetables	141.6	0.79	107.9	0.58	132.1	0.594	139.1	0.528	157.7	0.496	163	0.487	158.7	0.45	128.4	0.39
11 Processed fruits, juices, miscellaneous	77.3	0.43	78.8	0.43	90.6	0.407	115	0.437	265.4	0.835	307.1	0.918	173.5	0.5	169.5	0.51
12 Marine products	585.2	3.28	601.9	3.25	813.6	3.659	1126.4	4.278	1010.8	3.179	1128.9	3.373	1207.3	3.45	1038.4	3.13
13 Sugar and mollases	63.8	0.36	122.1	0.66	56.8	0.255	19.8	0.075	151.4	0.476	303.6	0.907	68.6	0.2	5.8	0.02
14 Meat and meat preparations	93.6	0.52	88.8	0.48	109.8	0.494	128.3	0.487	187.4	0.589	199.7	0.597	217.5	0.62	187.3	0.56
15 Others	181.4	1.02	174.6	0.94	290.8	1.308	363.6	1.381	530.8	1.669	633.1	1.892	740.9	2.12	595	1.79
Total exports	17865.4	100	18537.2	100	22238	100	26330.5	100	31795	100	33469.7	100	35006.4	100	33218.7	100

	Commodity	1999-00	%	2000-01	%	2001-02	%	2002-03	%	2003-04	%	2004-05	%	2005-06	%	2006-07P	%
	Agriculture and Allied Products	**5608**	**15.2**	**5973.2**	**13.4**	**5901.2**	**13.46**	**6710**	**12.73**	**7533.1**	**11.8**	**8474.7**	**10.14**	**10213.8**	**9.91**	**12514.6**	**9.91**
1	Tea	411.9	1.12	391.5	0.88	360.5	0.823	341.4	0.648	356.3	0.558	409.6	0.49	390.9	0.38	432.3	0.34
2	Coffee	331.1	0.9	259.4	0.58	229.6	0.524	205.4	0.39	236.3	0.37	237.9	0.285	358.8	0.35	435.1	0.34
3	Rice	721.4	1.96	641.8	1.44	665.6	1.519	1204.9	2.285	907	1.421	1506.5	1.803	1405.2	1.36	1555	1.23
4	Wheat	0	0	90.9	0.2	278.9	0.636	363.6	0.69	520.4	0.815	324.9	0.389	125.9	0.12	8	0.01
5	Cotton raw including waste	17.8	0.05	48.4	0.11	9	0.021	10.4	0.02	205.1	0.321	94	0.113	656	0.64	1348.5	1.07
6	Tobacco	232.8	0.63	189.8	0.43	169.4	0.387	211.4	0.401	238.6	0.374	279.2	0.334	300.6	0.29	371.7	0.29
7	Cashew including cashew nut shell liquid	567.9	1.54	449.5	1.01	376.2	0.858	426	0.808	371	0.581	554	0.663	585.8	0.57	553.8	0.44
8	Spices	407.9	1.11	354.1	0.79	313.9	0.716	342.1	0.649	336	0.526	419.1	0.502	477.9	0.46	690.1	0.55
9	Oil meals	378	1.03	447.6	1	474.5	1.083	307.3	0.583	728.7	1.141	707.2	0.847	1101.1	1.07	1216.1	0.96
10	Fruits and vegetables	148.4	0.4	184.6	0.41	221.1	0.504	245.5	0.466	389.9	0.611	398.7	0.477	481.9	0.47	664.3	0.53
11	Processed fruits, juices, miscellaneous	196.9	0.53	288.4	0.65	259.3	0.592	306.7	0.582	305.2	0.478	284.3	0.34	359	0.35	401.5	0.32
12	Marine products	1182.6	3.21	1393.8	3.13	1236.8	2.822	1431.6	2.716	1328.7	2.081	1439.8	1.724	1589.2	1.54	1743.6	1.38
13	Sugar and mollases	9.3	0.03	110.6	0.25	373.6	0.852	374.9	0.711	269	0.421	34.5	0.041	135	0.13	703.8	0.56
14	Meat and meat preparations	189.1	0.51	321.7	0.72	250.2	0.571	284.6	0.54	373.1	0.584	424	0.508	621.2	0.6	716	0.57
15	Others	813.1	2.21	801.2	1.8	682.8	1.558	654.3	1.241	967.8	1.516	1360.9	1.629	1625.3	1.58	1674.7	1.33
	Total exports	36822.4	100	44560.3	100	43827	100	52719.4	100	63843	100	83535.9	100	103091	100	126331	100

Source: Reserve Bank of India (Mumbai), *Handbook of Statistics on Indian Economy*, Various Issues.

Table 3

Share of Principal Agricultural Exports in Total Agricultural and Allied Product Exports, 1991-92 to 2006-07

(value in million US$)

	Commodities	1991-92	%	1992-93	%	1993-94	%	1994-95	%	1995-96	%	1996-97	%	1997-98	%	1998-99	%
1	Tea	491.5	15.3	337.2	10.75	337.7	8.38	310.7	7.35	350.1	5.756	292.1	4.26	504.9	7.62	538.4	8.922
2	Coffee	134.7	4.21	129.9	4.142	173.9	4.32	335.3	7.93	449.3	7.387	401.9	5.86	456.4	6.89	410.7	6.806
3	Rice	306.5	9.57	336.8	10.74	410.2	10.2	384	9.09	1365.7	22.46	893.6	13	907	13.7	1492.9	24.74
4	Wheat	51.5	1.61	3.5	0.112	0.1	0	13.5	0.32	109.6	1.802	196.7	2.87	0.1	0	0.3	0.005
5	Cotton raw including waste	123.7	3.86	62.8	2.003	208.4	5.17	44.5	1.05	60.8	1	443.5	6.46	221.1	3.34	49.2	0.815
6	Tobacco	152.9	4.77	163.7	5.22	147	3.65	81.1	1.92	133.6	2.197	213.2	3.11	288	4.35	181.1	3.001
7	Cashew including cashew nut shell liquid	274	8.56	258.5	8.244	334.2	8.3	397.2	9.4	369.9	6.082	362.9	5.29	378.6	5.71	387.8	6.426
8	Spices	151	4.72	135.8	4.331	181.4	4.5	195	4.61	237.2	3.9	338.6	4.93	379.3	5.72	388	6.43
9	Oil meals	373.8	11.7	533.5	17.01	740.9	18.4	572.6	13.5	702.1	11.54	984.6	14.3	924.3	13.9	461.5	7.648
10	Fruits and vegetables	141.6	4.42	107.9	3.441	132.1	3.28	139.1	3.29	157.7	2.593	163	2.38	158.7	2.4	128.4	2.128
11	Processed fruits, juices, miscellaneous	77.3	2.41	78.8	2.513	90.6	2.25	115	2.72	265.4	4.364	307.1	4.47	173.5	2.62	169.5	2.809
12	Marine products	585.2	18.3	601.9	19.19	813.6	20.2	1126.4	26.7	1010.8	16.62	1128.9	16.4	1207.3	18.2	1038.4	17.21
13	Sugar and mollases	63.8	1.99	122.1	3.894	56.8	1.41	19.8	0.47	151.4	2.489	303.6	4.42	68.6	1.04	5.8	0.096
14	Meat and meat preparations	93.6	2.92	88.8	2.832	109.8	2.73	128.3	3.04	187.4	3.081	199.7	2.91	217.5	3.28	187.3	3.104
15	Others	181.4	5.66	174.6	5.568	290.8	7.22	363.6	8.6	530.8	8.728	633.1	9.23	740.9	11.2	595	9.86
	Agriculture and allied products	3202.5	100	3135.8	100	4027.5	100	4226.1	100	6081.9	100	6862.7	100	6626.2	100	6034.5	100

(value in million US$)

	Commodities	1999-00	%	2000-01	%	2001-02	%	2002-03	%	2003-04	%	2004-05	%	2005-06	%	2006-07 P	%
1	Tea	411.9	7.34	391.5	6.554	360.5	6.11	341.4	5.09	356.3	4.73	409.6	4.83	390.9	3.83	432.3	3.454
2	Coffee	331.1	5.9	259.4	4.343	229.6	3.89	205.4	3.06	236.3	3.137	237.9	2.81	358.8	3.51	435.1	3.477
3	Rice	721.4	12.9	641.8	10.74	665.6	11.3	1204.9	18	907	12.04	1506.5	17.8	1405.2	13.8	1555	12.43
4	Wheat	0.1	0	90.9	1.522	278.9	4.73	363.6	5.42	520.4	6.908	324.9	3.83	125.9	1.23	8	0.064
5	Cotton raw including waste	17.8	0.32	48.4	0.81	9	0.15	10.4	0.15	205.1	2.723	94	1.11	656	6.42	1348.5	10.78
6	Tobacco	232.8	4.15	189.8	3.178	169.4	2.87	211.4	3.15	238.6	3.167	279.2	3.29	300.6	2.94	371.7	2.97
7	Cashew including cashew nut shell liquid	567.9	10.1	449.5	7.525	376.2	6.37	426	6.35	371	4.925	554	6.54	585.8	5.74	553.8	4.425
8	Spices	407.9	7.27	354.1	5.928	313.9	5.32	342.1	5.1	336	4.46	419.1	4.95	477.9	4.68	690.1	5.514
9	Oil meals	378	6.74	447.6	7.493	474.5	8.04	307.3	4.58	728.7	9.673	707.2	8.34	1101.1	10.8	1216.1	9.717
10	Fruits and vegetables	148.4	2.65	184.6	3.09	221.1	3.75	245.5	3.66	389.9	5.176	398.7	4.7	481.9	4.72	664.3	5.308
11	Processed fruits, juices, miscellaneous	196.9	3.51	288.4	4.828	259.3	4.39	306.7	4.57	305.2	4.051	284.3	3.35	359	3.51	401.5	3.208
12	Marine products	1182.6	21.1	1393.8	23.33	1236.8	21	1431.6	21.3	1328.7	17.64	1439.8	17	1589.2	15.6	1743.6	13.93
13	Sugar and mollases	9.3	0.17	110.6	1.852	373.6	6.33	374.9	5.59	269	3.571	34.5	0.41	135	1.32	703.8	5.624
14	Meat and meat preparations	189.1	3.37	321.7	5.386	250.2	4.24	284.6	4.24	373.1	4.953	424	5	621.2	6.08	716	5.721
15	Others	813.1	14.5	801.2	13.41	682.8	11.6	654.3	9.75	967.8	12.85	1360.9	16.1	1625.3	15.9	1674.7	13.38
	Agriculture and Allied Products	5608	100	5973.2	100	5901.2	100	6710	100	7533.1	100	8474.7	100	10214	100	12514.6	100

Sources: Reserve Bank of India (Mumbai), *Handbook of Statistics on Indian Economy*, Various Issues.

Table 4
India's Share in World Agricultural Exports

(per cent)

S. No.	Commodities	1991	1992	1993	1994	1995	1996	1997	1998	1999	2000	2001	2002	2003	2004	2005
1	Tea & mate	18.6	10.52	13.8	13.6	16	11.1	11.9	15.8	18.8	14	13.9	12.6	10.9	10.4	9.6
2	Coffee & its substitutes	1.6	1.25	2.2	2.4	2.8	2.7	2.4	2.6	3.4	2.3	2.6	2.3	2.4	1.8	2.5
3	Rice	7.6	3.39	8.6	6.6	18.9	12	12.6	15.9	20.1	10.2	8.4	18.1	12.5	16.4	15.8
4	Tobacco & its manufactures	2.3	0.38	0.7	0.4	0.6	0.3	0.7	1.5	2.4	0.7	0.7	0.7	0.8	0.9	0.9
5	Spices	8.7	64.1	10.1	9.1	9.3	11.2	11	11.4	2.8	10.3	10.3	8.5	7.7	8.2	NA
6	Feeding stuff for animals	2.3	2.51	4.2	3.1	3.4	3.7	4	2.3	0.7	2.3	2.1	1.4	2.8	2.4	3.7
7	Fruits and vegetables	0.7	0.7	1	1.7	1	1	0.9	0.9	1	1.3	1.2	1.1	1.1	1.1	1.4
8	Fish & its preparations	1.5	1.78	3.2	2.7	2	2.3	2.3	2.3	2.4	2.7	2.7	2.6	2.2	2.1	2.3
9	Suger and honey	0	0.5	0.4	0.2	0.8	2	1.6	0.1	0.1	0.9	0	2.4	1.6	0.3	0.8
10	Meat & its preparations	0.3	0.19	0.3	0.3	0.4	0.3	0.4	0.4	0.5	0.7	0.7	0.6	0.7	0.6	0.8
11	Ceraels & its preparations	0.9	0.33	1	0.9	2.7	1.6	2.1	2.6	3	1.5	1.4	2.8	2.4	2.9	2.5
12	Oilseeds & oleaginous fruit	0.8	0.2	0.8	0.7	1.2	1.1	1.1	0.8	1	1.7	1.5	0.9	1.7	1.3	1.4
	Total export	**0.4**	**0.6**	**0.6**	**0.6**	**0.6**	**0.7**	**0.6**	**0.6**	**0.6**	**0.7**	**0.7**	**0.8**	**0.86**	**0.9**	**1.1**

Source: Government of India, Ministry of Finance (New Delhi) , Economic Survey, various issues.

Table 5

Growth and Instability of Principal Groups 1991-92 to 2006-07

(per cent)

S. No.	Groups	1991-92 to 1998-99		1999-00 to 2006-07		1991-92 to 2006-07	
		G	I	G	I	G	I
1	Primary Products	11.11	1.61	17.97	1.07	9.13	2.13
2	Manufactured Products	11.61	0.88	16.59	0.72	12.01	1.03
3	Petroluem Products	-12.88	8.26	95.26	12.9	28.99	17.96
4	Others	15.62	2.81	30.04	3.22	24.19	3.66
5	Total Exports	11.22	0.94	19.47	0.8	12.46	1.33

Source: *Handbook of Statistics on Indian Economy*, RBI, Various Issues.

Table 6
Growth Rates and Instability Indices of Indian Agricultural Exports 1991-92 to 2006-07

(per cent)

S. No.	Items	Annual Compound Growth Rate			Instability Index		
		1991-98	1999-2006	1991-2006	1991-98	1999-2006	1991-2006
	Agriculture and allied products	**12.82**	**11.97**	**7.42**	**1.67**	**0.91**	**1.91**
1	Tea	2.82	0.904	0.47	4.22	1.43	3.01
2	Coffee	22.27	4.06	3.12	4.73	4.55	7.17
3	Rice	26.34	14.61	9.36	5.06	2.69	5.74
4	Wheat	-29.15	48.33	0.24	216.63	72.25	108.82
5	Cotton raw including waste	2.91	88.71	5.11	19.33	26.2	31.98
6	Tobacco	6.92	8.94	5.91	7	2.87	4.94
7	Cashew including cashew nut shell liquid	5.52	2.61	4.23	1.78	3.13	2.46
8	Spices	17.86	7.44	8.47	2.06	3.34	3.76
9	Oil meals	6.48	19.18	2.52	5	4.23	6.34
10	Fruits and vegetables	2.4	23.19	10.72	2.71	1.45	4.72
11	Processed fruits, juices, miscellaneous	18.05	7.85	10.45	7.66	2	5.42
12	Marine products	10.47	4.57	6.09	2.41	0.94	1.98
13	Sugar and mollases	-13.94	32.76	9.96	31.19	27.45	29.51
14	Meat and meat preparations	14.68	18.78	13.4	3	2.83	3.18
15	Others	24.27	14.06	14.28	3.48	3.16	3.92

Source: Reserve Bank of India (Mumbai), *Handbook of Statistics on Indian Economy*, 2007.

References

Balassa, B. (1978), "Exports and Economic Growth: Further Evidence", *Journal of Development Economics*, 5(2): 181-189.

Chand, Ramesh and S. C. Tewari (1991), "Growth and Instability of Indian Exports and Imports of Agricultural Commodities", *Indian Journal of Agricultural Economics*, 46(2): 159-165.

Coppock, J. D. (1962), *International Economic Instability*, New York: McGraw Hill.

Dattatreyalu, M. (1987), "India's Agricultural Exports", *Foreign Trade Review*, 22: 302-28.

_____, (1994), "Export Potential of Agricultural Commodities in the New Economic Environment", *Foreign Trade Review*, 29(1): 84-103.

Ghatak, S. and K. Ingersent (1984), *Agriculture and Economic Development*, Select Bank Service Syndicate, New Delhi.

Government of India, *Economic Survey*, Controller of Publication, New Delhi (various issues).

Goyal, S. K., R. N. Pandey and J. P. Singh (2000), "India's Agricultural Exports: Growth and Instability", *Foreign Trade Review*, 35(1): 32-46.

Krueger, A. (1989), "Asian Trade and Growth Lessons", *American Economic Review*, 80(2): 108-12.

Pal, Suresh (1992), "Agricultural Exports of India: Issues of Growth and Instability", *Indian Journal of Agricultural Economics*, 47(2): 185-193.

Pursell, Garry and Ashok Gulati (1993), "Liberalizing Indian Agriculture: An Agenda for Reforms", World Bank Working Paper, Policy Research Department, The World Bank, Washington.

Reserve Bank of India (RBI), *Handbook of Statistics on Indian Economy*, Mumbai (Various Issues).

Sengupta, S. K. (1986), *Export Prospects of Cereal, Fruits and Vegetables*, A Report by Federation of Indian Chamber of Commerce and Industry, Delhi.

Sharan, Vyuptakesh (1984), "Instability in Export Earnings, Export Concentration and India", *Foreign Trade Review*, 19: 143-50.

World Bank (1987), *World Development Report*, New York: Oxford University Press.

Chapter 6

Globalization and Gender: How to Move towards Gender Equality?

— Shilpi Tiwari and Shaily Tiwari

Abstract

Globalization has come into use in Asia in the last 10 years. It indicates that the world now is more interconnected than it was before. It has brought changes in the global economy-notably rapid movements of large volumes of money, increased volume of trade, through ICT. It has further helped to bridge the gender inequalities in employment and economic status of Asian women especially in India. The present paper aims to focus on these aspects and strengths of globalization and IT sector in bridging the gender disparities by increasing the technical education opportunities and IT accessibility to women. This paper is divided into five sections. In the first introductory section we made an attempt to discuss the relationship between globalization role of ICT and gender. The second section discusses review of gender and ICT current scenario. It will be followed by importance of ICT for women empowerment. The third section discusses the options that are available to reduce the inequalities-minimizing the damages of globalization and maximizing the opportunities of globalization. The third section discusses interstate pattern of expenditure on health and family welfare. The fourth section discusses the current situation of women and ICT providing illustrations of Asia and India. The last section of conclusion (5th) makes some specific suggestions and recommendations regarding the courses of action to ensure such an outcome.

Introduction

Globalization is a controversial term being defined in different ways. It has come into use in the last ten years. In fact it makes us wonder what is this force that has emerged on planet Earth to attract such attention? It indicates that the world now is more interconnected than it was before. It is a result of changes in the global economy—notably rapid movements of large volumes of money and increased volume of trade as well as changes in communications and in information technology. These trends are related in turn with a variety of political, cultural and educational changes. Globalization integrates the world economy through more trade and intensified factor mobility. Movement of people from one country to another links them to distant localities in such a way that local happening are shaped and in turn shape events occurring miles away (Giddens, 1994). Globalization implies weakening of the restrictions imposed by or inherent in a nation state. The 19th century had seen the weakening of the national barriers, as the movement of goods services, capital, and labour are much easier. The 20th century saw progressive liquidation of the colonialism and corresponding rise in the powers of the nation and state. We find that the mainsprings of globalization during this period were development in IT, which contributed more than anything else to the emergence of a "global village".

The UK Government's white paper on globalization of December 2000 highlighted, making globalization to work for the poor—aims to address—"there is no alternative" to globalization and we must learn to live with it. Not only that globalization creates unprecedented new opportunities for sustainable development and poverty reduction. This paper also recognizes that globalization poses threats to employment and livelihood and more intensive impact on the weaker sections and to the human security in general. However, we must have to learn how to live with it.

The UNDP's Human Development Report further substantiates this point and states that the public health has declined, it can be seen in the spread of aids, there is increasing environmental degradation, there is underemployment or unemployment which now accounts for one-third of the labour force of the world—one billion people according to ILO as the relevance of education, type of education in demand has changed drastically. Education is undergoing constant changes under the effects of globalization. The structure of education is being altered to enable it to compete in an open, global market, leading to the modification of education. Education institutions around the world are being forced to compete globally, by engaging in entrepreneurial activities to sustain themselves in an uncertain and competitive world. The strongest arms of the globalization are privatization and information technology. As women education and gender disparity in education in developing countries are already a major problem this has added fuel to the problem.

For women in Asia, given the skewed distribution of resources within households and communities, that makes not just access to health, but often basic survival itself and struggle. Female literacy in many Asian countries has always been lower in enrolment of higher education than boys. Thus the gender inequality, is already exists in Asia. Privatization of higher education and the introduction of self-financed courses in colleges and universities can be seen as the major impact of globalization on women. A high fee structure in private institutes and self-financed course would be detrimental to women taking admission at the tertiary level education. The already existing gender inequalities have reinforced more forcibly. Thus entry of women in technical education is becoming much difficult as a result the job opportunities for them are also shrinking.

Gender and ICT—Current Scenario

The present content of theoretical proposition is that the impact of globalization on gender is explicit and geared to gender discrimination and inequalities in terms of access to and control newly emerging forms of employment, especially in the IT and service sectors, the semiskilled or the unskilled ones have lost the control over their natural recourses (land, etc.), resulting in the loss of traditional livelihood and sustainability. Under such climate of economic transition towards global economy, the moot issue remains "the status of women" in changing labour market and how the contemporary capital and labour operate in the context of globalization from a feminist perspective, more so, the dynamics of power and capital distribution exerting gender discrepancies that are otherwise left invisible in the "male stream of theoretical" discourse.

While probing the above issues, the underlying assumption is that women have never received equal treatment of homogeneous category and, when united as gender, other factors like: class, ethnicity, religion have further divided them in terms of the age, ideology and sexual preferences. One has to keep these differences in mind while talking about "globalization and women" as indeed, one woman's forte might be another woman's loss. For instance, in the case of female migrant domestic helper in the countries like Middle East and Europe, an housewife gets service from a migrant domestic maid at the cost of exploiting "her" wages and working hours or sex (Ceilina, 2000). Therefore, it remains an illusive concept of economic "freedom" as described by the advocates of globalization and neo-liberalization who assert that women are expected to enter in many new job opportunities in new economic era, whereas the reality depicts that emerging new work opportunities laid out to them generate further exploitations and vulnerability.

In the service industries of banking, finance, and insurance, women are concentrated at the lower and less skilled employment levels. In India, for example, women made up 70% of the banking workforce by the middle of the last decade. Women's employment in the telecommunications industry in Malaysia reflects similar percentages. However, they tend to be data entry clerks, computer typists, or tellers. The percentages of women in electronic data processing and in management are low, ranging from one to 12% in India. According to Nancy Hafkin and Nancy Taggart in their study entitled "Gender, Information Technology and Developing Countries: An Analytical Study", although IT is a new field; a "gendered" division of labour is already emerging. In general, women tend to be concentrated in end-user, lower skilled IT jobs related to word processing or data entry, comprising only small percentages of managerial, maintenance, and design personnel in networks, operating systems, or software development. In brief the impact on women is mixed, i.e.:

1. The trade openness increased the share of women's paid employment but they are also the first to lose their jobs when economic crunches occur.
2. Women predominate informal subcontracting, which is on the rise, but this is associated with low wages and poor working conditions.

Thus, women also predominately prefer home based part- and tele-work that accommodates family care obligations but these jobs are precarious and poorly paid. But how to make this weakness into strength for the women is a major problem. In this context, in the following section we tried to discuss the Asian scenario by focusing on India illustatrtions.

Globalization in Asia with Special Focus on ICT India

Globalization refers to the international flow of goods, capital, labour, services, information, which has occurred in response to improved transport and limitless revolution in communication technologies, and the regulatory policies/economy restructuring policies adopted in many countries during the past two decades by realizing as the economy restructuring as a path for economic development. At first, the development paths adopted were just four Asian tigers. The next were South East Asian countries, which experienced very rapid growth of development and employment during last decade. Thailand, Indonesia, Malaysia and China also now join them. In the past few years the Philippines, and even Bangladesh have shown interest to follow them. This process of restructuring has made the nations to liberalize, and then privatize and globalize (LPG). The reforms in these countries are related to information technology, trade, industry financial, fiscal, agriculture sectors. These reforms have made tremendous impact on education and training either directly or indirectly. In some cases, it had a lethal effect and in some cases, it has done miracles and experienced rapid economic growth.

1. The trade openness increased the share of women's paid employment but they are also the first to lose their jobs when economic crunches occur.
2. Women predominate informal subcontracting, which is on the rise, but this is associated with low wages and poor working conditions.

IT could simply defined as "Technology to exploit information the most efficient way", it comprises computer science, telecommunications, electronics and computer applications. This also includes artificial intelligence, Robotics, numerically controlled machines, computer integrated manufacturing (CIM) Computer aided designs, etc..

Now India is beginning to see the culture of innovations and magic in hi-tech. The IT magic after globalization has not only made the software sector as one of the high value-addition and net foreign exchange earning industries, but has created a history of sort in the Indian stock exchanges. The strengths of the capacity of IT to generate, foreign exchange and employment has already caught the imagination of Indian businessmen, citizens, economists, educationists, planners and politicians. Thus globalization has made many changes in Asia in the last 10 years. It indicates that the world now is more interconnected than it was before. It is a result of changes in the global economy—notably rapid movements of large volumes of money, increased volume of trade as well as change in communication and information technology in each of these sectors. Last decade of economic reforms has touched different sectors, ranging from agriculture to international trade. Thus, there is an up rise of demand for IT related education. As a result e-learning centers, corporate universities, abundant computer coaching institutions, technical institutions and engineering institutions have grown tremendously in many parts of Asia particularly in India. Moreover, functioning of the government offices, in agriculture, education, industrial and business sector has also drastically changed. Many innovative IT related changes were taken place in these sectors. These changes has yielded better results and led to digital empowerment. However, the gender inequalities already existing gender inequalities in education and employment were aggravated by the process of globalization and the new technology movement., Thus in the context to explore how weakness of globalization can be made as strengths for women empowerment and reduce gender inequalities is discussed in this paper. Few illustrations of India are discussed below.

The Indian IT Industry and Women Employment (Illustration from India)

There are several employment opportunities in IT for young women who have had education and training in urban, English medium schools. The IT enabled services centres offer several opportunities to women. The IT enabled services require excellent verbal communication skills and pleasing personality. Data entry/data conversion needs typing conversion and strong written English communication skills. Medical transcription requires a good understanding of medical terminology, ability to understand English with different accents and good typing speed. Entry-level salaries range from Rs.3,000-10,000 a month. After four to five years of experience, medical transcriptions can look forward to Rs.14,000-

20,000 a month. The same is true for other jobs in this field. The age of entry is between 19-24 years. The minimum qualifications required are class 12. Call centres prefer women as they feel that women are better suited to voice-based projects.

A large number of women are joining the IT enabled services sector (Ramani, S. 2000). A large number of companies as GE, American Express, Standard Chartered Bank, Citibank, British Airways, Microsoft, AOL Time Warner, HP, Dell Computers, Prudential Insurance, Morgan Stanley, Mark & Spencer have call centres where a sizeable number of women are employed ranging from 35 to 65% (www.express it people.com). GE capital had 40 to 55% women employees in their various centres (Sandhya Sule, 2002). A study of an international call centre at Pune (Dutta, 2003) showed that 59% of employees were women.

As per NASSCOM estimates, women comprise 20-25% of total number of science and engineering graduates in the country. The number of software professionals has been rising continuously over the years. The number of software professionals increased from 6,800 in 1985 to 650,000 in 2003-2004 (NASSCOM, 2004). Women are joining the IT sector and their numbers are fast increasing in India.

In 1993, only 10% of workforce was women. In 1998, 18% of IT workforce was women, which was higher than the national average of 12%. In 2003, the proportion increased to 21%. The participation of women in IT is rapidly growing and is expected to go up to 35% in 2005. Hence, women are now occupying a prominent position in the labour force.

Women in India are employed in IT companies located mainly in cities as Bangalore, Poona, Chennai, Delhi , Hyderabad and Mumbai. More women are employed in southern regions of the country, where hiring of professionals was 41 percent as compared to eastern region at 6 per cent (NASSCOM, 2003). The women employed in IT belong to the younger age group. The overall median age of software professionals was about 25.6 years. 44 per cent of software professionals possessed over 3 years of work experience (NASSCOM, 2003).

Due to IT, women have employment options as flexitiming and work at home concept. Tele-tech India , a joint venture BPO company between Tele-tech and the Bharti Group, gives its employees a choice of four-day weeks instead of the normal five, hourly rates with a minimum number of work hours in a week. There are incentives for housewives and other part-time workers for 30-hour weeks.

Mumbai-based Datamatics Technologies, a BPO which processes data, women to work from home, 20 hours a week. This facilitates employment for married women, especially with small children. The employee strength is over 800 part-time workers as compared to only 500 permanent employees. Tracmail, a Mumbai-based business process outsourcing (BPO) company employs 2,000 people of which roughly 45 per cent of them are women who work 8.5 hour shifts, attending calls from clients across the world. A BPO company, Infowavz International, has one-third of its 800 employees as women. 24 × 7 Customer Service, a company based in Bangalore employs women in large numbers where the share of women employees increased from 25 per cent to 40 per cent in the last two years. ICICI OneSource, a company based in Mumbai has 2,400 employees, of which 60 per cent are women, in the age group of 22 to 27 years. There are more women employees in call centres in north and western India.

Workforce trends show that a large number of women are joining the ICT sector. What is the position of women in newly emerging areas of information technology? Has ICT provided suitable employment opportunities to women leading to women empowerment? The main objective of this paper is to examine the different ways in which in IT has benefited women in terms of employment. However, the extension of the market economy can have both positive and negative effects for women's situation and gender relations. Positive effects may include increased employment opportunities for women in non-traditional sectors, thus enabling them to earn and control income. This is potentially empowering and may contribute to enhancing women's capacity to negotiate their role and status within the household and society. Negative effects can include increased exploitation and dependency on direct engagement with the market and particularly on the vagaries of the market. In the past two decades, the relocation of labour intensive industries from advanced market economies to middle income developing economies has increased employment of women in the latter. Even though female employment remains concentrated mainly in low skill sectors and the gender wage gap shows no signs of disappearing, the rapid increase in the female labour force participation rate has a considerable positive effect on women's economic well being and that of their families. Nevertheless, the issue of the poor conditions under which many women enter the labour market needs to be consistently raised. The problem is particularly acute in sweatshops in the informal sector, which through arrangements such as sub-contracting and outsourcing became an integral part of the formal economy and has experienced an explosive growth in recent years. In the developed countries, on the other hand, as industries relocate elsewhere in search of cheaper labour and production, labour demand has been shifting towards relatively high-skill manufacturing, while employment growth in traditionally low skill sectors such as relatively low-skill sectors in textiles and apparel, where women workers predominate, has been declining. The impact of these trends as observed, in both developing and developed countries, on gender relations is still not too clear. Evidence from around the world on women's labour market participation and gender inequalities (e.g., wage gap, power relations, etc.) is still mix.

Importance of ICT for Women Empowerment

The present day is witnessing a rapid change from an industrial to a knowledge based global economy. A highly skilled labour force is the key to success in the knowledge economy (Skyrme 1997; Stiglitz

1999). In the knowledge era, "information technology" serves an integrated factor of production. The information and communication technologies have reduced the globe to a village. These technologies have created new opportunities for scientific progress, economic development, education and social change.

The IT industry has gained the status of the fastest growing industry all over the world. In Asia particularly India too, the IT sector has come to occupy a prominent position. The contribution of ICT is significant in terms of income and earnings, growth and employment generation (NASSCOM, 2002). An abundant pool of skilled manpower has facilitated the rapid growth of IT industry in India. Hence, the IT workforce has come to occupy an important role in the economy.

ICT has profound gender implications for both men and women in employment, education, training and other productive and personal development areas of life. What becomes clear from these discussions and case studies is that access for rural women will depend critically on where the technologies are located. The most efficient and beneficial use of ICTs is closely related to the kind of information produced and distributed, that is, information that directly supports women's activities and responsibilities. In order to facilitate access for women from various classes and sectors, ICTs will need to be located in places which women frequent and to which they have open and equal access, such as health centres, women's NGOs, women's employment centres and perhaps even places of worship. When women can understand and experience the benefits of ICTs, they are quick to use such technologies. Establishing telecommunication canters in local communities is also a potentially useful strategy, if gender obstacles to access to them by women are taken into account. Information production and distribution strategies will also be an important consideration in order to make the most of each point of access. They will need to be flexible, mixed media and multi-technology systems in order to reach the greatest number of women effectively. Further consideration should also be given to the social background of women. For example, because girls in many developing countries tend to leave formal education earlier than boys. Technical education should be started at an early level of education.

There are several opportunities arising for women out of the globalization of technologies: one among ICT biotechnology which can make some of the traditional farming role of women redundant leading to unemployment particularly among older and rural women. Imported biotechnologies are not always relevant to the needs and traditions of the communities but they can make it possible to codify and transfer some of the unmodified knowledge of local women to the global market. However, if uncompensated, the move deprives women the economic gains and royalty they should be entitled to. To make the most out of globalization, we must manage globalization better so that its downside is minimized and its benefits maximized.

The second opportunity is relocated service sector jobs from high-wage countries. A combination of personal computers, cheap software, and cost-effective connectivity has given rise to networking technologies. These networking technologies are bringing new job opportunities for women in vast numbers in the region particularly in English speaking countries, such as India and the Philippines. A wide range of service sector jobs (e.g., medical transcription, data entry, geographical information systems, back office clerical jobs, airlines ticketing, and customer care services) can be and are being located from high-wage OECD to low-wage Asian countries that have a steady pool of high quality women workers. These relocated jobs are called Remote Processing. Women are getting a substantial proportion (nearly 20%) of relocated software services in the region—in India, the figure is 20%; the figure is comparable in the Philippines. As it takes up a smaller amount of capital to start up businesses in remote processing work, women find new opportunities in self-employment as sub-contractors of global corporations.

Conclusions and Policy Implications

The advent of globalization and IT can change the concept of work, especially for women. It is expected that more women will enter this sector as the new emerging trend could allow women to work from home with Internet and telecom connectivity. Flexi timings and work at home would enable more women to join the labour force. It has been observed that companies like Datamatics have adopted this policy and it has proved to be a great success. Similarly, other companies should also use this policy. The concept of part time work will also go a long way in helping women. There should be provision of child care support as day care centres and crèches also. All these factors will go a long way in benefiting women. Women also predominately prefer home based, part- and tele-work that accommodates family care obligations but these jobs are precarious and poorly paid. But how to make this weakness into strength for the women is a major problem. It can be by improving technical education facilities for women or introducing technical education/ ICT related courses for girls at early stage might help to women certain extent. As we have seen in the case of India and Asian increase of women in IT related jobs and contributing to the family and national income. To reduce the gender disparities and empower the women. Women should form a significant portion of labour force. To help women, policies should be undertaken as to increase women's access to computers and internet. There should be provisions for setting up of more women's only access sites. Efforts should be directed towards improving women's skills and usage of new technology.

It is also found from the several studies that there is a wide gap between computer education and absorption in the labour market. This is due to the fact there is restricted mobility for women. Timings of work are also a problem for women. Factors as marriage, childbirth, childrearing and household responsibilities may prevent women from working full-time. Policies should be made to subsidise childcare. Transport facilities should be provided to women. If women had a break from work, there should be provisions for retraining in industry.

Steps should be taken to encourage women employees.

Noteworthy examples are companies such as Infosys, Wipro and I-flex of India. The Infosys Women Inclusivity Network (IWIN), conducts networking and mentoring sessions along with initiating policies, benefits and training via the group and there is a similar initiative within Wipro, called Women of Wipro (WOW). I-flex Solutions ensures that women are encouraged to join I-flex by having a woman representative on most its employment panels and has also run women-focused recruitment advertising campaigns.

References

Agarwal, R.(2000): Educated Women in the Urban Labour Market: A Study of Career Mobility Patterns of Women Professionals in Information Technology. Ph.D. Thesis. Zakir Hussain Centre for Educational Studies, School of Social Sciences, Jawaharlal Nehru University, New Delhi, Business Standard (2003). Calling on Women, more and more, *Business Standard*, 18 june, http://www.tracmail.com/news.asp?

Dutta, 2003): A Study of an International Call Centre.

Dong-Sook, S. Gills: Economic Globalization and Women in Asia: Challenges and Responses (http://www.isanet.org/noarchive/gills.html).

Mishra, P.(2003): Call Centre Jobs are not Monotonous, http://www. globaljusticecenter. org/papers2005 www.express% 20 it%20 people.com.

Nasscom (2004), "Knowledge Professional", National Association of Software and Services Companies, http://www.nasscom.org.

Solita Monsod Professor, University of the Philippines: Globalization: Challenges and Opportunities.

Ramani, S.(2000): IT-enabled Services: Growing Forms of Telework, E & PW, June 24.

Chapter 7

FDI and Globalization in India

— Babita Agrawal

Abstract

The Indian economy opened up in 1991 within the framework of liberal economic reforms. FDI inflows were stimulated in industry and services, so benefiting from the many comparative advantages of the country (human resources, emerging market). In 2004, FDI inflows officially amounted to US $ 5.3 billion. They mainly came from the United States and Mauritius and concerned industrial sectors.

In parallel, some Indian firms started to grow in importance and to invest abroad: they had the financial means, experience, and ambition to acquire international recognition and they were encouraged by the Indian government. FDI issued by Indian firms amounted to more than US $2 billion in 2004; it was principally addressed to developing countries and to Russia, however, the share of industrialized countries was on the rise, and manufacturing and non financial sectors accounted for the bulk of it.

Introduction

This paper focuses on FDI (foreign direct investment) as a vector of

Indian globalization. Recently, not only did India become a more frequent destination for FDI, but also, many Indian firms started to invest abroad on a very large scale with, sometimes, some stunning takeovers in industrialized countries. The reforms undertaken since 1991 in India have unleashed the potential growth of the economy and stimulated international trade, outsourcing and FDI. Changes have been so many that investors have started to take a fresh look at India. At the same time, some Indian firms have become global players.

India: A Latecomer to FDI

India's share in world FDI is minor, notably when considering its size. Indeed, the opening of the country is relatively new and the history of its FDI on a large scale very short.

Low Amounts of FDI

At first sight, India appears to be an "underperformer" as far as FDI is concerned. In India, as in most developing countries, inward and outward FDI are not easy to analyse because they are generally low and fluctuating. Data relating to FDI inflows (and probably to outflows as well) are underestimated because of their national definition and interpretation. The Reserve Bank of India (RBI) and the Secretariat for Industrial Assistance (SIA) which officially publish statistics have, since 1991, only reported the equity component of FDI. So, reinvested earnings[1] have not been taken into consideration while IMF[2] guidelines estimate they are part of FDI inflows. Indian data include neither the proceeds of foreign equity listings nor foreign subordinated loans to domestic subsidiaries. Overseas commercial borrowings are also disregarded, as well as some depository receipts over 10 per cent of the equity coming from foreign institutional investors (Srivastava, 2003). So,

1. That is, the part of foreign investor profits that are not distributed to shareholders as dividends and reinvested in the affiliates in the host country.
2 International Monetary Fund.

there is a lot of scope for improving India's FDI statistics in order to put them in line with international standards.

Officially, at the end of 2004, India's stocks of inward FDI amounted to US $38.7 bn, that is, only 0.4% of world stocks, and 1.7% of investments received by developing countries. These stocks represented 5.9% of Gross Domestic Product (GDP) in 2004, a very small ratio compared with developing countries average (26.4%). We notice however that Indian stocks were 23 times greater in 2004 than in 1990. In 2004, India held the 15th slot in terms of inward FDI stock among developing economies (WIR, 2005).

Table 1
FDI Inward Stock

(US $ billion)

	1990	2000	2004
World	1769	5781	8895
Developing Economies	364	1734	2226
India	1.7	17.5	38.7

Source: WIR, several years.

If the Indian position in world outward FDI is not very high, it has increased rapidly since 2000. At the end of 2004, India issued $6 bn of FDI. Indian stocks amounted to 1% of GDP in 2004, far from the average observed in developing countries (12.7%).

Table 2
FDI Outward Stock

(US $ billion)

	1990	2000	2004
World	1785	6148	9732
Developing Economies	147	869	1036
India	0.1	1.9	6.6

Source: WIR, several years.

Though Indian outward FDI was very low, growth has been very impressive, notably since 2000. In 2004, India held the 16th slot in terms of outward FDI stock among developing economies (and the 12th if we exclude tax havens such as Virgin Islands, Cayman Islands, Panama, and Bermuda) (WIR, 2005).

FDI is Gathering Momentum

The analysis of FDI inflows and outflows corroborates the trends previously observed as to their weakness, but it also points out the boom of Indian investments abroad since 2000. FDI received by India is quite recent: 42.4% of it has been carried out since 2001, with a year on year increase of 26.5 % in 2003 and of 23.3% in 2004. In 2004, FDI reached a record level of US $5.3 bn, and India held the 7th rank among developing countries to attract foreign investors (behind China, Hong Kong, Brazil, Mexico, Singapore, South Korea, and Chile).

Though the share of world investment received by India remains weak (0.6% on average over the period 1992-1997, 0.7% in 2003 and 0.8% in 2004), it is increasing. Furthermore, if we take account of distortions of data formerly mentioned, actual FDI is higher than officially assessed. If we only add reinvested earnings by foreign firms, FDI inflows have to be increased by about 1.8 billion US dollars in 2003 and in 2004. So, India would have received about 7 billion dollars of FDI in 2004.

Table 3
FDI Inflows

(US $ billion)

	1992-97*	1998	1999	2000	2001	2002	2003	2004
World	310.9	690.9	1086.7	1387.9	817.6	716.1	632.6	648.1
Developing economies	118.6	194.0	231.9	252.4	219.7	155.5	166.3	233.2
India	1.7	2.6	2.2	2.3	3.4	3.4	4.3	5.3

*Annual average.

Source: WIR 2004 and others.

The growing trend in FDI inflows is also pushed by greenfield investments. The amount of Greenfield FDI has risen by 82.8% in 2003 with 457 projects, and by 50% in 2004 with 685 projects (WIR,

2005). As for the M&As by foreign firms, they amounted to 949 million dollars in 2003 and to 1,760 million dollars in 2004 (WIR, 2005).

Table 4

Cross-border Mergers & Acquisitions in India

(US $ million)

Year	1997	1998	1999	2000	2001	2002	2003	2004
Sales	1.520	361	1.044	1.219	1.037	1.698	949	1.760

Source: WIR 2004 and 2005.

Data available for 2005 lets us suppose that FDI received by India is on an ascendant trend: it increased by 35% over the period April-October 2005, thus approaching the target of 7.5 billion dollars in 2005-06, set by Mr Kamal Nath Commerce Minister[3] (IBEF, Feb. 2006).

Table 5

FDI Flows as a Percentage of GFCF in 2004

	Inward	Outward
India	3,3%	1,4%
China	8,2%	0,2%
Developing countries	10,5%	4,2%

Source: WIR 2005.

Indian FDI outflows surged to 2.2 billion dollars in 2004; it was a record level. Indeed, if it represents only 0.3% of world FDI outflows and 2.6% of outflows issued by developing countries, the progression of Indian investments has been really spectacular since 2002 when they reached 1.1 billion dollars, while they amounted to around 100 million dollars during the previous years.

---

3 With auto and mining sectors expected to attract huge funds.

Table 6
FDI Outflows

(US $ billion)

	1992-97*	1998	1999	2000	2001	2002	2003	2004
world	3238.2	687.2	1092.2	1186.8	721.5	652.2	616.9	730.2
Developing economies	51.3	53.4	75.5	98.9	59.8	47.8	29.0	83.2
India	0.09	0.04	0.07	0.15	0.12	1.1	0.9	2.2

*Annual average.

Source: WIR 2004 and others.

Indian FDI outflows issued in 2002, 2003, and 2004 represented two-thirds of Indian stocks of FDI at the end of 2004. In 2004, Indian FDI outflows amounted to 1.4% of the Gross Fixed Capital Formation: it was less that the average in developing countries (4.2%), but more than the ratio prevailing in a country such as China (0.2%). In 2004, India held the 7th rank among developing countries for its investments in foreign countries (behind Hong Kong, Singapore, Brazil, Taiwan, South Korea and Mexico). It is particularly interesting to put in parallel the evolution of Indian FDI inflows and outflows.

Chart I
FDI: Inflows and Outflows (bn US $)

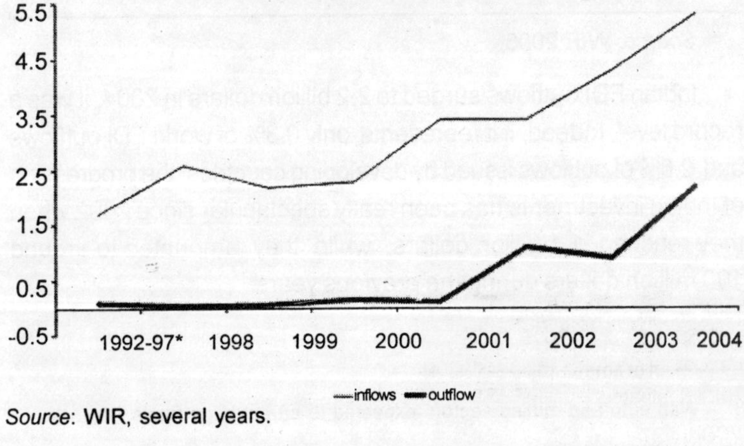

Source: WIR, several years.

India received 5.3 billion US dollars of FDI in 2004, but it issued 2.2 billion US dollars of FDI abroad: so the later represented 41.5% of the former. This is quite an astonishing result, as in developing countries FDI outflows are generally very low. That shows that Indian firms are going global very rapidly. Furthermore, it is very likely that FDI outflows are underestimated (UNCTAD, 2005), either for fiscal reasons, or because the Indian firms investing abroad under declare the amounts they invest.

India was Kept Out of World FDI until 2000 but It is Becoming a Global Player

Several reasons can explain the "weakness" of inward and outward FDI registered until recently. Being a developing country with very low GDP per capita, many illiterate people and poor infrastructures, India could not attract FDI. On the one hand, developing countries only attract foreign investors when they own raw materials or natural resources, but that was not the case with India. On the other hand, Indian firms stayed confined in their country to do business because they had neither opportunities nor financial and technical means to invest abroad and because such operations were not really well regarded by the government.

Furthermore, India implemented after its independence (1947), an inward looking strategy including planning, nationalizations, an import substitution policy, where tax structure was complex and FDI conditionally tolerated (for internal needs and with minority shares). Indeed, some industrial partnerships were historically concluded between Indian firms and TNCs: Tata and Daimler Benz in the 1950's, Bajaj and Piaggio (Vespa) in 1960 and Kawasaki in 1983; also Mahindra formerly collaborated with International Harvester and American Motors, Modi with Continental and Xerox, ... However Coca-Cola and IBM were expelled from India by Indira Gandhi in 1973, because they did not want to reduce their ownership stake to 40%. The success of the first JV established in 1984 between an Indian and a foreign firm (Maruti and Suzuki) was not really welcome, even if it is now considered a great success.

If some measures of de-licensing were taken in 1985 and 1986 by Rajiv Gandhi, it is mainly in 1991 that Indian opening to foreign investment occurred, in parallel with the liberalization of the economy. Private and foreign firms were permitted to invest in activities previously reserved for the public sector. FDI was allowed not only for the domestic market but also for exports; investment ceilings where raised, policy environment and procedures were significantly simplified and streamlined[4], and FDI abroad by Indian firms became also conditionally possible. That was finally beneficial to the Indian economy which started to emerge progressively, with, however, inertia.

Liberalizing has been combined with world globalization, thus benefiting from the international context of deregulation, lower transport costs and rapid expansion of internet. Growing international labour division and the fragmentation of TNCs also proved beneficial. Since 2000, India has kept pace with some of the more conspicuous developing countries, such as the Asian Dragons, Brazil and China. India is a more and more active partner in regional arrangements and agreements such as ASEAN[5], Gulf Cooperation Council, BIMSTEC[6], South Asia Free Trade Area, Indian Ocean Rim Association for Regional Cooperation, SAARC[7]. . . . In addition, India has signed, since 2000, many bilateral investment and trade agreements as well as double taxation treaties with an increasing number of countries (notably with other developing countries, but not exclusively): that stimulated exports and investments, all the more because, in parallel, the opening of the country was confirmed (elimination of many quotas, reduction of customs duties[8]).

---

4 Until 1992, all foreign investments in India and the repatriation of foreign capital required prior approval of the government, and the Foreign-Exchange Regulation Act rarely allowed foreign majority holdings.

5 Cambodia, Laos, Malaysia, Philippines, Singapore, Thailand, Vietnam, Myanmar.

6 Including since 1997, Bangladesh-India-Myanmar-Sri Lanka-Thailand Economic Cooperation, and Bhutan and Nepal since 2004.

7 South Asian Association for Regional Cooperation.

8 Such a trend was besides reinforced by the end of the textiles and clothing quotas (UNCTAD, 2005).

FDI is nowadays perceived by the government as a way to stimulate development, growth, and to create new resources. FDI is freely allowed in many sectors[9] with automatic approval[10], freedom of location and choice of technology. Imports and exports, repatriation of profits, dividends, and capital are also free[11]. On top of that, intellectual property rights are guaranteed.

Since November 2005, FDI is allowed up to 100% in most activities under the automatic route[12]. The government also aims to attract foreign investments by setting up special economic zones[13], science parks and free trade and warehousing zones[14]. The Indian Investment Commission is charged with the responsibility of wooing investors[15]. Foreign investment is particularly sought after in power generation, telecommuni-cations, ports, roads, petroleum exploration/processing, and mining. A ten-year tax holiday is offered to companies engaged exclusively in scientific R&D with commercial applications. On the other side, FDI by Indian firms abroad is more and more encouraged and perceived as a way to enhance the competitiveness of firms and to assert the power of India around the world.

Foreign trade also increased, although its share in world exports remains low: 0.8% for merchandize exports (rank 30) and 1.7% for services trade in 2004 (rank 16). In 2004, exports grew by 30% for merchandizes to reach $75.5 bn[16] and by about 70% for commercial

---

9 Sectoral ceilings remain in some activities.

10 Initially, FDI's approval relied on matching exports and dividend repatriation. In July 1991, this approval became automatic in thirty-four industries designated high priority, up to an equity limit of 51 per cent.

11 Recently, foreign-equity ceilings in aviation services, private banks, non-news print publications and the petroleum industry have been adjusted.

12 That is, without any prior approval.

13 For instance, export oriented units and units in export processing zones benefit of tax holiday (100 per cent) for five years.

14 In free trade warehousing zones, FDI are permitted up to 100%.

15 Also, the Foreign Investment Promotion Board is a one-stop service centre and facilitator for FDI.

16 Gems and jewellery, engineering goods, petroleum products, ores & minerals, and chemicals and related products were the key drivers of India exports.

services to reach US $39.5bn (WTO, 2005): software and IT-enabled services came with such a growth.

Since the end of the 1990's, the dynamism of services and high tech sectors have contributed to modernize the Indian economy and to boost international trade and investments. Policies implemented have been decisive to support information and communication technology industries, as well as the pharmaceutical and biotechnologies sectors. Leading IT firms shaped in the 1980's (such as Tata Consulting Services, Wipro, Infosys), benefited from a fiscal advantages, and a favourable environment thanks to the creation of Public Research Centres (in Army, in Telecommunications) and of software technologic parks. The role played by the NASSCOM (National Association of Software and Service Companies) since 1988 acting as a catalyst to the growth of the IT industry is worth being mentioned. It contributed to facilitate trade and business in software and services, and to encourage research and education in India. NASSCOM acted simultaneously as an advisor, a consultant and coordinating body, with representatives on various committees in the Government of India.[17]

So doing, India became well known all around the world for its services and software activities. Between the beginning of the 1990s and 2005, computing and information technology services registered an annual growth rate of 8-9%. In 2005, it accounted for 5% of Indian GDP. Such dynamism created hundreds of thousands of jobs and given self-confidence to a new generation of industrialists and entrepreneurs to compete globally. It also attracted many MNCs which started to outsource their business process in India.

If some Indian companies established partnerships with foreign firms as early as the middle of the 20th century, the bulk of them go back to 10 years ago, with the booming of FDI, JV,

---

17 In December 2005, the NASSCOM included 950 members (among them, 150 are global companies from the US, UK, EU, Japan and China) accounting for over 95 per cent of the revenues of the software industry in India.

subcontracting, outsourcing (software, call centres, financial services, ...)[18] which contributed to modernize productions facilities, to promote significant technology transfers and to improve performance. Indian research was stimulated[19], thus creating local demand for new services and high technology industries[20] (WIR, 2005).

In parallel, foreign firms gave to Indian companies an opportunity to meet with international levels and production standards (quality and safety) and to acquire new capabilities. Indian firms also had the opportunity to get information about foreign markets. Lastly, these relations prompted competition in local markets where Indian firms used to operate, until 1991, in a protectionist context. Progressively, some of them were able to become formidable international competitors.[21]

India has a well-established major manufacturing sector that spans almost all areas of activity. Despite revolutionary changes in the business environment, many old family groups have remained at the forefront and maintained their hold over their companies with dexterity. Their successors are more and more well-educated and well-versed in the art of management; most of them generally studied in the USA, in the United Kingdom, or in other European countries. The capitalist culture of enterprises such as Tata, Birla Kirloskar, Mittal, Mahindra, Mafatlal, Walchand, Mahindra, Bajaj, Singhania, is deeply rooted. It is

---

18 It has been estimated that as soon as 2000, 160 enterprises among the Global 500 had externalised their IT services and that in 2005 they were almost 400 (Boillot, 2005).

19 For instance, Indian pharmaceutical companies such as Dr. Reddy Laboratories and Ranbaxy have R&D alliances with Novo Nordisk, Novartis and GlaxoSmithKline.

20 Texas Instruments, the first TNC to be allowed to establish a wholly owned software affiliate in India in 1986 not only inspired other TNCs to set up operations in the country but also spurred the growth of the indigenous software and business services industry (WIR, 2005). In many ways, foreign investors have opened new job opportunities for Indian researchers in the interface between science and business.

21 For instance, Videocon conquered the opportunity to buy a branch of Thomson TV thanks to a former production agreement with Matsushita.

interesting to notice that besides these old and prosperous family groups, many other renowned Indian companies have been created in the last few decades: for instance in the case of Ranbaxy incorporated in 1977, of Dr. Reddy's (1984), of Videocon (1988), of Wipro, created in 1945 but which started to work in information technology in 1982 (for the Indian market first). Also, some Indian firms are true start-ups recently incorporated, and, in some regards, global born: they often operate in the field of the new technologies, that is the case of Infosys, of Moser Baer, KPIT, Satyam, HCL Technologies, ... All these firms have technical skills and required capabilities to act on a global level.

Who Invests in India and Why?

1. The United States is the First Investor

Most of FDI inflows come from a few countries. Between 1991 and 2005, investments of 10 countries accounted for 71 per cent of FDI, the main investor countries being the USA, the Netherlands, Japan, and the United Kingdom.

According to data relating to the period 1991-2005, Mauritius is the biggest source of "foreign" direct investment. But even if India and Mauritius have close political links and close bilateral relations rooted in common kinship, culture and interests (about 70 per cent of the population of Mauritius is of Indian origin), data are biased. Mauritius has low rates of taxation and an agreement with India on double tax avoidance regime. For these reasons, some multinationals set up companies in Mauritius before going to India. Investments from Mauritius in India are operated by Indian firms, either public[22] or private[23] .

22 For instance, it is the case of : Life Insurance Corporation, New India Assurance, State bank of India International, Bank of Baroda, Indian Oil Corporation, and so on.

23 It is the case, notably, of Infosys, Ajanta pharma, Apollo Tyres, Pentafour, Arvind Mills, Ashok Leyland, and so on.

Table 7

Top Investing Countries in India, According to FDI Inflows 1991-2005

(US $ billion)

Country	Aug. 1991 March 2002	2002-03	2003-04	2004-05	2005-06	Cumulative Inflows Aug. 1991- Nov. 2005
Mauritius	6.632	0.788	0.567	1.127	1.760	10.874
USA	3.188	0.319	0.360	0.668	0.356	4.891
Netherlands	0.986	0.176	0.489	0.267	0.068	1.986
Japan	1.299	0.412	0.078	0.126	0.098	2.013
U. Kingdom	1.106	0.340	0.167	0.101	0.196	1.91
Germany	0.908	0.144	0.081	0.145	0.052	1.33
Singapore	0.515	0.038	0.037	0.184	0.164	0.938
France	0.492	0.112	0.038	0.117	0.008	0.767
Sth Korea	0.594	0.039	0.024	0.035	0.057	0.749
Switzerland	0.325	0.093	0.045	0.077	0.064	0.604
Total FDI Inflows	23.829	3.134	2.634	3.754	3.348	36.704

Source: RBI (Reserve Bank of India), 2006 February.

Apart from Mauritius, the United States is the first investor in India: it contributed about 13 per cent of total inward FDI between 1991 and 2005. Both countries have close relations: the United States is the largest trading partner of India[24] and a broad Indian community lives in it.

Far behind the USA, Japan (5.5% of FDI inflows received by India), Netherlands (5.4%), United Kingdom (5.2%) are significant investors. Germany follows (3.6%), then Singapore (2.6%), France (2.1%), South Korea and Switzerland. The European Union's FDI in

24 In 2004, principal US exports were diagnostic or lab reagents, aircraft and parts, advanced machinery, cotton, fertilizers, ferrous waste/scrap metal, and computer hardware. As to major US imports from India, they included textiles and ready-made garments, Internet-enabled services, agricultural and related products, gems and jewellery, leather products, and chemicals. Bilateral trade in 2004 was 21.7 billion of US dollars.

India is higher than that from the US. FDI from Netherlands, United Kingdom, Germany, and France, registered between 1991 and 2005 accounts for 16.3% of the total. In 2004-2005, Mauritius has still again been the main investor with 30% of total inward FDI, followed by United States (17.8%), then by Netherlands (7.1%), Singapore and Germany.

2. Manufacturing Sectors Attract the Highest FDI Inflows

Between 1991 and 2005, FDI received by India was mainly related to manufacturing, notably sectors such as electrical equipment (including computer software and electronics) which received 22.5% of FDI inflows, transportation industry (14.4%), telecommunications (13.2%), fuels (11.6%), and chemicals (8.7%). Services accounted for 13.4%. In recent years, some sectors such as electrical equipment, services, drugs and pharmaceuticals, cement and gypsum products, metallurgical industries have had the wind behind them insofar as more than the half of FDI regarding them was made after 2002, compared to an average of 39.4% for all sectors.

Table 8

Sectors Attracting Highest FDI Inflows (1991-2005)

(US $ billion)

Sectors	Cumulative FDI	Inflows 1991 -2005
Electrical equipement	4,862	2,734
Transportation Industry	3,124	1,110
Services	2,908	1,462
Telecommunications	2,863	0,624
Fuels (power, oil refinery)	2,514	0,416
Chemicals (other than fertilizers)	1,887	0,538
Food processing industry	1,173	0,222
Drugs and pharmaceuticals	0,946	0,552
Cement and gypsum products	0,746	0,483
Metallurgical Industries	0,624	0,393

Source: Reserve Bank of India.

Since 2002, services hold the second rank in attracting FDI. Business services (IT, software, financing, insurance, real estate, etc.) are gathering momentum, in parallel with the "tradability revolution" in services in the world. India is the main destination for off-shoring of most services as back-office processes, customer interaction and technical support, R&D[25] (WIR, 2005). Indian services are more and more sophisticated with higher price tags (reading medical X-rays, analyzing equities, processing insurance claims). According to data provided by OCO Consulting (2005), India is, by far, the country which attracted the greatest number of projects in IT and software. Since 2002, of 1913 projects observed, it attracted 519[26], that is, 27%[27].

Chart 2

IT & Software: Top Locations by Number of Projects, Jan. 2002- Aug. 2005

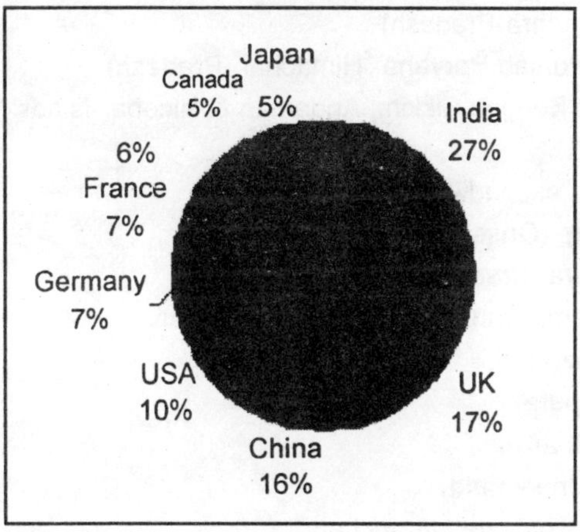

Source: OCO Consulting (2005).

25 Among them, we find, abstracting and indexing, call centres data entry and processing, electronic publishing, mailing list management, secretarial services, technical writing, telemarketing, web-site design, interpretation of medical scans, flight reservations, and so on (WIR, 2004).

26 Among them we find notably investments by Microsoft, Oracle, Syntel, SAP and Cybernet Software Systems.

27 However, during the same period, China seems to have attracted the largest ones in terms of job creation, with Satyam Computer Services and Bell Net each adding 3,000 jobs.

3. The Developed States of the Indian Union Attract the Largest Part of FDI

Foreign firms choose to locate their activities in the most developed areas of the country and, if possible, in poles of competitiveness when they exist.

Table 9

FDI Inflows According to Areas from 2000 to 2005

Regional Office and State Covered by FDI	%
New Delhi (Delhi, part of Uttar Pradesh and Haryana)	25.9
Mumbai (Maharashtra, Dadra and Nagar Haveli, Daman & Diu)	21.2
Bangalore (Karnataka)	7.6
Chennai (Tamil Nadu & Pondicherry)	6.0
Ahmenabad (Gujarat)	3.3
Hyderabad (Andhra Pradesh)	3.2
Chandigarh (Punjab,Haryana, Himachal, Pradesh)	1.6
Kolkata (West Bengal, Sikkim, Andaman & Nicobar Islnds	1.3
Panaji (Goa)	0.6
Kochi (Kerla, Lakshadweep)	0.4
Bhubaneshwar (Orissa)	0.3
Bhopal (Madhya, Pradesh, Chattisgarh)	0,2
Guwhati (Assam, Arunachal, Pradesh, Manipur, Meghalaya, Mizoram, Nagaland, Tripura)	0.05
Jaipur (Rajasthan)	0.02
Patna (Bihar, Jharkhand)	0
Kanpur (Uttar Pradesh, Uttranchal)	0

Source: Regional Offices of RBI.

Eight Regional Offices received more than 70% of Indian FDI inflows[28]. New Delhi and Mumbai and their surroundings include

28 Previous data have been reported by 16 Regional Offices of RBI as related to FDI received by them from January 2000 to November 2005. They concern amount of FDI of about US $20 bn. However, states have not been identified for 28% of FDI received.

almost the half of FDI received by India since 2000, with respectively 26% and 21% each. Far behind, are the areas of Bangalore and Chennai (with respectively 7.6% and 6% of FDI inflows), then places surrounding Ahmenabad and Hyderabad (about 3% each). All the previously mentioned areas include the main diploma-granting technical institutions and the most of diplomas awarded by private training Indian institutions.

It also appears that some areas are specialised. For instance, most software companies are in Mumbai and Bangalore[29], where Indian industry originally developed; but they are also developing quickly in Delhi and its surroundings as well as in Andhra Pradesh and Tamil Nadu. As to the main poles of competitiveness, they are mainly concentrated in the South on the axis Madras-Bangalore, and in the area of Delhi (Gurgaon, Noida).

4. Indian Comparative Advantages

India is becoming an attractive location for global business on account to its buoyant economy, its increasing consumption market, and its needs in infrastructure and in the engineering sector. To date, India is becoming a favourite destination for foreign enterprises. According to experts and TNCs managers, it is just ranked behind China and behind or on equal terms with USA (WIR, 2005)[30]; this trend was again recently confirmed by AT Kearney's FDI Confidence Index[31] (IBEF, 2006). TNCs invest in India to improve competitiveness and profits by means of cutting costs and

29 Previous data have been reported by 16 Regional Offices of RBI as related to FDI received by them from January 2000 to November 2005. They concern global amount of FDI of about 20 billion of US dollars. However, for 28% of FDI received, states have not been indicated officially.

29 Today, in Bangalore, there are apparently more data-processing engineers than in Silicon Valley.

30 In the responses from experts, China is the favourite destination (85%), followed by United States (55%) and India (42%). In the responses from TNCs, China comes first (87%), followed by India (51%) and USA (51%).

31 This index tracks investor confidence among global executives to determine their order of preferences.

to take a step in the Indian market. India has many comparative advantages for TNCs.

Though low literacy and education rates could suggest that labour is not skilled enough, it is not the case when human resources are normalized by the population size. Indeed, Indian skills in research, product design, and customisation of services are acknowledged. India is one of the largest pools of scientists, engineers, technicians in the world, more particularly in information technology, with competitive wage levels when compared to those of industrial countries[32] and the use of English in business and in technical and managerial education.

The contribution of Indians of the Diaspora to human resources is noteworthy. Until the end of the 1990's, this Diaspora was still rather resented for its success abroad; but it is no more the case. The government sees it as a potential source of skills, of entrepreneurship, of knowledge and of capital. It is even creating conducive conditions to favour its return: the idea is to turn the original "brain drain" into "brain gain"[33]. As a result, more and more Indians expatriated in industrial countries (mainly in United States and United Kingdom) start to come back to work in foreign affiliates or local companies; some of them creating their own business[34]. Furthermore, these last years, qualified workers went less abroad, seeing their country as a land of opportunity.

In the 1980s, some foreign companies such as Texas Instruments (semiconductor design) and Astra-Zeneca biopharmaceuticals were pioneers in research activities in India. They were followed in the 1990s by groups such as Motorola (telecommunications software), Microsoft (computer operating systems), ST Microelectronics (semiconductor design), Daimler-Benz

---

32 India includes about 3 million of scientists and engineers, and 360,000 engineering graduates per year.

33 There was a time when nearly top 70 per cent of the IIT (Indian Institute of Technology) pass-outs were going abroad, but the latest data shows that the percentage is down to 30 per cent.

34 In Bangalore, for example, some 35,000 non-resident Indians have lately returned with training and work experience from the United States (WIR, 2005).

(avionics systems), and Pfizer (biometrics). Nowadays, more than 100 TNCs[35] run research activities in India and their number is growing fast.

The availability of qualified workers, the existence of internationally reputed R&D institutes (Indian Institute of Technology, Indian Institute of Science, Indian Institute of Chemical Technologies, Centre for Drug Research), and the emergence of many Indian firms as service providers or as partners[36] contributed to attract TNCs in India to perform R&D.

On account of its cost advantages, India is nowadays the third destination[37] for R&D, just behind China and USA (WIR, 2005). It also benefits from the fact that the kind of R&D that is suited for expansion in developing countries is not very different from that which may be kept at home (WIR, 2005).

Being the second most populous country in the world, India is also attractive for market-seeking FDI. Half of the population is under 25 years of age. India's consumer market is growing quickly (with an average over 12 per cent a year)[38]. Living standards are rising, a vibrant middle class estimated to 300 million—with spending power is emerging in the cities, and infrastructures needs are tremendous.

Specificities of Indian Investment Abroad

Negligible until the beginning of the 1990s, FDI outflows from developing countries have grown faster over the past 15 years than those from developed countries (WIR, 2004). The emerging of Indian

---

35 For instance, we can quote General Electric, Intel, Cisco, Hewlett-Packard, IBM, Lucent, Boeing, ZTE, Huawei (China), Flextronics (Singapore), or pharmaceutical companies such as Eli Lilly, Glaxo SmithKline, Novartis, Sanofi-Aventis.

36 Indian software companies such as TCS, Wipro and Infosys, have alliances with Ericsson, Nokia and IBM.

37 For instance, in the pharmacy industry, it has been estimated that the cost of clinical development was 45% of the corresponding work in a developed country (Goldman Sachs, 2005; WIR, 2005, India is a very efficient and short way to test drugs for consumers because clinical trials are time-consuming, expensive and ethically difficult.

MNCs, following those of China and of Asian NPI, has to be placed in such a trend.

1. A Favourable Context

In many ways, India is outstanding among outward investors from developing countries: a few Indian firms invested abroad at the beginning of the twentieth century; they mainly went in developing countries. Mafatlal (textile) invested as early as 1920 in Uganda in a cotton-spinning. Birla invested in Africa in the 1950s and in South Asia east between 1965 and 1981. Kirloskar created its first JV in Africa and South East Asia in 1971, and Ranbaxy set up its first JV abroad in Nigeria in 1977, and so on.

But Indian FDI took a new course in 2001-2002 when it became more diversified, involving a larger number of companies and countries. Buyouts performed by them would have been unthinkable several years ago. The government encouraged outward FDI and overseas M&As[39]. Even public enterprises were at the forefront of these investments. Since 2000, Oil and Natural Gas Corporation (ONGC) has set up large businesses abroad (notably in Russia on in Angola) and Indian Oil Corporation (IOC) invested massively in Libya in 2004-2005.

Many Indian firms have ownership-specific advantages which spur on their investments abroad. Furthermore, Indian enterprises have comfortable financial means and can afford to invest abroad. This investment is funded by former profits, banking loans and stock markets.

India has a great number of experienced and competitive companies with capabilities in a large area of activities, from raw materials to the most cutting edges of services. They are not satisfied

---

38 Personal computer penetration is 9 per 1,000 persons. The cellular mobile market is expected to surge to over 70 million subscribers by fiscal year ending 2005 from the present 67 million users. The country has 54 million cable TV customers.

39 For instance, in January 2004, the Indian government removed the ceiling of US $100 million on foreign investment by Indian companies and raised it to equal their networth.

with exporting or being passive partners of foreign firms, they aspire to become global players.

2. *Indian Firms Go First in Developing Countries but the Share of Industrial Countries is Increasing*

Most of Indian FDI is going to other developing countries and Russia. Between 1996 and 2004, these countries received about 70% of it. Such a trend can be easily explained by the numerous proximities (geographical, social, economic), and by the need to secure Indian natural resources (industrial, energetic, agricultural), many of them being located in Africa, in Latin America and in Russia. The share of Asia has been increasing these last years: Hong Kong, Singapore, and Vietnam, taken together, accounted for 9% of total Indian FDI. This share is probably growing again in the coming years while China is becoming one of India's largest trading partners.[40] As for industrial countries, its share has been booming since 2000. North American and European countries respectively accounted for about 16 and 11 percent of Indian FDI abroad between 1996 and 2005. Indian firms are increasingly attracted by the US and EU.

Ten countries account for 86.1% of approved Indian FDI abroad since 1996.

Russia accounted for 19.9 per cent of total cumulative Indian FDI outflows due to oil and gas industries.[41]

The United States is the second destination of Indian FDI: it received 16.3% of it between 1996 and 2005. It is one of the most favourite destinations of Indian FDI.

Two tax havens, Bermuda and British Virgin Islands, account together for 11 % of cumulative Indian FDI, followed by Mauritius (8%).[42] Such privileged ranks are in relation with the important Indian

---

40 The top IT Indian services players have already invested in China.

41 With, notably, the acquisition of Sakhalin Oil field by the Oil and Natural Gas Commission (ONGC).

42 The double taxation avoidance treaty between India and Mauritius have encouraged Indian firms to practice "round trip" investment through Mauritius and other tax haven countries to take advantage of the tax benefits enjoyed by overseas investors (WIR, 2005).

Table 10
Country-wise Approved Indian Direct Investments in Joint Ventures and Wholly-owned Subsidiaries, Main Countries

(US $ million)

	Ap1996-March 2002	2002-03	2003-04	2004-05	2005-06 (Aug. 05)	Total
Russia	1748.68	0.15	1.43	1076.17	1.068	2827.450
USA	1540.83	185.27	207.14	251.73	135.83	2320.780
Mauritius	618.34	133.35	175.59	149.38	55.9	1132.56
Virgin Isl.	776.53	3.27	4.92	131.41	14.71	930.84
Bermuda	232.63	28.95	142.46	221.26	2.6	627.9
Sudan	—	750	162.03	51.55	43.13	1006.71
U.Kingdom	410.62	34.53	138.48	71.85	120.09	775.58
Hong Kong	445.12	14.8	16.15	73.64	22.22	571.93
Singapore	152.96	46.79	15.85	239.03	19.49	474.12
Australia	6.99	94.97	92.87	158.76	28.97	382.56
Netherlands	157.92	15.92	30.18	30.65	124.56	359.23
UAE	110.24	12.6	32.07	41.85	61.30	258.06
Vietnam	228.79	0.06	0.04	0.06	0	228.95
Oman	204.88	0.35	1.51	5	1.7	213.44
China	38.8	30	27	15	44	153

Source: Reserve Bank of India.

Diaspora living in Mauritius and also with some round tripping investments and financial transfers [43]; however, some "true" commercial and manufacturing investments do exist[44].

With 6.5% of Indian FDI outflows, Sudan also appears as a favourite destination. This rank is related to many investments in the oil sector. However, its share is not regular according to the years.

The United Kingdom is the sixth destination of Indian FDI (5.5% of outflows). It is a privileged destination, in relation to former colonial and human networks, and on account of the use of English by Indian businessmen.

43 We previously noticed that Mauritius was the main "foreign" investor in India.

44 For instance, these last years Indian firms set up in Mauritius new spinning mills, a disaster recovery centre (Infosys), and so on.

All in all, Indian FDI in Russia, Sudan and other developing countries is mainly boosted by the research of raw materials and energy, while FDI in the United States, the United Kingdom and other industrial countries is either driven by market targets or by access to know-how and technology. As to FDI in Bermuda, Virgin Islands and Mauritius, they are mainly stimulated by financial goals.

3. *Manufacturing Industries and Non-financial Services are Prominent*

Manufacturing and non financial services account for the bulk of Indian investment abroad. Between 1999 and 2005 (as of August), manufacturing industries globally represented 59% of outward FDI, and non financial services 30%. In 2004 and 2005, the share of manufacturing was very high (72.2% and 68.8% respectively). In 2005, the trading sector held the second rank (12.2%), and non-financial services the third one (12.1%).

Table 11

Industry Distribution of Approved Indian Outward FDI, Fiscal Years 1999-2005

(US $ millions and %)

Fiscal Year	Manufac-turing	Financial Services	Non-financial Services	Trading	Others	Total
1999-00	535.8	4.3	1130.7	58.3	2.3	1731.5
2000-01	370.7	16.6	876.5	89.2	29.1	1382.2
2001-02	2210.9	48.6	565.5	139.2	62.3	3027.0
2002-03	1056.7	1.8	280.2	69.9	63.7	1472.2
2003-04	756.6	35.1	438.8	76.9	134.1	1450.5
2004-05	2026.4	9.2	548.2	69.1	151.33	2804.3
2005-06 (Ap.-Aug. 05)	627.4	16.0	110.9	111.0	47.0	912.5

Source: Reserve Bank of India.

Pharmaceuticals, software and IT-related services have been the main drivers of Indian FDI abroad. As early as 1975-1990, Indian FDI outflows in services went to Singapore, Thailand, Sri Lanka and

Malaysia. By the 1990s, most of Indian FDI in services concentrated in developed countries, mainly in the United Kingdom and the United States (UNCTAD, 2005). However, some investors moved into selected developing-countries, especially China, South-East Europe and in the CIS.[45] Indian call centres and business-process outsourcing companies started to set up foreign affiliates in countries such as the Philippines and Mexico (WIR, 2005). By 2004, the top 15 Indian software and related service companies had all invested abroad, and many TNCs (software, pharmaceutical) had global R&D operations: they focused on serving their customers in specific areas and on the acquisition of know-how.

4. The M&As Road

In recent years, cross-border M&As have become a new mode of overseas market entry for Indian companies in many activities, and, for some of them, a key part of their growth strategy: today, while they benefit of an optimistic climate, some Indian firms go aggressively after M&As in industrial countries.

According to a recent study by Grant Thornton (2006), between 2001 and 2005 (until August), Indian companies were involved in 4690 overseas M&As in the world. These deals have been prominent in the IT software services and pharmaceutical industries, and many of them have been made in Europe (50% of deal value in 2005), and in North America (24% of deal value in 2005). The United States and the United Kingdom have been the countries that garnered the more important outbound deal share. If the number of Indian purchases has fluctuated according to the years and to the opportunities, the trend is largely increasing.

Table 12

Cross-border Mergers & Acquisitions— Indian Purchases

(US $ million)

Year	1998	1999	2000	2001	2002	2003	2004
Amounts of purchases	11	126	910	2,195	270	1,362	863

Source: WIR 2004, and 2005.

45. Commonwealth of Independent States.

In 2005, according to Neha Kaushik (2005), overseas Indian acquisitions could have topped 4.5 billion US dollars, compared to about 2 billion in 2004. They were often made by small and medium size companies and their average amount was about 30-40 million US dollars. By acquiring a partnership with a foreign firm abroad, Indian firms try to circumvent their difficulties. Setting up a subsidiary, attempting to grow organically and establishing one's brand in a new country, is quite difficult for an Indian firm, notably in industrial countries where markets are mature. M&As promote an accelerated acquisition of production facilities and capabilities, and access to strategic assets (know-how, technology, market niches, international brand names, R&D). M&As are a good way to gain a ready access to new markets (with a good approach to local consumers) and to new sales networks. M&As facilitate growth, obtaining additional products, more revenue, more labour force, more economies of scale. For instance, the ability to add employees and to broaden their range of products and services helps Indian firms to get new customers and to acquire, as quickly as possible, a critical mass and greater credibility.

Interestingly, the big ticket deals are not only driven by the technology sector but also by traditional sectors such as pharmaceuticals, telecommunications, auto components and other manufacturing activities. Indeed, when an Indian firm buys out a foreign company, success is not quite guaranteed. A relatively easy entry on a foreign market does not mean it will be smooth sailing for the acquirers.

First, Indian companies are relative newcomers to the game of cross-border acquisitions: many of them are on a learning curve and, so, can be mistaken. It is possible they feel destabilized by the economic and social environment of the host country (cultural and legal differences). Second, the Indian firms using the M&A route to conquer new markets are not certain to be successful because they generally purchase companies which are unprofitable (it is usually the reason why they are for sale). Generally, the success or

Table 13

Some of the Biggest Acquisitions by Indian Companies in 2004 and 2005

Indian purchaser	Company purchased - Place of FDI
ONGC	Sakhalin, Russia; Royal Dutch Shell, Angola; a Refinery in Sudan; an oil filed in Brazil, ...
Indian Oil Corp.	a large oil block in the Sirte Basin of Libya
Tata Steel	Nat Steel (Singapore), Millenium Steel Company - Cementhai Holding (Thailand) ($130 million)
Tata Chemicals'	Brunner Mond Group Ltd., United Kingdom ($110 million)
Reliance	Flag Telecom (USA); Trevira (Germany)
Ranbaxy	RPG Aventis (France)
Infosys	Expert Formation (Australia
Wipro	Nerve Wire, USA
VSNL	Tyco Global Network (USA)
Videocon	Thomson - division picture-tube, France ($289-million)
Apeejay Surrendra	Premier Foods (tea), United Kingdom (138 million)
Matrix Laboratories	Docpharma NV Belgium (for $263 million), Mchem in China, 43% stake in Swiss firm Explora
Videsh Sanchar Nigam	Teleglobe International Holdings Ltd USA
Dr. Reddy's	Betapharm, Germany
United Phosphorous	Advanta, Netherlands
Sun Pharma	Able Labs, USA
Continental Engine	Vege Motors, Netherlands
Sundram Fasteners (SFL)	Peiner Umformtechnik, Textron Deutschland Germany
Bharat Forge's (BFL)	FAW Corporation (forging industry, automotive), China
	Carl Dan Peddinghaus Gmbh, Germany
Mittal Steel	ISCOR, South Africa

failure of M&A deals depends on the acquisition cost and on the way the integration is made.

However, most Indian purchasers are optimistic insofar as their acquisition entails synergies between, on the one hand, new local distribution networks abroad which boost their sales and, on the other hand, low-cost manufacturing based in India and the possibility to achieve higher scales of production. Some Indian firms notice that many Western companies have their own financial problems increased by stringent labour and environmental regulations prevailing in their country: this is very true in Europe where "the costs of compliance add significantly to overall manufacturing costs" (Darel, 2006).

It is sometimes considered that it is easier to set up a greenfield facility in the United States, while the M&A road is preferred in Europe (WIR, 2005). In the coming years, Europe is likely to remain a hunting ground for Indian companies seeking to acquire firms, particularly since its economy is growing slowly, "sellers are numerous and the valuations are low" (Neha Kaushik, 2005).

Conclusion

Opening and FDI have really created new opportunities for India's development and boosted the performances of local firms as well as the globalization of some of them. Such a trend has undeniably raised Indian's stature among developing countries.

However, the potential of the country to catch up the levels of the leading economies in the coming decades, often touched on, is not quite guaranteed. India has an extremely hard job to perpetuate its advantages, to achieve further productivity gains and to ensure that all segments of its population participate in the income growth. The challenge that India has to take up is, in many regards, close to that of China. What is sure it is that, because of their size, of their capabilities and of their ambitions both of these emerging countries have the possibility to alter the international economic landscape over the coming generation.

References

Boillot, J.J. (2005), "L'Inde dans la mondialisation économique ", in Questions Internationales, L'Inde, grande puissance émergente, n°15, September-October 2005.

Boillot J.J. (2006), "L'économie de l'Inde", Collection Repères, La Découverte.

CNUCED (2005), "Les nouveaux IDE en provenance des pays en développement", Questions de politique générale concernant l'investissement et le développement, Conseil du commerce et du développement, Commission de l'investissement, de la technologie et des questions financières connexes, Genève, 7-11 mars.

Darel, P. (2006), "The Indian MNCs", January, IBEF (Indian Brand Equity Foundation) www.ibf.org

Drawat (2005) "Foreign Direct Investment & Developing Communities, *Universal Journal Economic Times* (2006)" Brain Drain on Reverse Gear to India, March, 08 Grant Thornton (2006) http://www.gt-india.com/downloads/DealtrackerAnnual_06.pdf site

Huang, Yasheng & Tarun Khanna (2006), "Can India Overtake China?", China Now Magazine, March 23, http://www.china nowmag.com/business.htm

IBEF (Indian Brand Equity Foundation)(2006), www.ibef.org

Jaffrelot, C. (2005), "L'Inde moderne: un produit de longue durée", in Questions Internationales, L'Inde, grande puissance émergente, N°15, September-October 2005, McKinsey Quarterly (2004), "A Richer Future for India", the *McKinsey Quarterly*, December 13 Neha Kaushik (2005), "Overseas Indian Acquisitions Set to Top $4.5 b in 2005 ", *Hindu Business Line,* 26 December.

OCO Consulting (2005), "L'Inde, grande puissance émergente", Questions Internationales, n°15, September-October.

RBI (2006), Reserve Bank of India, www.rbi.org.in

Satya, Madan (2006), "L'Inde, un géant encore entravé", Les Echos, 20 February

Srivastava, S. (2003), "What is the True Level of FDI Flows to India?" *Economic and Political Weekly*, February 15.

Upadhya, C. (2004), "A New Transnational Capitalist Class? Capital Flows, Business Networks and Entrepreneurs in the Indian Software Industry", *Economic and Political Weekly*, 27 November 2004.

World Investment Report (WIR), 2004 and 2005, United Nations, Genèva World Bank (2006), www.worldbank.org

8 *Chapter*

Globalization: Its Impact on Human Living

— Tushar Singh and Preetee Arpita

Gone are the days of individual, isolated continents, nations and states. The world map now represents more of a single, unified globe. The world has shrunk incredibly to an extent where nothing is out of reach, be it trade, travel, education, medicine or entertainment. Welcome home the era of unification—the era of globalization. It is a word which has pervaded nearly all important aspects of human life. The use of the concept of globalization has found favour among economists since the 1980s, but gained larger popularity only during the later part of the 1980s and 1990s. It is not something new, though. Since thousands of years people and governments, followed by corporations have traded amongst themselves via land and sea routes. A noted example is the famed Silk Road across Central Asia. Added to the trade were discoverers such as Vasco da Gama and Columbus who helped connect different, isolated lands of the world by means of their discoveries of new and unknown lands.

Although in the present times it has a wide variety of connotations, the notion of globalization finds its origin in the field of economics and trade practices, where it was first conceived of and applied. "At its most organic and fundamental level, globalization is about the monumental structural changes occurring in the processes of production and distribution in the global economy" (Cogburn, 1998). Thus on a broad economic level, globalization may be understood as a process which is marked by an increased openness and reciprocity between governments and peoples of the world, which created an environment conducive to greater interaction and integration among different nations, their governments, people and industries, driven by international trade, foreign direct investment, capital flows, migration, and the spread of technology.

What globalization has managed to do to us is an effect which can be noticed and felt without even trying. The walls between nations have fallen. There is connectivity greater than ever that could have been possibly imagined fifty years back. We have a stronger nexus between countries. There is an increased awareness of and interest in international affairs of importance. The national divide that separated countries has dissolved, boundaries have been blurred. They only exist on the geographical maps, in a physical sense alone. The development of technology, especially information technology has indeed brought together the far flung consumer and the service provider to boost business by manifolds. And as might be observed, it is a phenomenon which has had a radical effect not only on the fiscal elements, but has far reaching and long term impacts on the cultural, social, psychological and political lives of countries. The changes in the political and economic scenario may be immediately visible. However, to be able to gauge the influence it has on the mindset of a nation, it takes some serious thought, reflection and a careful comparison of the past with the present life both at home and abroad. Moreover, it is a change which does not manifest as an immediate consequence of globalization strategies, but may take a considerable amount of time to make its presence felt. For culture is an entity rooted firmly in a people's existence, and takes time to alter, transform or even perish.

Globalization has gained a highly controversial nature in time.

Pro-globalization arguments emphasize the benefit it allows to developing countries, whereas the anti globalization stand endorses the view that it has only helped multinational corporations enhance their profit more and more, at the expense of local enterprises, culture and values. Coupled with this comes the political edge that richer countries have over the poorer, peripheral ones—the latter are becoming increasingly dependant upon the former due to their monopolized possession of advanced expertise and technology. We are also witness to the disproportionately large power chunk that lies with the so called corporate giants, challenging even the government of a state in its strength, which can have unhealthy consequences for national growth and prosperity. The debate continues, for resolution of a conflict where the pros and cons seem to even each other out, at least apparently, is tough. International linkages owing to a globalizing economy and world are here to stay. With far reaching chain reactions which metamorphoses practically all walks of life. And hence, it would help to understand better our own lives, by assessing the importance globalization has in our national existence and its impact on our individual as well as collective life—both positive and negative.

Globalization is not just fiscal. There are far more areas in modern human civilization than one can imagine that it has found relevance to. We are affected and influenced by it and in many instances, even without awareness. So ingrained is the nature of some of its consequences for us. The most obvious domain is the industrial sector. The entire world has transformed into a global market for products and services from all nations for the international consumer. The next most conspicuous domain it has touched is the political one. There has been a growing trend of creation of transnational bodies which act as a world government, for example, the United Nations, which regulates relationships among nations and the power balance in terms of human rights and obligations.

On another note, the poorer and weaker nations are subjected to subtle and at times very obvious forms of subordination by their stronger counterparts, which is again a political consequence of globalization. Because of the global receptivity and reciprocity, countries like China are emerging and evolving, and may come on par with super power such as the United States in the near future. Informational globalization refers to the much advanced state of the flow of information and its bolstered accessibility and availability, practically in any remote corner of the globe. The sphere of human existence which is most profoundly affected by globalization trends is the indigenous culture. The intermingling, modification and even transformation of cultural practices and beliefs are but a most natural change brought about by the growing openness between different lands. Ecological globalization, being the next form of globalization, concerns itself with the environmental changes created by the increased industrial activities, which is often accompanied by pollution, long term climatic changes and so on, which cannot be solved without international cooperation. Another highly relevant feature of globalization for psychological interest is its social aspect. It is now much easier for people to migrate to and from their homelands in search of greener pastures, than was ever before.

Nothing in this world is available in black and white. Globalization also comes with its own shades of grey. However, it is difficult to judge whether the advantages outweigh the disadvantages or vice versa. It is a notion which can by simultaneously identified with the force of two powerful and contradictory dynamics: fusion and fission, as Ramonet states in his article. Its integrative side has managed to overhaul the efficiency of the world economy, by roping in greater employment and raised standards of living, evidenced by the mushrooming of call centers in the past decade (Everthing.com, 2008). The larger picture looks overwhelmingly optimistic. Nations are growing richer, wealthier, and prosperous. But its disintegrative aspect has done more damage than good. It has done very little to bridge the gap between the rich and the poor. And it has encouraged an aggressive competitiveness among the corporations of the world, which sometimes overrides all virtue and value. The following space is devoted to attempt a reflection on and assessment of the benefits of the topic of interest in this chapter, with a view to creating a ground for a deeper comprehension and appreciation of what globalization has done to the national psyche.

Economic Boom

The first boon of globalization that shines bright is the liberation of the economy. Free trade is in, which has ushered in a whole new era of what is so fondly called the "economic boom". This is one of its primary focal regions, backed by the economic belief that unrestricted trade is imperative to maximization of efficiency, growth and profits experienced by an economy. The formation of the G8, General Agreement on Tarrifs and Trade (GATT), empowerment of organizations such as the International Monetary Fund (IMF), the World Bank (WB) and World Trade Organization (WTO) are all efforts made towards introducing a just world economy. Most economists agree that poverty is linked to growth; on average, for every 1 point of real Gross Domestic Product (GDP) contraction, poverty increases by 2 points. Hersh & Weller (2002) conducted a large study of nearly 200 countries from 1961 to 1999. This study revealed that the majority of countries which showed high growth had governments dedicated to free trade, whereas most of those countries in which the economies shrank (especially those with severe contractions) had implemented protectionist policies. All of this indicates to the colossal financial gains made by nations who kept their doors open to foreign investors and buyers (Bhagwati, 2004). And India hasn't been lagging any far behind. She has seen the forces of globalization ever since the days when she served as colony to the Mughals, Turks, Afghans, the Europeans, French and the English. The staggering growth of various sectors like the Business Processing Outsourcing (BPO) industry, Knowledge Processing Outsourcing (KPO), retail and insurance have experienced a major impetus. The resultant gigantic expansion of employment opportunities for the work force in India is unprecedented. Brands have now gone global. Multinational brands like McDonald's and Coca-Cola have become household names in Indian middles class circles. Brands like Nike and Dell no more come with a halo around their names. The average Indian can also avail of their services like any other. What was luxury only a few years back has now become more than a "created necessity" due to the influence of globalization on households. This in turn, has raised the standard of living for many—one of the universal goals of any growing economy.

Employment

To quantify and offer concrete evidence of such positive economic restructuring, it may be cited here that In 1991, the country's GDP growth rate had dipped to a snaillike 1.1 per cent. However, today, successive prime ministers have started calling for 7-8 per cent growth. Furthermore, in the early 90s, inflation was at 17%. Now the government is worried when it crosses 7%. The software and services export market have touched a all new high in the nation (Shenoy, 2007). The government offers least resistance and interference in the modus operandi of the free markets. This in turn maximizes efficiency and gains. Another edge that this phenomenon has added is privatization of existing public sectors, which improves organizational effectiveness. With the advent of technology, the investment in terms of the number of workers has been brought down by a staggering proportion. What was once manual is now electronic. The whole world can be operated by mere touch of buttons. This has resulted in massive downsizing of employees, who are replaced by computers and machines—making the same work, faster, more accurate and economical. There is emergence of a buoyant private sector with industries like Tatas, Ranbaxy, Mahindra & Mahindra, etc., becoming conglomerates. India has shot into the global limelight and has become conspicuous on the world map owing to the massive success of corporations like these. Such companies not only assimilate foreign capital and know-how but also display the ability to withstand MNC competition and becoming global players themselves (Shenoy, 2007).

Greater freedom and choice now exists among the workforce in India. The favourite Indian notion of a "government job" as a symbol of security, permanency and social prestige is now giving way to a wide variety of employment. The basic mindset itself is in transition—a real change at the grassroots level. Traditional, one-track thinking is gradually giving way to flexibility and tolerance to accept novelty and difference. To name a few, BPOs, the medical transcription industry, the field of clinical research, biotechnology and pharmaceuticals are emerging as the new age employing sectors. These fields are new and innovative, and unlike the IT/Engineering sector, are not saturated yet, which means that they hold immense capacity to absorb the increasing number of youth that passes out of professional colleges and universities year after year. Apart from the employability that they offer, there is also far more freedom among the employable to choose from a variety of work. Switching jobs is also easy, given the new scenario, where there is an ever increasing need for working hands and minds in the nascent transnational corporations. A forward move can also be marked in the levels of remuneration given to the young employees who work for the private segment. In order to lure and retain badly needed employees, corporate companies do not mind shelling out decent pay packets to their employees. Substantial incentives and perks are also offered to check truancy and attrition rates. All this put together, makes for a huge advantage for the working class today.

Information

Another lead for the country again comes from the global connectivity and system of information partaking transnationally. The number of globally situated NGOs have seen a major ascent in the recent years. Many such non-profit organizations, based abroad, have entered into partnerships with developing states such as India. Such organizations, backed by their superior infrastructure and strong funding, have the ability to invest time, and resources, with an aim to aid the development of remote, impoverished corners of the nation. Many associations like the CRY and UNICEF have worked marvels in the areas of education, human rights, women and child care, provision of basic life amenities such as potable water and basic medical treatment.

Knowledge

Implications of globalization for knowledge, education and learning are also immeasurable. Indigenous language literature and technical know-how travels freely all over the world. Information flow is no more unidirectional or bidirectional, but multidirectional. The best illustrations to support this development are the operations of corporate giants Nike and Dell. For its manufacturing, Nike depends on more than 700 locations around the world, where its factories are set up. Dell Inc., an American-based computer and computer peripherals company develops, manufactures, markets, sells and supports machines all over the world. And such wide and diverse areas of operation are integrated by its global web or partnerships with the rest of the globe. China, Malaysia, Poland, Brazil and many other nations serve as its manufacturing plants. The United States is the point where the parts finally reach and are merely assembled and branded. India, with her intellectual repertoire, now has the opportunity to showcase her talents outside and also to enrich her knowledge by incoming contributions from other nations. This helps produce a work force which is scientifically and technically superior to what existed in the past.

Agriculture

Globalization has also come as a blessing in disguise for the poor Indian farmer. It has helped transport Indian agricultural produce to Western markets, where it is valued higher. Indian mangoes, safed musli (Indian Viagra) and other medicinal plants are in great demand outside the country. At present the government is allotting upto Rs.1

crore to a section of the farmers in Nalgonda and Mahabubnagar districts in Andhra Pradesh, to encourage cultivation of medicinal plants [for exports]. Efforts are also on by a few Indian research institutes to help assist small scale farmers, in collaboration with international development agencies (Pimbert & Wakeford, 2002). "The Bio Energy Research Institute (BERI) and the International Development Enterprises (IDE), have implemented a new irrigation project to solve the plight of small landholders. Farmers are also being trained in more advanced and scientific ways of agriculture. For this, diffusion of information is often facilitated by international organizations and NGOs, which have branches all over the world (farmingsolutions.com).

Education

The education sector has also responded to globalization in a big way. The number of schools and educational institutions which have seen private ownership are burgeoning, and almost turning corporate. Such schools have managed to run on extremely high levels of professionalism, expertise and performance and have greater accountability to parents for proper education of their child. The use of latest, state-of-the-art equipment and approached to teaching have made a world of difference to the concept of education. In addition, the student has the advantage of exposure to a wide range of perspectives and viewpoints to knowledge and facts, which offers much food for thought. This has an obvious advantage—the backbreaking burden of literacy that our government forever combats, is now shared by able bodies. Education has a new face now. Courses can be completed and degrees earned over the internet now, amidst the comforts of home and convenience of flexible study timings. This makes higher education more accessible, especially to those who work and pursue studies simultaneously. Such a trend breaks and renders futile the notion of time, space and boundaries. The awareness and literacy that comes through exchange of data and advanced communications over various digital networks and learning communities like internet blogs, emails, and social networking websites have created an information revolution in itself. It encourages self-reliance in the student to acquire and utilize knowledge. This also boosts self-esteem and confidence of being able to do something new by oneself, without the help of elders and parents. The current trend is also heavily in favour of establishing official tie ups between native universities with those abroad, with an intention of cultural as well as informational exchange—a hallmark of globalization process. This helps widen the students' horizons and expands her outlook on the world. An ability to work in alien conditions and circumstances, in teams comprising heterogeneous members teaches the student tolerance and respect for novelty, difference and value adaptiveness.

Family

An important layer of societal functioning is the family life, structure and dynamics. All those changes discussed previously, have significant direct and symbolic effects on the functioning of the family. The average level of family income and expenditure has increased. With greater employment options, generally all members of the family unit are found to be working. There are two interdependent points to be made in this context. First, with a general raise in the national economy, coupled with increased exposure to and contact with superior lifestyles of the rich and affluent, the average middle class family is starting to set its ambitions very high, and is desirous of a glamorous lifestyle which is popularized by the inter-connectedness of the higher ups and the middle class in the interactive, global world of today's. Temptations are high and countless. From rising multiplex movie theatres to ultra-stylized shopping malls, every single establishment comes at a big price. Glamour is the ultimate temptation in the materialistic and consumerist society that we are relentlessly turning into. The next step thus takes the shape of an aim to earn the most the family can, so that it may acquire the capacity to spend in proportion and finally, the ability to adopt that coveted lifestyle. This ensures optimum realization of the individual family member's skills and training, and their financial productivity and contribution towards running the household. So, in a way each member is accountable for their share of work.

This also allows members a greater spending power. The young adults in the family can easily find suitable jobs which can earn them their pocketmoney. Part time jobs which are available aplenty on the internet, are just a mouse click away. It gives one the freedom to work any time, from anywhere, and for durations as desired.

A fallout of the economic upliftment of the middle income groups due to globalization has been the dissolution of the joint family system. The collective life, which was once the strongest of identities of India, is slowly fading out of existence. Family life in the past almost unanimously denoted to a roof housing at least three generations of a single family. Modern times have a seen a contradicting trend, wherein couples choose to live away from parents and relative, opting for separate accommodations. A perspective which would see such a move as beneficial, lies in the need for more privacy, autonomy of decision making and avoidance of the inescapable difference of opinions and arguments arising out of the coexistence of a multitude of members within the joint family life. The stressful work routine makes recreation and leisure a rarity for couples. They prefer to spend whatever little free time that they manage on weekends, with each other, in the privacy and quiet of their own homes. Members of nuclear families have greater freedom to live a life on their own terms, than by those dictated by elders of the house, which is very often in clear opposition of the young couples. The liberty and self-determination that is experienced in such family systems augments a sense of responsibility in the members. From fixing leaking taps to rearing children, every single need has to be taken care of by constituents of the family themselves. And hence there is greater accountability for each member's share of work.

Another attraction of the nuclear family is its superior spending capacity. The number of people sharing the household income is dramatically lesser than in a joint system, which makes sure that individual member gets to satisfy most of his needs, and in a befitting manner at that.

In the absence of interaction with relatives, children also receive parents' exclusive attention, which goes to foster the emotional and psychological bonding between them. The family is small and compact. There is more quality time spent together, which cements the attachment and friendship between the two sides, making for a very healthy, secure and stable environment for growing up.

Another powerful area of changing dynamics in the nuclear family system is the power equation between the husband and wife, which carries implications for authority sharing by both genders in the larger purview of human life and interaction. With both spouses working, the disparity graph between men and women is taking a nosedive. Women now constitute nearly half of the work force, moving into fields traditionally labelled "masculine", challenging and recreating the age old feminine gender role identity. Such a trend evens out the control and influence that both the counterparts have over each other and in planning family affairs at large and the crucial decision making process. A very constructive upshot which follows is the creation of an androgynous family structure, wherein the traditional and rigid divide between the rights and duties of the man and the woman of the house is undergoing a revolutionizing change. Chores related to running the family are becoming neutralized in terms of their values of masculinity and femininity. The lines are blurring. Men and women both share the labour of managing the house. This promotes an equitable, power balanced and nourishing relationship between couples and also sets ideal role models for the children to learn from and emulate.

Migration is also an important additive factor in the dwindling of the joint family, though with its own accompanying package of benefits. And very often, the beneficiaries are the families back in the immigrant's hometown. There has been a growing trend in youngsters to move out to different cities in order to pursue higher education and eventually to make a living. This necessitates their staying away from family. However, the brighter side is that such immigrants add considerably to their home economy. It is known that Filipinos abroad remit approximately US $7 bn to the Philippine economy. Filipinos, being extremely family-centered, would above all remit earnings to the family left behind. The standard of living of these families would improve considerably, and their status in the community elevated commensurate to the remitted green bucks. Another very practical reason which makes existence of the joint family in cities a near impossibility is the soaring real estate prices (Hefti, 1997). It is a colossal task to find accommodation to fit three generations under one roof in the age of sky high rents and exorbitantly valued property. Physically, smaller number of family members means more living space, which also facilitates larger mental space and peace.

Social Structure

One aspect of globalization which deserves special mention is its miraculous influence on minimizing the adverse effect of social constraints such as age, sex, religion, caste and the like. Migration of people within the nation, in search of greener pastures elsewhere has brought down the cultural divide within the nation to a great extent. The omnipresent psychological wall between what is called "north India" and "south India" has started to show signs of crumbling, finally. The bigger metropolitan cities are home to a cultural assortment of people, traditional customs, beliefs and multiple mini worlds in themselves. A festival like the Holi which was typically a north Indian ceremony, has now percolated down south. Festivities and celebrations are also turning global, within the country, which may be seen as a path to cultural union among the diverse territories. The gender divide has also started to shatter. Conventional stereotypes and beliefs associated with what men and women can do, is now changing. Just as many women as men can be found working. Night shifts are no more a taboo for working women. It is a change at a very fundamental level in the mindset of the whole nation, which has allowed greater freedom to women to come out and tempt their fates. There is better acceptance of women who do not conform to the traditional feminine gender role. One of the biggest beneficiaries of the globalization movement is thus the womenfolk.

Culture

Human society is inherently a dynamic entity. Members join, migrate and transform over generations. A cultural practice revered yesterday becomes obsolete today. There cannot be a better illustration than culture to support the notion that the only consistency in life is change. Culture is not static; it grows out of a systematically encouraged reverence for selected customs and habits. As Indians, we are experiencing rapid metamorphosis of our indigenous culture as a result of a myriad of influencing factors such as globalization and mighty innovations in communications, transport and infrastructural amendments (Rothkop, 1997).

The notion that culture affects human behaviour is, of course, hardly new. And cultural ramifications due to the effects of globalizing are not new for us as a nation. The English colonization, which is one form of globalization, has helped us get rid of many social evils and inhumane practices such as the Sati Pratha and the prejudice against English language and education. They helped promote English language in Indian education and thus widened the scope of education to include knowledge from all over the world. English, being the *lingua franca* in today's world, one cannot fail to see the benefit of educating school students in the English language, right from the beginning. The present day India best represents a melting potpourri of different cultural beliefs and values. She exhibits a formidable capacity to absorb, assimilate and adopt what is foreign. Globalization is synonymous with the word connectivity. With global communication and transmission of ideas to and from the country by various agencies such as the print and electronic media, travel and tourism, international collaborations and partnerships at the corporate and government levels, we now have an overwhelmingly wide exposure to lifestyles and societal customs of other nations. We have picked up and retained many elements of other cultures foreign to us, which is manifest in the way we dress (fashion), in the manner we use language, education, sports and entertainment. The rapidly multiplying and immensely popular reality shows like the Indian Idol (a reproduction of American Idol), Kaun Banega Crorepati (an Indian replica of Who Wants to Be a Millionaire) on the television are products of such a tendency of the masses towards generation of what may be termed a transnational, global culture. Such shows provide a platform for showcasing talent, which is otherwise never brought to light. It has helped many ordinary mortals to shoot up into the limelight, while inspiring many others to follow suit. One of the most recent events with maximum potential to portray what globalization can do to the world was the IPL league of Cricket matches. Teams have been formed by selecting players not only from different official national teams, but from across the world. Players come together as cohesive units, irrespective of their divergent nationality, and official team membership at their hometowns. The only allegiance is to the team, not to a country, where lay the cricket team's traditional loyalty once. This is a truest and most vibrant representation of the consequence of globalization—transcending boundaries of nations, territories and even patriotism.

Physical and Mental Health

The health sector has also witnessed gigantic leaps ahead. Many hospitals in various cities now perform the most complicated surgeries and treatment procedures, unheard of before in the country. According to the Roemers' analysis, trans-national exchanges have facilitated the diffusion of technological innovations such as effective methods of contraception, techniques for obtaining safe drinking water, low-cost refrigeration, efficient transport and communication technologies, and new therapeutic agents that can effectively treat leprosy, schistosomiasis, trachoma, onchocerciasis (river blindness), and many other diseases (Roemer & Roemer, 1990). There is increased trade in the field of food materials, goods and medicines that has implied a greater availability of health care facilities. The increased use of modern information technology (internet, e-mail) hag greatly advanced the speed of health related communication. The information and knowledge related to health care services are freely available via internet and other means of communication. Tele-health and telemedicine facilities have ensured availability of health care services for inhabitants in any part of the globe. Relevant information can now be disseminated from wherever the experts are stationed, without having to move physically in order to seek consultation.

Globalization has also benefited the psychological health care services. The rapidly spreading technologies are a definite blessing for us. The introduction of telecounselling, cybercounselling and webtherapy has attracted considerable attention in recent years. These technologies has permitted mental health professionals to allocate repetitive computational and instrumental tasks to computers and other modern economical and time saving gadgets so that they are able to focus exclusively on the unique aspects of people's problems and to help them to enhance their psychological state of well-being.

Hi-tech inventions and discoveries have helped to inform and enrich fishing practices by providing information relating to prices, markets and weather forecasts (Economist, 2001). According to Okasha (2005), Globalization has contributed to a growing emphasis on the implementation of international protocols in psychiatric training, mental health policy and the protection of human rights of mental patients. It has also resulted in a through examination of the concept of social capital and its influence on the mental health of various segments of a population. Listed below are some of the areas where modern technology has helped boost the quality of services rendered to people.

Internet-based CRT Tools	Potential Uses by Counselors
1. Electronic mail (e-mail)	Therapy; marketing; screening; client/therapis correspondences for scheduling, inter-session monitoring and post-therapeutic follow-up; client record transfer; referrals; intake; homework; research; and professional collegiality (Bowman & Bowman, 1998)
2. Websites/homepages	Marketing/advertising; information dissemination; and publications
3. Computer videoconferencing	Therapy; homework; referrals; and consultation
4. Bulletin board systems/listservs newsgroups	Consultation; referrals; resources for information; and professional / collegiality (Bowman & Bowman, 1998)
5. Computerized simulation	Supervision and skills training
6. Databases/FTP sites	Research; information resources for therapists; self-help libraries; client record transfers; and assessment and analyses
7. Chat rooms/electronic discussion groups	Group therapy; self-help; and support
8. Software	Skills training; self-help; and homework

Adapted from Sampson, Kolodinsky, & Greeno, 1997, except where noted.

Conclusions

Globalization has come with both benefit and losses. The comprehensive review presented here clearly shows the importance and benefits of globalization not only for India but also for the world at large. It should be clear to all that the increasing importance of globalization can not be underestimated or ignored. And neither does it deserve to be. In more than one way, globalization is the need of the hour. However, care has to be taken that the positive force of globalization reaches all, in a manner that is fair and reasonable. The developing world should be more prepared to welcome the correlates of the phenomenon and to be selective enough about it to make sure that the evils associated with it do not offset its positive value for us as a nation. A healthy tradeoff has to be found and sustained. World organizations, national governments, and NGOs should work together to mitigate inequalities among sections of the global society that we inhabit and is so much a part of our quotidian lives. Only countries which have effective social practices can in a true sense, reap the payback of globalization.

References

Bhagwati, J. (2004). "The Human Face of Globalization." *Global Agenda,* 2, p. 74.

Bowman, R. and Bowman, V. (1998). Life on the Electronic Frontier: The Application of Technology to Group Work, *Journal for Specialists in Group Work*, 23 (4), 428-445.

Cogburn, D. L. (1998). Globalization, Knowledge, Education and Training in the Global World. *Conference Paper for the InfoEthics98*, *UNESCO*. http://www.unesco.org/webworld infoethics_2/eng/papers/paper_23.htm

Economist (2001). *Globalization.* London: Economist/ Profile.

Farming Solutions. Available: *http://www.farmingsolutions.org/*

Globalization. Retrieved from *http://everything2.com/node/1706146.* on 27/05/2008.

Hefti, A.M. (1997). Globalization and Migration. Presentation at Conference *"Responding to Globalization",* 19-21 September, 1997, Zurich.

Hersh, A. & Weller, C. E. (2002). Free Markets and Poverty. *The American Prospect,* 13 (1), 1-14.

Okasha, A. (2005). Globalization and Mental Health: A WPA Perspective. *World Psychiatric,* 4 (1), 1-2.

Pimbert, M. & Wakeford, T. (2002) Prajateerpu: a Citizens Jury/ Scenario. *Workshop on Food and Farming Futures for Andhra Pradesh, India.* IIED & IDS, 2002, http://www.iied.org/pdf Prajateerpu. pdf

Roemer, M. & Roemer, R. (1990) Global Health, National Development, and the Role of Government. *American Journal of Public Health*, 80, pp. 1188-92.

Rothkop, D. (1997). In Praise of Cultural Imperialism? Effects of Globalization on Culture. *Foreign Policy*, June 22, 1997, pp. 1- 10.

Sampson, J., Kolodinsky, R., & Greeno, B. (1997). Counselling on the Information Highway: Future Possibilities and Potential Problems. *Journal of Counselling & Development,* 75, 203-212.

Shenoy, P.D. (2007). Globalization: Its Impact on Labour in India. Paper presented in a seminar *on "India and Globalization "* India Habitat Centre, New Delhi, Feb. 1,2007.http://www.ris.org.in India_Globalisation_Its%20Impact% 20on%20Labour% 20in%20India_P%20D%20Shenoy.pdf

Chapter 9

Globalization and Development—Potentials and Pitfalls in 21st Century

— Aurnob Roy

Abstract

This paper examines the conditions under which globalization improves the socio-economic prospects in developing countries. It is often claimed that the impact of globalization depends crucially on domestic policies. Accordingly, the expectation is that, in the presence of well designed domestic policies and institutions, globalization will spur economic growth and promote job creation. The purpose of this paper is to examine the validity of this premise, based on a review of available studies. The paper notes that there is no simple-minded link between globalization and development. Some developing countries have engaged in freer trade and investment policies, and yet results have been disappointing so far. By contrast, some successful performers have not adopted orthodox liberalisation policies. The paper looks into possible explanations behind country heterogeneity in the response to globalization. These include different national policies, the role of international rules and standards and the pace and nature of the globalization process itself. Paradoxically, the latter is often an omitted factor, and yet, according to the paper, it plays a crucial role. Importantly, it puts forward a research agenda which would usefully shed light on how developing countries can successfully be engaged in the international economy.

Introduction

This paper will review the recent economic literature on globalization, examining its implications for the overall prospects of growth and employment creation in developing countries. A particular concern is whether the majority of these countries, rather than only a small minority as at present, will be able to harness the opportunities created by globalization to accelerate their economic development. This takes a different approach from the mainstream literature on the relationship between globalization and development.

That literature has focused largely on cross-section and country studies of the impact of globalization on growth, poverty, income distribution, and employment in developing countries. The overarching question is whether globalization has been good or bad for developing countries in terms of these impacts. A common method is to compare outcomes across countries with different degrees of engagement in the global economy. Subsumed within this is, of course, the issue of whether more open policies towards globalization have led to superior outcomes.

Not surprisingly, proponents of globalization have often used the results of some of these studies to preach the benefits of greater economic liberalization. A fair reading of this literature will, however, reveal that such a stance is not fully justified. There are divergent results from empirical studies on the impact of particular aspects of globalization and there is an ongoing debate over the policy conclusions that can validly be drawn from this literature.

Moreover, much of the mainstream literature also implicitly suggests that all developing countries can benefit from globalization if only they adopt the right policies and create effective institutions for economic and political governance. Thus the fact that only a small minority of developing countries have so far succeeded in enjoying the benefits of globalization is put down to deficiencies in national development efforts. In other words, the main claim is that the successful countries have adopted orthodox liberalization policies while the laggards have not.

Important as this issue is, it is not likely to constitute the whole answer. It has, of course, been disputed by those who point out that a number of the success stories have not in fact adopted orthodox liberalization policies, while many of the unsuccessful countries have done so, but to no avail.

In any case it is implausible that differences in domestic policies and institutions can be the whole answer to the puzzle of why only a minority of developing countries have succeeded in the global economy. It is therefore important to discover additional explanations, particularly since a crucial requirement for creating a better world is for very many more poor countries to embark on the path of rapid development. An interesting candidate among the possible an alternative explanation is the very nature of the globalization process itself. Are there structural features and deficiencies in the current process that make it inherently difficult for more countries to succeed in joining the global economy on beneficial terms? If so, then we need to identify these failings and find ways to redress them.

The issue of the effects of globalization on the prospects for development is highly topical. An important strand in the general literature implicitly suggests that new developments in the global economy have indeed created vast new opportunities for all developing countries. This literature focuses on the impact on the advanced countries of new developments such as the rise of off-shoring in service sector jobs and rapid growth in China and India. The doomsday tenor of the more popular discussion of these issues clearly implies that many more developing countries are now better placed than ever to experience a take-off in development.

It is clearly important to assess the validity of such a prognosis as part of a broad attempt to understand the real opportunities and constraints to generalized development that are brought about by the current process of globalization. To this end it has been necessary to review not only the literature that has fuelled this media interest—on the economic threat to advanced countries unleashed by globalization—but also a wide-ranging literature on other aspects of globalization such as the growth of global production systems in agriculture, manufacturing and services; financial globalization; global income inequality; the rise of a global labour market; international migration; and the implications of the increasing interconnectedness of nations for global ethics. These literatures remain largely separate and attempting to draw out common implications from them for the development prospects of poor countries has been particularly interesting, and we hope useful exercise.

New Dimensions of Globalization

The Expanding Scope

The globalization of the world economy has continued at a steady pace over the past decade. The shares of international trade, investment and financial flows in world output have all continued to rise. This reflects in large part an expansion in conventional flows of these items. An important new development, however, is that this is by no means the whole story. The scope of globalization has also been expanding significantly with the emergence of new items as well as new forms of international economic transactions. This change has potentially wider ramifications than a simple quantitative expansion in the standard indicators of globalization. A central element of this widening scope of globalization has been a change in the nature of international trade. The Ricardian theory of international trade was based on the then prevailing reality that trade consisted of the exchange of final goods such as primary commodities and simple manufactured items between nations. The extent of trade was limited by the fact that it was generally necessary to make goods close to the point of consumption. This constraint has since been broken by declining transport costs and by successive technological breakthroughs.

As a result both the volume and scope of international trade have expanded vastly. A first stage in the process was the emergence of trade in intermediate goods when the production of manufactures began to be fragmented vertically. With falling transport costs particular parts of a manufacturing process could be separated out and located in different countries to take advantage of differences in labour and other costs. Although there are few figures at the aggregate level, "the intra-industry share of manufacturing trade has increased significantly since the late 1980s across many OECD countries".[1] Between 1996 and 2000 intraindustry trade accounted for more than half of total trade in manufactures in 22 out of the 27 OECD countries for which data were available. In addition, *intra-firm* trade accounted for one-third of goods exported from Japan and the United States in 1999. "Moreover, given the increasing importance of foreign direct investment relative to both world trade and output, it is likely that the importance of intra-firm trade has increased at the global level . . . there are some middle-income countries where intra-firm trade accounts for a high share of their bilateral trade".[2]

The latest phase has been described as the "great unbundling" since it has now become increasingly possible to fragment activities within a factory or an office to a finer level.[3] Even specific tasks within an enterprise can now be outsourced when this is warranted by cost differentials whereas previously it was only possible to do this in the case of more aggregated clusters of the production process.

This was followed by the rapid growth of trade in services. Trade in all commercial services (which includes traditional services such as transportation and travel) grew at the rate of 11 per cent per annum between 2000 and 2006 compared to 5 per cent per annum between 1995 and 2000. Within this overall growth, trade in "other commercial services" (which includes communication services, computer and information services, financial and other business services) doubled in value between 2000 and 2006 and now accounts for half of total commercial services exported in the world.

Furthermore, within this category of "other commercial services" the "fastest growing sectors were computer and information services (17 per cent growth), insurance (14 per cent growth) and other business services (13 per cent)".[4]

Overall, trade in commercial services now accounts for one-fifth of total world trade in goods and services. By comparison trade in agricultural products accounts for only 9 per cent of global trade. The enabling effect of successive waves of technological change has been the underlying factor behind these developments. While it is true that trade, investment and financial liberalization also played an important role in advancing globalization, its scope could not have expanded without the new possibilities opened up by technological breakthroughs. The declining cost of transportation was sufficient to fuel the expansion of trade in physical goods. However, trade in intermediates, intra-industry trade and global production systems only became possible with the emergence of new low-cost information and communications technologies. These made the coordination of multinational production systems feasible. The effects of these new possibilities for coordinating multinational production were first felt in the manufacturing sector. These new technologies expanded the scope for the vertical fragmentation of production and the relocation of parts of the production process across borders in order to exploit differences in labour costs. This was done through increased FDI flows from the advanced countries to produce labour-intensive intermediate goods in low-wage economies. This led to the emergence of both consumer-driven and producer-driven global production systems for manufactured goods. Consumer-driven systems consisted of the production of branded retail consumer goods such as garments and footwear through a system of global subcontracting to firms in developing countries. Multinationals controlled the production and distribution system, with the higher valued-added parts of the process such as design, advertising and retailing being retained in the advanced countries.

Producer-driven systems, on the other hand, consisted of the intra-firm production of specific components of a manufactured good through subsidiaries transplanted to low-cost locations. The products were then trans-shipped for final assembly and distribution; this process was reflected in the growth of both intra-firm trade and trade in intermediate goods.

For developing countries, both parts of this emerging global production system represented new opportunities for industrialization, the export of manufactured products, and employment creation. This was largely viewed as a boon in spite of concerns raised by critics over the labour exploitation and unequal exchange which they blamed on the economic power wielded by MNCs. In contrast, for the advanced countries, the same process was widely viewed with growing anxiety. A primary reason was the perception that manufacturing, and jobs, were being lost to developing countries. While the process was obviously profitable to the MNCs involved and also represented, from an economy-wide perspective, a desirable shift out of labour-intensive activities in which the advanced countries no longer enjoyed comparative advantage, there were clear losses to the workers involved.

The first wave of relocating production and jobs in the manufacturing sector has now reached a mature phase and, to that extent, the anxieties it provoked have subsided. The share of manufacturing in GDP and total employment has declined sharply in the advanced countries.[5]

Much of what was obviously ripe for relocation has already gone. While the underlying dynamics of shifting comparative advantage dictates that the process will continue, it will do so at a much slower pace than previously. However, a new threat of relocation has surfaced in the form of what has been termed the off-shoring of service sector jobs.

As was the case in the relocation of labour-intensive manufacturing, technological developments paved the way for this new phenomenon. The spread of the infrastructure of fibre optic cables to many parts of the world increased global connectivity, and was additionally facilitated by the increasing use of standard software and operating systems across the world.

Furthermore, the increased supply of scientists and engineers in several key developing countries such as India and China created a global supply base of the skilled labour that was required. The pre-conditions were thus in place for the off-shoring of service sector jobs.[6] Beginning with simple repetitive tasks such as data entry and processing, and call centres, the process of off-shoring has since worked its way up the skill chain to include a range of business services and complex professional tasks. Although the extent to which this has occurred is still limited, these new forms of off-shoring have triggered alarm in the advanced countries about an impending massive loss of skilled service-sector jobs. Global trade flows and the competition for jobs unleashed by them can now operate through both physical and virtual channels.

Forces Driving Increasing Linkages

This expanding scope of globalization means that the array of economic interrelationships among countries has grown. Over and above this, other factors are also creating a general tendency for the economic fates of nations to become more closely interconnected. We consider two of the most important of these factors — structural inequalities within the global economy and global tensions over the distribution of income.

Structural Inequalities

Two structural inequalities are fuelling this greater interconnection. One is the persistence of large income gaps between advanced and developing countries. The other is the related and equally large gap in the capital-labour ratios between these two groups.[7] Beginning with the latter gap, the Penn World Tables provide data on capital stock per worker for about 60 countries for the years 1985 and 1992. The data show that the capital-labour ratio for the G-7 countries was US$ 31,000 in 1985. In contrast it was US$ 1,900 for the seven sub-Saharan economies for which data were available, giving a 16:1 ratio between the rich and poor countries in the sample. By 1992 this ratio had increased to 28: 1 as a result of an increase in capital per worker in the rich countries and a decline in the sub-Saharan countries. A similar picture is true of India, albeit to a much smaller extent. The ratio of capital per worker between the G-7 countries and India increased from 18.2:1 in 1985 to 18.4 :1 in 1992. The corresponding situation for the only two middle-income industrializing Asian economies for which data were available was that the ratio remained unchanged between 1985 and 1992.

This gap in the capital-labour ratio is a reflection of both the much larger population size and the lower average income of developing countries. Some 5.5 billion people live in the developing countries compared to 1.2 billion in the advanced countries. Similarly, workers from developing countries constitute the bulk of the labour force in the world. Until recently most of the labour force in developing countries was engaged in subsistence agriculture and the informal sectors of the respective economies. These activities were at best only loosely linked to the global economy.

There has, however, been a significant increase in the number of workers from the developing world whose jobs and incomes are now connected to the global economy through trade and investment flows. This has been depicted as a dramatic increase in the size of the "global labour market". In this new context, the large gap in the capital-labour ratio between rich and poor countries assumes much greater significance than hitherto.

Globally, the increased involvement of China, India, and other developing countries in the world economy has resulted in a huge increase in the potential supply of unskilled labour. These workers bring with them little physical capital and thus increase the relative abundance of labour as well as the relative scarcity of capital. Although we should not exaggerate the extent to which this new entry of unskilled labour has actually occurred, the trajectory is nonetheless clear.[8] The gap between rich and poor countries in terms of per capita GDP is even greater than the gap in terms of capital stock per worker. The ratio between the average per capita incomes of the 20 richest countries and the 20 poorest was 37:1 in 2000.[9] This gap has also been increasing steadily for several decades. The per capita income of all developing countries expressed as a per centage of that in the advanced countries fell from 18 to 15 per cent between 1950 and 2001 in spite of the fact that Asian developing countries have been closing the gap since 1990.[10] The latter implies that for Latin America and Africa the gap widened considerably more than the average for all developing countries.

It will of course be objected that the use of such simple ratios of average incomes (unweighted by the population of countries) gives a misleading picture of the extent of global inequality.[11] If we do weight average incomes by population then we see some closing of the gap in average incomes between rich and poor countries from around 1990.[12] But it is important to note the reason for this change. It is almost entirely due to the rapid growth of China and India, two very populous countries that raised the population-weighted average income figures for the developing world. "It is this growth in these two countries, the transformation of China from desperately poor to poor, and the transformation of India from desperately poor to extremely poor...that has for the first time in at least two centuries narrowed the proportional gap between rich and poor".[13] Indeed, "'in the absence of the influences of China and India the pattern of improvement in inequality and poverty reduction would instead have been one of worsening".[14]

The reason for this worsening is that most other developing countries have done much less well than China and India. There are 49 other countries that are classified by the World Bank as low-income and they have a combined population of almost half that of the two giants. Most of these countries have fared very poorly in terms of economic growth and have diverged further and further from the income levels of the advanced countries.[15] In addition, a significant number of middle income countries have also fallen behind, albeit to a lesser extent.[16] If we think in terms of the number of countries that were in the group where average incomes were converging then a striking fact of the period between 1950 and 2000, in contrast to earlier phases of globalization, was that "the convergence club both expanded and contracted massively, as many economies joined, but also for the first time many economies dropped out. . . over the past two decades many countries have fallen behind not just relatively but absolutely in terms of both income levels and structural development".[17]

Given that our main concern is the implication of the current phase of globalization for the economic prospects of developing countries as a whole, it is valid to focus on the nation state as the basic unit of analysis rather than on proportions of the total population of the developing world. Development policies are framed at the national level regardless of population size. Taking a systemic view of globalization, a key issue is how its current nature affects the development prospects of different groups of countries. While the high growth in China and India is a cause for celebration from a cosmopolitan standpoint and does make for a better world in a number of important ways, it should not in itself reduce concern over the fact that so many developing countries are still falling behind the advanced countries in terms of income levels.

Moreover, from a systemic perspective the essential fact is that income gaps are widening between the advanced countries and a large majority of developing countries. These gaps are what will drive the dynamics of globalization in terms of the flows of trade, FDI, other financial flows and international migration. In this context it is also important to note that even if we include China and India among developing countries, *absolute income gaps* between advanced and developing countries will continue to increase for a long time to come. "While the relative world income distribution may not have changed much over recent decades and stands a chance of remaining relatively stable in the near future, we can be absolutely certain that absolute income gaps will continue to grow for at least one or two generations".[18] This is likely to tempt "the elite in poor countries to push for more unequal economic policies' and also 'create increased incentives for migration of both educated and unskilled labour from poor to rich countries".[19]

These structural features of the global economy heighten what has been described as a clear tendency towards "global labour arbitrage".[20] In other words, there are vast new opportunities for businesses to profit from exploiting the current large price differences across national labour markets. The wide gap in capital-labour ratios and wages is likely to prevail or even widen given the significantly higher rates of population and labour force growth in the developing countries compared with the advanced countries. This not only creates huge incentives for workers from developing countries to emigrate; it also poses equally strong incentives for enterprises in the advanced countries to intensify the search for possibilities to reduce costs and maximize profits through the relocation and outsourcing of production. Thus even though actual international migration remains limited, the inherent "law of one wage" can still exert its influence through the increasing mobility of jobs because of the expanding scope of globalization.[21] In a sense these channels can be seen as alternative ways round the fact that the labour market remains the least integrated of global markets; wage gaps in labour markets remain much larger than price gaps in product and financial markets.[22]

This global labour arbitrage illustrates our opening observation about the wider ramifications of the expanding scope of globalization. Much of the anxiety in the advanced countries emanates from the basic fact that the increased possibilities for global labour arbitrage now pose an increasing challenge to jobs and wage levels for a larger segment of the labour force. The biggest change is that the service sector, until recently insulated because it was largely non-tradable, is now also vulnerable to the forces of global labour arbitrage. In short, the expanding scope of globalization and the deep structural inequalities in the global economy are working together to intensify the underlying dynamics of global labour arbitrage.

Global Tensions over the Distribution of Income

Another important source of increasing inter-connectedness is through the distribution of global income. A basic rationale for globalization is that it raises global GDP. While not all agree that this is the case, it is still reasonable to say that some countries and social groups within countries have enjoyed a significant increase in income as a result of globalization. The problems associated with globalization in fact reside not so much in the issue of whether there has been a net overall increase in global income but more in how the income gains associated with globalization have been distributed. These distributional tensions are important at both the global and national level.

From a global perspective it would be a useful heuristic device to think of world GDP in terms of a basic division between income that is clearly linked to globalization and that which is not (or is only marginally so). Since with increasing globalization the first component of global income is the predominant and much more dynamic source of growth, most of the distributional tensions centre on this. A basic part of these tensions is over inclusion and exclusion from this dynamic source of global income growth.

From a cosmopolitan perspective, the fact that many less developed countries are still largely excluded from this income-generating circuit is a cause for great concern. Globalization may well yield income gains that clearly pass a global welfare compensation test, that is, the income gains of winners could potentially more than compensate for the losers. This is a meaningful test in the context of nation states with well-developed institutions for the redistribution of income, since actual compensation is feasible. Thus workers in such countries who have lost out from globalization can be, and often are, compensated. However, at the global level a compensation test is meaningless. Short of more effective global governance, the fact that income gains are large enough to fund compensation is of little comfort to countries that have lost out (either from participation in the global economy on unsatisfactory terms or through being excluded from it) since there are no actual compensation mechanisms.

There are also serious distributional tensions along other important axes. First, there is the long-standing North-South distributional issue that is intensified in the current context of globalization. A topical aspect here is anxiety in the advanced countries that the current phase of globalization has opened the Pandora's box of "catch up" by the South, with the consequential erosion of their current economic predominance. This has been provoked largely by the rapid growth of countries from the South which have successfully integrated into the global economy, especially when these include giants such as India and China. Apart from the obvious geopolitical fact that sustained growth at current rates would lead to growing economic and political power for India and China, there are two other major anxieties. One is the fear that rapid growth in these countries has also been accompanied by a rapid growth of the absolute numbers of scientists and engineers.[23] This fact, combined with the continuing transfer of technology through FDI and off-shoring, has raised the spectre of a coming challenge to the dominance of the advanced countries in their last economic bastion of high technology and high skilled industries.

We discuss below the likelihood that such a scenario will unfold in the near future. Be this as it may, we still have to recognize other current distributional tensions between North and South. One is the issue of income distribution within the expanding global production system. The divide here is between Northern "winners" and Southern "losers". In the first category are Northern MNCs who are often accused of earning super-normal profits through their considerable market power, as well as Northern consumers who benefit from low prices.[24] In the other category are Southern sub-contractors of the MNCs who face severe competition and insecurity and Third World workers who make up the exploited bottom of the global production system. While the issue of how to shift income distribution within global production systems is the rallying cry of anti-globalization movements and underlies arguments for product labelling, ethical trade and corporate social responsibility, there is also a basic issue of development strategy involved.

This relates to the question of whether it makes any sense to seek participation in the global economy on these unequal terms. A purely economic calculus would indicate that the answer depends on a comparison between the economic outcomes of participating and the counterfactual of not doing so. The case has been made that such a comparison would favour participation, given the lack of meaningful alternatives for a poor country. This aside, the key, issue from the perspective of a developing country is whether participation in this global production system can serve as a stepping-stone to wider development options. This involves questions of industrialization strategy such as whether there are effective policy instruments to promote greater learning by local firms, entry or upgrading into higher value-added lines of production and, above all to raise productivity and hence wages.

Apart from this great North-South distributional divide, there are also other axes of contention within both the advanced and developing countries as well as among developing countries as a group.

Within the industrialized countries, a major new source of tension is the emerging divergence of interests between capital and labour that has been provoked by the new globalization. In the context of new opportunities for global outsourcing and off-shoring, profit-maximization on a world scale is now the main driver of corporate strategy. This has different distributional implications from profit-maximization on a largely national scale. In the latter case the interests of capital and labour were largely congruent as captured in the saying that 'what is good for General Motors is also good for the US (and its workers). Competitive success in both domestic and foreign markets meant greater profits but also more domestic jobs and rising productivity and wages. In contrast, profit-maximization on a global scale may no longer carry any guarantee of these benefits for workers.[25]

This is because a new type of divergence between private and social benefits has now arisen. A key element is the transfer of jobs to lower cost locations but this is not all. Owners of general and technological knowledge now also stand to gain from the exploitation of these assets on a global scale, strengthening the incentive for greater transfer of technology to developing countries. This works through the direct establishment of production facilities in the South as well as through sub-contracting, franchising, and licensing arrangements. All this increases the scope for spill-over and learning effects to strengthen the technical capabilities of potential economic rivals. This is the real basis of the concerns in the advanced countries about a possible loss of the comparative advantage that they currently enjoy in the skill and technology intensive industries to emerging rivals such as India and China.[26]

From a developing country perspective, however, a cause for concern should be the fact that these developments have not increased the relative demand for their most abundant factor of production, unskilled labour. Contrary to the predictions of the Hechsker-Olin theorem that growing trade with the industrialized countries will raise the relative demand for unskilled labour, skill premiums have in fact increased in many developing countries. Several explanations have been advanced for this phenomenon.

One is that increasing trade and investment flows are spreading skill-biased technological change to the developing countries.[27] Although the direct evidence so far is only partial there are grounds for believing that this may in fact be occurring. A closely related explanation is that trade and investment flows increase the incentives for producers in export and import-competing industries to adopt more skill-intensive technologies.[28] The competition for export markets pushes exporters to adopt newer and invariably more skill-intensive techniques of production.

The same applies to import-competing firms who have to preserve or strengthen their position in domestic markets in the face of increasing competition from imports. At the same time, foreign investment is usually the vehicle for introducing more skill-intensive technologies as it sets up or sub-contracts production in developing countries. Finally, the transfer of production from the advanced countries to developing countries tends to increase the skill-intensity of production in the latter countries. Production that is outsourced occurs at the margin of what constitutes the least skill-intensive jobs in the advanced countries. Yet these very same jobs are likely to be relatively skill-intensive from the vantage point of the developing countries that now come to host them. This is true of both manufacturing and service sector jobs, but with the added twist that the latter which are now being outsourced also include some that are skilled even from the advanced country perspective.

This new tendency towards increasing wage differentials between skilled and unskilled workers in developing countries has also to be viewed in the context of the great gap between North and South in terms of capital-labour ratios. Over and above the disturbing fact that current levels of FDI and other capital flows do not appear to be sufficient to close this gap, there is now the fact that neither increased openness to trade nor the transfer of capital and jobs that occurs is necessarily helping to boost the relative demand for unskilled labour in developing countries. Instead, “there appears to be a widespread tendency for wage and income inequality to increase in the wake of trade liberalization and contemporaneous developments such as the increase in trade in services and intermediate goods, increased flows of FDI and outsourcing, and the diffusion of skill-biased technical change. The increase in the relative demand for skilled labour is a global phenomenon that often leads to an increase in wage inequality”.

This phenomenon has important implications for employment policies in developing countries since the corner-stone of these policies has been the attempt to increase the demand for unskilled labour in order to maximize the rate of growth of productive employment. At the same time labour markets in these countries are also being confronted by other challenges. A key one is that several factors are tending to generate greater turbulence in labour markets. For instance, the recent literature indicates that labour market adjustments following trade reform occur not only between sectors but also within sectors, thereby increasing the extent of job reallocation.

This implies that jobs are at risk in all sectors and not, as conventionally thought, only in the import competing ones. Similarly, as more industries become footloose small shifts in costs can cause comparative advantage to shift abruptly from one country to another, implying an increase in labour turnover. In addition, in globally integrated production systems fixed cost activities are concentrated in the industrialized countries while variable cost activities are concentrated in developing countries. Since output shifts are driven mostly by changes in variable costs the volatility of output and employment will be higher in developing countries.]

References

1. OECD: *Economic Outlook 71*, Paris, 2002, p. 159.
2. *Ibid.*, p. 163.
3. R. Baldwin: *Globalization:The Great Unbundling(s)* (Prime Minister's Office, Finland, Aug. 2006). See also G.M. Grossman: *The Rise of Offshoring:It's not Wine for Cloth Anymore* (Paper for Federal Bank of Kansas Symposium, Jackson Hole, Aug. 2006).
4. WTO: *World Trade Report*, Geneva, 2006, p. 39.
5. A. Blinder: Offshoring: The Next Industrial Revolution? in *Foreign Affairs* (2006), Vol. 85 (Mar./Apr.).
6. R. Dossani and M. Kenny: "The next wave of globalization: Relocating Service Provision to India".
7. Penn World Tables: Capital Stock per Worker (accessed through http:/ datacentre2.chass.utoronto.ca/cgibin/pwt/jump?t=1).
8. R. N. Cooper: *How Integrated are Chinese and Indian Labour into the Global Economy?* (Washington D.C.
9. World Bank: World Development Report 2000/01 (Washington, D.C.,

2001), .*Development* (2007), Vol. 35, No. 5, May, Bank, mimeo, Feb. 2006.

10. B. Sutcliffe: "World Inequality and Globalization" in *Oxford Review of Economic Policy,* Vol. 20, No.1, 2004.
11. There is a lively literature on the pros and cons of alternative measures of global inequality, the trends they reveal and the extent to which globalization explains the observed outcomes. Three useful reviews of this literature are B. Milanovic: *Global Income Inequality: What It is and Why It Matters* (World Bank Policy Research Working Paper 3865, Mar. 2006), P. Svedberg: *World Income Distribution: Which Way?* (Institute of International Economic Studies, Stockholm, Seminar Paper No.724, Sep. 2003), and K. H. O'Rourke: *Globalzation and Inequality: Historical Trends*, paper for Annual World Bank Conference on Development Economics, May 2001.
12. J. Bradford Delong: *The World's Income Distribution: Turning the Corner?* (University of Berkeley, Feb. 2001).
13. *Ibid.*, p. 2.
14. A. Berry and J. Serieux: "All about the Giants: Probing the Influences on World Growth and Income Distribution at the End of the 20th Century" CESifo Economic Studies, Vol. 50, No.1, p.155, 2004, p.155.
15. P. Collier: *The Bottom Billion. Why the Poorest Countries are Failing and What can be Done about it* (Oxford University Press, 2007).
16. E. Leamer: "A Flat World, a Level Playing Field, a Small World After All, or None of the Above?" in *Journal of Economic Literature*, 2006.
17. S. Dowrick and J. Bradford Delong: *Globalization and Convergence*, Paper for NBER Conference on Globalization in Historical Perspective, Santa Barbara, California, May 2001.
18. P. Svedberg, *op. cit.*, p. 26.
19. *Ibid.*, p. 29.
20. S. Roach: *Perils of a Different Globalization* (Morgan Stanley Equity Research, Mar. 2006).
21. D. Colander: "The Long-run consequences of Trade and Outsourcing", in *Challenge* (2005), Vol. 48, No. 1, pp. 94-103.
22. R. Freeman: "People Flows in Globalization", in *Journal of Economic Perspectives* (2006). Vol. 20, No. 2.
23. R. B. Freeman: *Does Globalization of the Scientific-engineering Workforce Threaten US Economic Leadership*? (NBER, Working Paper 11457, June 2005).

24. J. Heintz: "Low-wage Manufacturing and Global Commodity Chains: A Model in the Unequal Exchange Tradition" in *Cambridge Journal of Economics* (Vol. 30, 2006).
25. R.E. Gomory and W. J. Baumol: *Global Trade and National Interests* (MIT Press, Cambridge Mass., 2000).
26. P. A. Samuelson: "Where Ricardo and Mill Rebut and Confirm Arguments of Mainstream Economists Supporting Globalization", in *Journal of Economic Perspectives* (2004), Vol. 18, No. 3, pp. 135-146.
27. E. Berhman and S. Machin: "Globalization, Skill-biased Technological Change and Labour Demand; in E. Lee and M. Vivarelli (eds.), *Understanding Globalization, Employment and Poverty Reduction* (Palgrave McMillan, 2004).
28. D.J. Robbins: *The impact of Trade Liberalization upon Inequality in Developing Countries, A Review of Theory and Evidence* (International Policy Group, ILO, Geneva, 2002, mimeo).

Chapter **10**

Paradigm Shift in the Foreign Trade Strategy to Trade Blocs

— Arun Bhadoria

Introduction

Though agriculture continues to be the mainstream of Indian economy, yet its contribution in total export of the country is not very encouraging. After the introduction of economic reforms in the country the situation has changed altogether. It is widely accepted that in the initial phase of economic reforms manufacturing sector received a greater weightage as compared to agricultural sector. The things were not so serious till agriculture was not brought on the main agenda of World Trade Organization (WTO). It was because of two reasons. Firstly, the import intensity of agriculture sector was not so high and secondly, this sector was considered to be less significant for the purpose of earning foreign exchange. However, after the establishment of WTO the issues pertaining to agricultural sector in general and agricultural exports in particular have drawn the attention of both researchers and policy-makers. It is significant to note that the agenda on agriculture of WTO has great bearance upon the agriculture production of developing countries including

India. It is a fact, which has drawn the attention of policy-makers to take suitable policy measures for safeguarding the interest of Indian farmers. Not only that but this is also very important in the context of raising overall growth rate to the tune of 9 percent (as achieved successfully in the last year) or more as targeted in subsequent Five Year Plans (FYP), for which it is necessary to raise growth rate in agricultural sector to the level of over 4 per cent, which is despite of holistic efforts trembling around 2 per cent and luckily touched 3.2 in the first quarter of last financial year, i.e., 2007-08.

Agriculture in post-WTO era has become strategically important for India. Besides, it's traditional importance, it can be a potential foreign exchange earner. But it all depends on the fact, how well we can reap the benefits of WTO regime. The WTO agreement on agriculture is stipulated to bring agriculture effectively for the first time under the discipline of the multilateral trading system. The trading arrangements evolved by WTO are a judicious mix of indicated, suggested and restricted measures. The agreement on agriculture under WTO has far reaching effects on Indian agriculture. The basic objectives of this agreement were to initiate substantial progressive reduction in support and protection resulting in reforms in world agriculture trade so as to make it more purposive and more transparent. Besides solving the traditional problems of Indian agriculture, it has to be made more competitive in the liberalized trading system. There is therefore, a need to inject the elements of productivity and efficiency in agriculture production. Unless we do this, we cannot prepare ourselves to reap the advantages of liberalized trading system. It is this fact, which has put agriculture on the centre stage of policy and planning framework.

In the ninth and eleventh FYP document, agriculture growth occupied the highest priority. The objectives of reducing the incidence of poverty and removal of unemployment were sought to attain primarily through accelerated agriculture growth. The focus has, however, shifted from growth in agriculture to sustainable development of agriculture. An emphasis has been made to increase the rate of gross value addition in agriculture and making its terms of trade favourable. Similarly the approach paper of tenth FYP lays greater emphasis on agriculture production. While there has been greater emphasis on enhancing the productivity of agriculture at domestic front, efforts are also being made to create exportable surplus in agriculture. According to ninth FYP, 16.68 million tones of food grains and 4.25 million tones of oilseeds, 123.5 million kg of tea and 220 million kg of coffee were the targets for creation of exportable surplus in the plan period. Greater emphasis has been laid on those areas, which have great potentials for exportable surplus production and globally competitive.

The subject of agriculture export in WTO era has emerged as a matter of concern for both researchers and policy-makers in India and elsewhere. There have been mind-boggling discussions and political parlays on the issue, for what should be the Indian line of action in New International Economic Environment. There is a unanimous view of all concerned that adequate policy measures are the first and foremost requirement so as to make Indian agriculture globally competitive. India has been a founder member of WTO and leading signatory to all the important agreements including on agriculture under WTO. There is no way to step backward. It is therefore of paramount interest to analyze the issues relating to agriculture exports of India under WTO. It is significant to note that agro-food production constitutes a large share in agriculture production. It is also considered to be a potential foreign exchange earner for the country. Therefore, the study of agro-food exports of India could be of vital interest to planners and policy-makers.

The bugbear that had engulfed Indian psyche on account of rising intervention of WTO regulations have now seems to be subsiding. This attributes to the fact that Indian economy has been sailing quite smoothly through the crossroads of promising imbibitions of growth in economic activities and expanding service sector and successful to raise its million's voice to account its claim to be self-reliant. After reaching to 2008 without crumbling due to the modalities pertaining to agreement on agriculture, the panic of subjugation under the threat of World Trade Organization's (WTO's) agreements have disappeared as ministerial conference of Singapore has failed to break the deadlock between two sections of traders and no guess can work that what way should it adopt. However, it is high time to learn lessons to survive future crisis as have experienced in yesteryears. For instance it will be worth-thinking that globalization is here to stay. And this meant to affect every activity in society. Taking positive approach to counter floodgates of development on account of globalization may be the winning strategy for any developing country. In the light of above, the hypotheses and scapegoats of unidentified dangers either have proved wrong or have disappeared from the scene. At this juncture, it would not be wise to talk about the false-hood of *swadesi*. The issue now is what form globalization should take whether encourages the expansion of international trade and investment. The most convincing fact is that WTO would hold the cradle for the future international trade and we have to find the way most feasible for working in WTO era. Under the purview of WTO, Agreement on Agriculture (AoA), Multi-Fibre Agreement (MFA), Trade Related Intellectual Property Rights (TRIPs) and Trade Related Investment Measures (TRIMs) have emerged one of the most controversial and challenging issues, which have remain main cause of confrontation between member states at many occasions and in which member countries are extremely polarized. The challenges facing the South Asian region due to the process of globalization and its implications for the agriculture sector are enormous characterized by high trade distortions and protections. We must celebrate our success in attracting the attention of developed countries towards the unity of developing countries.

But we should not forget that developing countries are not strong enough in front of developed countries. We must initiate the process of shaping our future strategy to fight the boomerang. We need to assess how much is at stake for us in agriculture. Does it matter if developed countries become reluctant to negotiate further and adopt their imperialistic style of dealing with developing or Third World countries?

This paper is an effort to analyze the opening of new avenues in agriculture exports in WTO era. The Part-I of the paper critically examines the WTO agenda of agriculture reforms in the first decade of new millennium. This paper also takes full account of India's trade relations with rest of the world during last few years. Part-II discusses trends of Agricultural Exports with trade blocs and other Less Developed Countries (LDCs). Part-III laid stress on the need to harness vast potential of Agro-food Export from India in post Cancun. Next part analyzes the emerging prospects of multilateralism over bilateralism or vice-versa.

PART-I : Cancun: A Great Divide?

The fifth Ministerial Conference of the 146 members WTO held at Cancun in Mexico was supposed to carry forward the negotiations put in the Doha Ministerial meet and set the tone for the future events. Though it could not make any stride in the contentious issues pertaining to the developing countries especially India, Brazil, etc. Moreover, it failed to negotiate even on those issues that were supposed to be settled before January 2005. Needless to mention that the launch of the Doha Development Agenda negotiations gave a big boost to the multilateral trading system and it was important that Cancun should have delivered on the promises that were built into the Doha negotiations. The Meet could not develop consensus amongst its members. This all happened due to the fact that Cancun Ministerial Conference turned out to be a ministerial of alliances for the developing world. The G-17 (group of developing countries formed to support on the issues pertaining to agriculture) became G-21 and finally emerged as G-22 including India, China, Brazil and South Africa. Meanwhile several other groups also formed following the same line of making blocs. Nevertheless, the Cancun brought about an attitudinal change in the developed countries for the developing world as they were caught unaware with the level of preparedness and unity of their developing counterparts. However, need of the hour is to look into the matter. Does it matter if developed countries become reluctant to negotiate further and adopt their imperialistic style of dealing with developing or third world countries? India would analyze its trade prospects with ASEAN, SAARC and all the other trade blocs. Thus the Cancun Ministerial can be termed as a "Great Divide".

India and other constituents of G-22 would welcome the WTO for being the main avenue to provide necessary framework to facilitate multilateral trade. The rule of WTO is mandatory in order to ensure success of multilateralism over regionalism and bilateralism. But the emergence of trading blocs during the Cancun Meet is a sign of conflict that may persist. In this context India would have to follow the policy of wait and watch as to encash positive repercussions, if any, as it has been in the form of Business Process Outsourcing (BPO). In the mean time India must assess its potential in all the sectors in general and agri-business in particular.

PART-II : Future Prospects of India's Agri-business with Rest of the World

Trends of Agricultural Exports with Major Trade Blocs

Inception of WTO in 1995 opened the floodgates to the global trade. Overnight countries had to devise suitable strategy to negotiate with the incoming flow of crossroads from all corners. All of them who were part of GATT automatically turned to be members of WTO. Those who weren't part of any such forum/bloc have felt great difficulty to devise suitable trade related strategy. Nevertheless they were also ignorant about their most traded commodities and did not know where their potential lies most. India, however was the member of GATT and have decided to join the WTO quite obviously, has never thought before seriously about most traded commodities and their potential which could be utilized to find its place in the global trade.

India had been trading with almost all the big/small countries of the world. Agricultural exports had a vital place in India's trade relations. Initially we were quite comfortable with whatever we were exporting. But soon with the opening of floodgates we realized that this could not be sustained for long unless we do not improve quality of our product and take a big leap in food processing industry. Moreover, rapid growth of agro-food based exports by south East Asian countries in food processing and other agricultural-allied activities forced India to think about its own potential. Debate over the usefulness of agri-business became centre of all discussions and negotiations nation-wide and later on of course internationally. The realization of its hidden potential was apparently a good sign of change in our approach.

Agreement on Agriculture (AoA) under the aegis of WTO charter opens up debate on various modalities of exports of agricultural products. Market access, tariffication and protection have found special mention in the draft of AoA. As per the modalities shown in the draft, developing countries find it very difficult to trade with rest of the world freely. This draft clearly refutes theory of multilateralism and tries to establish the idea of Most Favoured Nation (MFN) and Non Tariff Barriers (NTBs). Consequently, countries like India involved themselves as a part in the formation of various trade ambitious groups such as G-22, G-33 and G-15, etc. At this juncture it is quite appropriate to work out trends of trade with all the major and minor trade blocs and even with those who are not the part of any blocs. India would also have to analyze its trade prospects with ASEAN,

SAARC and all the other trade blocs. This is appearing from the fact that terms of trade are not improving with ASEAN and volumes of export have drastically reduced over the period of few years. As contrary to it terms of trade have improved quite fabulously with OECD. This is however to be noticed significantly that no improvement in total export has been seen even in case of OECD. But as far as NAFTA is concerned both terms of trade and volume of exports have shown noticeably favourable signals. Terms of trade with SAARC nations have appeared favourable but these figures do not have any significance for agri-business in India until it has separate trade bloc. Moreover, figures of trade with SAARC do not reveal complete fact about the trade in agro-food products. If we look at product wise export data, we find that almost same number of commodities is being exported to every bloc. This certainly approves idea of multilateral trade relations. However, to observe the trade efficiency it was desirable to observe the trend of exports to major trade blocs in last few years, especially after 1998-99. This would present a good picture of impact of WTO after the said year signifying transitional year.

Keeping this in mind, analysis of the trade relations and performance of India's exports with different countries and trade blocs over few years is desirable. The data reveals that terms of trade are most favourable with SAARC and NAFTA while terms of trade are favourable with OECD and EU except ASEAN. However, the data for exports with the same blocs for the year 2000-03 unveils surprising fact that indices of exports are in favourable direction with ASEAN and some countries from SAARC. Terms of trade have improved quite fabulously with OECD but no improvement in total export can be seen with the same. But as far as NAFTA is concerned both terms of trade and volume of exports have shown favorable signals (Table 1).

Terms of trade with SAARC nations have appeared favourable but these figures do not have any significance for agri-business in

India. It will become clearer if we have a look at top market destinations for agro-products throughout the world. OECD provides market for 173.3 per cent of major agro-products as selected by APEDA. EU (110 %), NAFTA (56.67%) are included in OECD (Table 2). Therefore, India would have to go to world market blocs especially EU, NAFTA and OECD as they happened to be large product destinations for India's agro-food products in general and agro-processed food products in particular (See Appendix). Though former Prime Minister Mr. A.B.Vajpayee had envisaged the establishment of free trade blocs SAFTA (see notes) but its constitution is still not clear and has not been proposed yet. Detailed analysis reveals the fact that downward trend with some countries of EU is the outcome of problem of quality and standards, which can be overcome. While with some countries of EU, NAFTA and OECD it was only relative difference not the absolute as the total volume of exports have risen from 0.67 per cent to 0.84 till 2003-04, which have led to the difference in absolute sense. The most appealing fact revealed by this discussions is that trade has received favourable trends from the countries of Middle East Asia like Kuwait, UAE and Iran over the few years. Agri-Export Zones (AEZs) for Potato at Agra (Uttar Pradesh, India) have exported most of its potato to UAE (Dubai) while AEZ for Onions and Vegetables in Karnataka and Andhra Pradesh are continuously trading with Sri Lanka. This may emerged as an separate trade blocs and may be named as West Asia Free Trade Area (WAFTA) or Middle East Free Trade Area (MEFTA).

Direction of Trade: Country-wise, Product-wise:

To make our discussion more authentic we finally take into the account the performance of India's trade with major countries in the last few years computing indices of exports and imports as well. Discussion with indices of exports revealed that exports to NAFTA are a good deal while with those countries that are not the part of any trade blocs are favourable too. While import indices revealed that EU, OECD and other countries are the best destinations for trade. This clearly states that India will not take the risk to go out of negotiations with countries of NAFTA and would also concentrate upon regional trade. Product-wise India is trading with all countries irrespective to any specific country. Though the types of commodities being traded are of traditional type and not fully processed. This bare fact for instance put future of India's agri-business on dark side as India is processing very small volume of its total produce while Malaysia is processing 83 per cent. This is why some experts refute the view of Free Trade Area by calling them Flop Trade Agreements.

Appropriate Stand in WTO Regime for Trade

For the last four years the whole debate during all the ministerial conferences, other meetings and summits has centred on the various types of subsidies as mentioned in the AoA. These subsidies are meant for extra protection given to the farmers and cultivators to avoid unwanted interference and competition. So far subsidies provided by the Indian Government so far, these do not come under questionable limit as mentioned in AoA. This is, however, a different but relevant matter that the pattern to raise subsidies is highly questionable in Indian context, which calls for policy-makers to review the functional objective behind these subsidies. Subsidies should not be indiscriminately to various odd sections of the community rather they must be devoluted with a view to give incentives to the farmers for their hard work. The basis, character, forms and procedure of providing subsidies at present actually allow a vast opportunity to traders and suppliers to corner sizeable money from public exchequer. Obviously more rationalized and productive subsidies can offer opportunities and avenues for higher earnings and thereby uplifting their quality of life. But such a drastic move requires a very strong political will. This would certainly boost the morale of masses and of course then they would be in position to elect good and efficient public representatives. Around Rs. 4,000 crore go waste every year just on account of subsidies. Moreover, well-off consumers, middlemen and traders salt this huge sum away. That ultimately causes burden on taxpayers. The system that is not beneficial to any one in real terms, not even to the poor whom it is claimed for.

The trade performance over last few years clearly reveals that exports are not healthy as transaction cost is not favourable. Policy-makers recognize that transaction cost is sliding from 19 per cent to 22 per cent on the value of exports. Consequently on the policy front, the ministry flags as urgent the issues of rebating all possible duties, levies and taxes suffered by exporters and making export promotion schemes WTO compatible. Raising concern over the transaction cost one should not forget that tariffs, levies, custom duties are major concern of developing world with developed countries. If we are making our products export compatible, others should counter it. Provided that Non Tariff Barriers and Most Favoured Nation type barriers should not put any hurdle. In case they continue, countries like India would have no option but to find its remedy by keeping all options open to trade with regional blocs.

Domestic and Regional Concerns

There has been complete shift in the policies since the adoption of economic reforms after 1994-95. Agriculture and allied sector are now being considered as potential foreign exchange earner. Earlier less than fifty per cent populations were economically active but this number has risen to 61 per cent over the last decade. Though we lag far behind than that of China (69 per cent economically active population) but being largest democracy and largest agriculture sector we have huge prospects for agri-business in India. Per agriculture worker value addition is Rs 397 while it is as high as Rs. 34,727 in USA, Rs. 19,930 in Germany and Rs. 28,665 in Japan. We must take care of competition with rest of the world in general and South

Asian region in particular. We have observed India's trade with major trade blocs all over the world.

If we look at the percentage of agro-products processed in the countries in this region then it becomes clear that India has to go long way. In Thailand 30 per cent food products are being processed while this is 78 per cent in the Philippines and 80 per cent in Malaysia. Though Philippines is not the part of SAFTA but this has close bearings upon the trade relations of the countries in this region.

PART-III : Need to Harness Vast Potential of Agro-food Export from India in Post-Cancun

The prospects for the trade in this sector are not dull as compared to the other sectors. Government has given it top priority in Tenth Plan and has estimated that the production of fruits and vegetables and other processed food products would reach 80 per cent of the total quantity of food grains produced in India by 2010. The present status of food processing industry though seems to be very minimal as it has very low level of contribution in food processing. These figures do not show the exact and exclusive picture of total food processing potential in India. In fact, India's food processing industry includes large number of agro-food product, which comes from agriculture and allied sector. Among these diversified product line several products have shown huge potential of export demand and hence good source of earning foreign exchange. Such products and their sub-sectors are being described here.

1. India exported fruits and vegetables worth Rs. 5,240 million in 1997-98. The horticulture production was around 100 million tones and FDI stood at nearly Rs. 8,000 crore.
2. India's current level of meat and meat-based exports is around Rs. 8,000 million. FDI is around Rs. 5,000 million, which happens to be 50 per cent of total investment in this sector.

3. India ranks fifth in the annual egg production.
4. Milk and milk products performed with 4 per cent growth at the time of worldwide recession (growth rate was –2).
5. FDI in fisheries was of the order of nearly Rs. 7,000 million.

Moreover, the processing food industry ranks fifth in size in the country representing 6.3 per cent of GDP. It accounts for 13 per cent of the country's exports and 6 per cent of total investment. The estimated size is at US $ 70 million, including 22 billion of value added products.

PART-IV : Multilateralism vs. Bilateralism

In the recent past India has enjoyed the expansion of its service sector. India has recorded sound development in Information Technology (IT), BPO-ITES, medical transcription and application software. On the other hand, China has emphasized on the improvement in its manufacturing sector. Though both the countries have largest manpower in the world, but they are nurturing their manpower in the field where they finds comparative advantage. India prefers self-reliance by developing its inner strength and want to least dependent on FDI while China is receiving $ 50 bn FDI every year compared to only $ 4 bn FDI in India. Consequently India does record slow growth but sustained. Indian Economy is developing steadily and will certainly improve its manufacturing sector. However, she has to seek advantage of being agriculture-based economy. If we look through the statistics of export competitiveness of Indian crop we find that traditional crop seldom appear cost competitive in international market (See notes). While cereal crop are not found cost-competitive, processed food products and edible oils are appearing as most internationally demanded products. This is therefore we must encourage processing of agro foods. We should not forget that despite of being 1 billion, processing insignificantly. However, we are exporting to every major trade blocs. Establishment of Agri-Export Zones have opened new horizons of processing long range of agro-food products like gherkin, strawberry, potato, mango, etc. Moreover, we have been already doing quite well in several products like milk, meat, onion, etc. This is therefore India is on advantage to practice agri-business in post-Cancun. India certainly going to have advantage in agri-business provided she adopts a sound strategy and policy framework and planning for the same. In this scenario, India must not forget its identity and previous policies. She has never favoured unilateralism and bilateralism (as indicated from trade relations with major trade blocs) in trade relations. India must develop its infrastructure to support the agri-business and would negotiate for true multilateralism in WTO (see notes). At the same time India would maintain the pace of developing inter-regional trade in South Asian region, as it will promote its economic, political and social interests.

Notes:

1. Out of total agro products, APEDA (Agro-Processed Food Products Export Development Authority) has selected 30 products for development. APEDA prepares the record of total exports at regular intervals and provide the requisite information.
2. SAFTA (South Asian Free Trade Area) (as same as NAFTA), in the Ministerial Meet at Islamabad, Prime Minister Mr. A.B.Vajpayee proposed SAFTA in which member nations would form a trading bloc and would engage themselves in inter-regional trade.
3. Export competitiveness of most of the commodities in India has undergone significant changes during 1990s. At the time of inception of WTO international agricultural prices were moving on a rising trend, which however showed a decline in trend after 1997. Indian Rice was found competitive

throughout while wheat and coarse grains were not found fit. Soya bean is found export competitive. Domestic Resource Cost indicates that wheat and maize are efficient import substitutes.

4. Indian Premier Man Mohan Singh has stated at Jakarta that India is standing for all the issues concerned with developing world but it would seek neutral attitude and would welcome true globalization.

5. The Indo-Thai FTA (ITFTA) has been in effect from September 2004. The SAFTA and ITFTA can be compared with regional trade blocs of US (NAFTA) and EU. Amongst FTAs the key issue is whether the economies of the countries entering into an FTA complement or compete with each other. In fact, when these FTAs were signed, there was a commitment from the government that issues like anomalies in the duty structure would be resolved before the FTAs are implemented.

6. Mr. Rahul Bajaj, Chairmen Bajaj Auto writes in *Times of India* that FTAs are the sign of global trade and are appearing quite favourable in USA, etc. For the successful FTA it is necessary that member countries should have suitable and soothe climate, which is not found in this region. FTA may not be very promising until our handicaps are removed.

7. As per the editorial of *Times of India*, about 20 years ago, then Prime Minister Rajiv Gandhi reckoned that only about 15 per cent of the money intended as subsidies actually reached the poor. Farmers can be given food stamps (a kind of food currency) that can be used to buy only specific eatables.

8. According to Ministry of Commerce, India's exports are on a high growth path. But are now faced with huge challenges including poor infrastructure and high transaction cost.

9. Commerce and Industry Minister, Mr. Kamal Nath has recently said that Non-Tariff Barriers (NTBs) are cause of concern. The barriers, which are other than health and safety related obviously, driven by commercial interests. Generalized System of Preferences (GSP) will also bother if India is not a part of it.

References

Drafts for Ninth and Tenth Plan from Handbook (2003), Kitab Mahal, New Delhi.

Bhargava, Sunil (2003): "WTO & Cancun Conference", *Journal for Chartered Accountants in India*, New Delhi, Dec.

Bhaumik, T.K (2003): "WTO, South Asia and Related Issues", *Liberal Times*, Vol. XI, No. 2, pp. 36-37.

Bajaj, Rahul (2005): "Flop Trade Agreements-Exports need policy impetus, not low tariffs", *Times of India*, April 28, New Delhi.

Bajaj, Rahul (2005): "Flop Trade Agreements: Exports Need Policy Impetus, Not Low Tariffs", *Times of India*, New Delhi, April 28, p. 14.

Editorial (2005): "Thought for Food: Scrap Subsidies, Top up incomes", *Times of India*, New Delhi, March 15, p. 14.

Times News Network (2005): "Exports Buoyant but Face Bumps Ahead", *Times of India*, New Delhi, June 24, p. 18.

Nath, Kamal (2005): "India Warns against Dividing Developing Nations at WTO", CII Conference; *Times of India*, Tuesday, New Delhi, March 15.

Statistical Outline of India (2002), Tata Services Limited, Mumbai.

Annual Report (2003): Food Processing Industry in India, www.google.com

Ibid.

Sen, Amitabh (2003): "Food Processing Industry in India", Google.com

Ibid.

Jhunjhunwala, B. (2005): "Success of China: Don't Scared", Daily Amar Ujala, April 19.

Ramesh Chand, (2001): *Trade Liberalization, WTO and Indian Agriculture-Experiences and Prospects*; Mittal Publications, New Delhi.

Bhargava, Sunil (2003): "WTO & Cancun Conference", *Journal for Chartered Accountants in India*, New Delhi, Dec.

Bhaumik, T.K (2003): "WTO, South Asia and Related Issues", Liberal Times, vol XI/ no 2, p.p-36-37.

Sen, Amitabh (2003): "Food Processing Industry in India", Google.com

Table 1

Trade with Major World Blocs

(In US $ Mn)

Trade Blocs	1994-95		1999-2000		2000-01	
	Export	Import	Export	Import	Export	Import
ASEAN	1902	1940	2192	4919	2836	3864
SAARC	1215	177	1396	398	1925	432
EU	7319	7580	9349	10989	10379	10320
NAFTA	5367	3212	9114	4046	10156	3244
OECD	15976	15512	21841	22863	24246	20576
Total*	35396	35973	49382	57816	56241	42495

Source: Statistical Outline of India, 2002-03.

* Total of trade from all blocs throughout the world.

Table 2
Percentage of Commodities Marketed in Major Trade Blocs

Major Market Blocs	Types of Products	Percentage Share
ASEAN	13	43.3
SAARC	21	70
EU	33	110
NAFTA	17	56.67
OECD	52*	173.3

Source: APEDA and List of trade Blocs.

*. OECD includes several countries, which are the part of either EU, SAARC, and any other trade blocs and it is true for EU and others. Therefore figures are not exclusive.

Table 3
Direction of India's Trade with Various Countries throughout World

Name of Country	Percentage Contribution			Exports Imports		
	1999-2000	2000-2001	Index	1999-2000	2000-2001	Index
USA (NAFTA)	22.7	22.8	100.44	7.7	5.5	71.43
Germany (EU)	4.8	4.3	89.58	4.0	3.3	82.50
Other European Union (EU)	14.3	13.2	92.31	12.1	8.9	73.55
UK (EU)	6.0	5.4	90.0	5.8	6.4	110.34
Japan (OECD)	4.5	4.3	95.55	5.0	4.3	86.0
Russia	2.5	2.1	84.0	1.3	1.1	84.6
OPEC	10.6	10.5	99.05	23.8	6.0	25.21
Other East EU (EU)	0.5	0.4	80.0	0.4	0.5	125
Asia (ASEAN & SAARC)	20.4	20.1	98.52	17.5	13.7	78.21
Other Less Developed Countries	4.8	5.1	106.25	5.0	4.0	80.0
Others	8.9	11.8	132.58	7.7	46.3	601.29

Source: Economic Analysis 2000-2001, Ministry of Finance, GOI.

Table 4

Comparative Analysis of Trade with Major Trade Blocs

Countries	Trade Blocs	No. of Products Exported to	Value of Exports (lakh Rs.) (2000-01, 01-02, 02-03)	% to the Total Exports
Pakistan	SAFTA*	19	21303.8 10069.3 3312.61	2.31 0.99 0.24 ↑
Bhutan	-do-	9	76.079 1132.061 3127.175	0.008 0.11 0.23 ↓
Sri lanka	-do-	28	27046.492 28887.713 28334.363	2.94 2.84 2.05 ↑
Nepal	-do-	29	4974.520 5589.287 9161.388	0.54 0.55 0.66 ↓
Bangladesh	-do-	26	77177.371 105901.059 149728.740	8.38 10.41 10.83 ↑
Maldives	-do-	25	3037.00 3032.00 3208.00	0.33 0.30 0.23 ↓
France	EU	27	12671.121 9293.281 12877.946	1.38 0.91 0.93 ↑
Spain	-do-	25	6852.296 6823.240 7762.849	0.74 0.67 0.56 ↑
Germany	-do-	27	18211.785 14984.548 21576.353	1.98 1.47 1.56 ↑
Netherlands	-do-	27	18541.71 15558.77 17421.77	2.01 1.53 1.26 ↑
Belgium	-do-	25	8203.170 7648.783 9249.105	0.89 0.75 0.67 ↑

UK	-do-	28	55616.285	6.04	↑
			42526.451	4.18	
			46731.200	3.38	
Italy	-do-	24	6381.554	0.69	↑
			6470.007	0.64	
			5701.934	0.41	
Portugal	-do-	19	965.00	0.11	↑
			649.00	0.16	
			922.31	0.07	
USA	NAFTA	28	77077.884	8.37	↑
			60841.168	5.98	
			90419.109	6.54	
Canada	-do-	28	9499.811	1.03	↑
			8263.042	0.81	
			10043.899	0.73	
Indonesia	ASEAN	27	23295.0	2.53	↓
			37422.19	3.68	
			90369.27	6.54	
Singapore	-do-	27	9543.53	1.04	↓
			15143.00	1.49	
			18129.02	1.31	
Malaysia	-do-	27	57827.442	6.28	↓
			71186.363	6.99	
			102102.201	7.38	
China	-do-	29	4403.00	0.48	↓
			8078.19	0.79	
			8808.97	0.64	
Hong Kong	-do-	28	3324.71	0.36	↑
			4033.25	0.39	
			2782.20	0.20	
Korea	-do-	26	13429.31	1.46	↑
			10541.00	1.04	
			11609.53	0.84	
Japan	OECD	26	7912.564	0.86	↑
			8912.671	0.88	
			9822.212	0.71	
Australia	-do-	27	4686.110	0.51	↑
			4991.153	0.46	
			5943.174	0.43	

Kuwait	WAFTA**	28	32793.035 29343.826 27947.578	3.56 2.89 2.02	↑
UAE	-do-	28	73082.938 75801.656 78675.726	7.93 7.45 5.69	↑
Iran	-do-	19	6139.523 8169.408 5494.046	0.66 0.80 0.40	↑

Source: DGCIS, Annual Volume, apeda.com.

*Proposed to constitute by 2006.
**May be created.

List of Types of Products

1. Floriculture— floriculture (01) and fruit and vegetable seeds (02)
2. Fruits and vegetables— fresh onions (03), other fresh vegetables (04), walnuts (05), fresh mangoes (06), fresh grapes (07) and other fresh fruits (08).
3. Processed fruits & vegetables—dried & preserved vegetable (09), mango pulp (10), pickles & chutneys (11) and other processed fruits & vegetables (12).
4. Animal products foods—buffalo meat (13), sheep/goat meat (14), poultry products (5), dairy product (16), animal casing (17) and processed meat (18).
5. Other processed food—groundnut (19), guar gum (20), jaggary & confectionery (21), cocoa product (22), cereal preparation (23), alcoholic beverage (24), miscellaneous preparation (25) and milled product (26).
6. Cereals—basmati rice (27), non-basmati rice (28), wheat (29) and other cereals (30).

List of Product Destinations

Name of Blocs	Nations	Number of Products	Code Number of Products
NAFTA	USA	16	28
	Canada	01	28
EU	Italy	02	24
	France	02	27
	Germany	06	27
	Belgium	01	25
	Netherlands	07	27
	UK	12	25
	Spain	02	28
	Portugal	01	19
ASEAN	Indonesia	03	27
	Singapore	02	27
	Korea Rep	01	26
	Malaysia	04	27
	Hong Kong	02	28
	China	01	29
OECD	EU	33	29
	NAFTA	17	28
	Australia	—	27
	Japan	02	26
SAARC	Sri Lanka	09	28
	Bhutan	—	9
	Pakistan	02	19
	Nepal	01	29
	Maldives	—	25
	Bangladesh	09	26

Source: APEDA.

Chapter **11**

Globalization and Its Impact on Child Labour

— Pooja Singh

Abstract

This paper is an attempt to examine the impact of globalization on child labour. Globalization has positive effect on child labour. In the process of globalization FDI, liberalized trade, capital flows, technology changes the local labour market, which increases the earning opportunity available to poor household in developing countries. Poverty creates child labour. Due to poverty parents are unable to provide for basic formal education to their children. So when globalization improves the income of improvised household this additional income helps parents reduce the work loads of their children and send more of them to school. Therefore in age of globalization household above its subsistence threshold allowing it to reduce or eliminate reliance on income generated through child labours.

This paper is divided into 6 parts first part is introduction which describes the scope and objective of this paper. The second part shows the trends of child labour in India which present the scenario of socio and economic background of children in India. The third part is how can globalization affect the child labour both Indian and global context. The fourth part is empirical evidence on globalization and child labour the fifth part deals with exploration from this evidence and the last part is conclusion which discusses the main finding of this paper.

Introduction

This paper analyzes the relationship between globalization and child labour. The effect of globalization on child labour is a central issue in the globalization debate. Proponents of globalization argue that free trade increases income and therefore decreases the incidence of child labour. If households send their children to work not out of greed but rather subsistence, then increases in income may push the household above its subsistence threshold, allowing it to reduce or eliminate reliance on income. Poverty creates child labour in India.

The most important cause of child labour in India is wide-spread poverty: Nearly one-third of India population subsists below the poverty line, because of poverty the parents wants their children to fend for themselves as soon as they can if not generated enough surplus to support the family. The poor parents who do not have sufficient income are in need of the earning for their children. The parents forced to send their children in the labour market to earn wage income.

Due to poverty the household are unable to provide for basic formal education to their children. As a result the parent's are compelled to send their children to take up wage employment to the detriment of the children health education and general well being. Also the parents do not underscore the future of their children due to illiteracy and ignorance.

However, several recent studies have found that poverty creates child labor. A new study examining child labour in over 4,000

Vietnamese households during the 1990s suggests that when globalization improves the income of impoverished households, this additional income helps parents reduce the workload of their children and send more of them to school.

Magnitude and Trend of Child Labour in India

The complex issue of child labour is a development issue worth investigating. The notion that children are being exploited and forced into labor while not receiving education crucial to development concern many people. India is a largest example of nation faced by the problem of child labour, estimates cite figure of between 60 and 115 million working children in India which is highest number in the world Millions of children in India enter the labour market at an early age and in large number. In 1991 census estimates out of about a total of 200 million children in the age group of 5–14 years some 11.28 million children are child labour and it is 5.37% of the total no. of children.

The census count as workers only those children below the age of 14 years who are engaged in gainful economic activity. Since not all the work done by children is remunerated the census figures appear to be underestimates. Unlike the census most other estimates include all children engaged in work, productive or otherwise, whether paid or unpaid, at any time of the day within or outside the family.

The International Labour Office estimates that at least 250 million children between the ages of 5 and 15 are working. This prevalence of child labour upsets many people in rich countries. As a result, governments in Europe and elsewhere have imposed or threatened to impose trade sanctions that restrict the sale of goods from developing countries. The stated aim of these sanctions is to force developing countries to take steps towards the elimination of child labour.

What is Child Labour

According to Convention 182, the work is done by child in the age of 5-14, except their physical development, basic education and entertainment related needs can be called child labour.

In November of 2000, ten children earning around $11 per month burned to death in a garment factory in Bangladesh. The exits from the factory were chained shut. Images of children chained into factories, sold as slaves, or forced into prostitution stain the popular imagination about child labour. Fortunately, while many children work in the developing world, relatively few experience such atrocities.

Politicians in developing countries like to define child labour as work that impairs the development and well-being of children. Economists prefer a less subjective definition. Economists view child labour as the economic activities in which children participate. This definition includes slavery and prostitution, but it extends to the types of activities that children regularly participate in throughout the developing world.

In 1999 and 2000, UNICEF interviewed children across 30 developing countries. UNICEF discovered that factory work is rare. Only 3% of children work outside of their household for pay. Unpaid domestic work is more common than is work for pay. UNICEF found that 2% of boys and 5% of girls perform unpaid domestic work for households other than their own. However, most working children are employed in their own household, helping with household duties or the family's farm and business.

Consider the typical 14 year old girl living in rural Nepal who was interviewed in a recent labour survey. She works about 35 hours per week. She spends 19 hours of that time working in agriculture for her family, and 9 hours helping her family with household work. She does not work for pay, and she does not attend school. An array of activities occupies the rest of her time. Gathering firewood and collecting water are two of her more time consuming tasks.

While economists and politicians differ in their definition of child labour, economists differ among themselves in how they define the economic activities of children. The first wave of child labour studies only considered work for pay, work in a formal household business, and work in agriculture. More recently, economists have begun to recognize that ignoring household activities limits their ability to understand how children spend their time. For example, if a parent leaves the household to work for a local employer, a child may take over many of the parent's household roles. Ignoring time spent by children collecting wood and water, tending to animals, preparing foods and meals, or caring for family members would imply that a child spending two hours a day in agriculture works more than the child labouring twelve hours a day filling in for an absent parent.

Why Do Children Work?

Social scientists vary in how they view a parent's decision to send a child to work. The debate revolves around how parents in developing countries view child labour. In one view, parents want their children to work. Perhaps parents even have children in order to send the children to work. This view implies that parents take advantage of any earnings opportunity open to children. So long as parents benefit more when the child works than when the child goes to school, child labour persists. Improvements in living standards may do nothing to ameliorate child labour.

An opposing view believes that parents in developing countries do not differ from parents in rich countries in how they view child labour. Researchers have observed that parents in poor countries generally say that they would rather their children attend school and work less. So why is child labor so pervasive? For the simple reason that impoverished households need their children to work.

Households that cannot meet their basic needs depend upon

the income of their children for survival. Without the income from working children, parents in poor households may have to choose which children to feed. Moreover, schooling is expensive in most of the developing world. Thus, it is not uncommon to see some children working so that their siblings may attend school. If governments could somehow prevent children from working, we might see less schooling rather than more, because the loss of income from working children would make schooling even more unaffordable.

A casual cross-country comparison supports the view that child labour stems from poverty. In the world's poorest nations with per capita incomes below US $1,500 in 1998, it is not unusual to find over 30% of children working. In contrast, child labour is rare in countries with per capita incomes above 7,000 US dollars. Per capita income of the US in 1998 was approximately US $30,000. Thus, parents in countries that are not even a quarter as wealthy as the US are able to keep their children from having to work.

This cross-country evidence on the link between child labour and poverty is supported by a recent study in Vietnam that examines how the economic activities of children evolve as household incomes change. The General Statistical Office of Vietnam and the World Bank followed over 4,000 households during Vietnam's economic boom in the 1990s. Participation rates in child labour declined by over 25% in rural Vietnamese households between 1993 and 1998. The declines in child labour were largest in the households experiencing the largest growth in living standards during Vietnam's boom. Income growth was largest in poor households. Overall, the study finds that improvements in living standards can explain 94% of the decline in child labour for households near the poverty line in Vietnam. Thus, the evidence from both across and within countries suggests that children work because of poverty. When incomes increase, children stop working.

How can Globalization Affect Child Labour?

Globalization in its literal sense is the process of globalizing, transformation of some things or phenomena into global ones. It can be described as process by which the people of the world are unified into a single society and functioning together. This process is a combination of economic, technological, socio-cultural and political forces. Globalization is very often used to refer to economic globalization that is integration of national economies into the international economy through trade, foreign direct investment, capital flows, migration, and the spread of technology.

In the age of globlization India get new technology, increased foreign investment and new jobs opportunity. This new jobs opportunity decreased the magnitude of chid labour in India, because globalization increase the employment and earnings opportunities available to poor households in developing countries. So changes in local labour markets from globalization decrease child labour.

Globalization can enhance employment and earnings in developing countries because of inflows of foreign investment or increases in the value of a developing country's export products. When a country opens to international markets, foreign investment often (but not always) enters the country. This leads to increases in the demand for local labour and hence higher wages. In addition, many of today's developing countries have comparative advantage in agriculture, and integration into international markets may increase the price of the export product to international levels. Thus, trade liberalization may increase employment and wages in these agricultural export sectors.

Alternatively, globalization induced improvements in earnings opportunities can reduce child labour. If poverty drives child labour, children work either for the income from work or because they cannot afford school fees. When one child makes more as a result of globalization, other children may be able to stop working and attend school. Moreover, increased parental earnings may help parents reduce the work that children perform. Parents can buy substitutes for goods previously produced by children, or they can use their increased income to substitute for the money previously earned by children. Hence, globalization can help parents in poor countries stop child labour without foreign intervention.

Of course, critics of globalization question whether globalization increases the earnings opportunities of residents in poorer countries. Globalization increases a country's exposure to foreign competition. This may force inefficient firms in import-competing industries out of business. Regardless of the long-term benefits of this reallocation of resources, in the short term, these adjustments may create difficulty for some households with children.

A second argument against the link between globalization and increased earnings opportunities claims that globalization encourages the entry of foreign multinationals and that they depress the earnings opportunities and wages of local workers. This can happen if foreign companies wield non-competitive market power in local markets. Anecdotes of this type of "bad" behaviour of firms are common in the popular press. Serious researchers have taken the time to collect data on every single manufacturing plant in a vast array of countries. Every one of these studies based on complete manufacturing information finds that foreign firms actually pay higher wages than do local firms after researchers control for other firm characteristics.

Not only does globalization affect earnings opportunities in developing countries, but globalization also increases the ability of rich countries to influence policy in the world's poorer nations. As developing countries integrate into the world economy and increasingly rely on export markets to sell their products, rich countries can use the threat of trade sanctions to coerce policies that attempt to curtail child labor. In December 2001, EU Trade Commissioner Pascal Lamy announced that EU foreign ministers have approved a preferential tariff scheme for countries that adhere to ILO labour standards including child labour. Both the Clinton and Bush administrations have voiced a commitment to a similar policy, and in 1999 the US imposed quotas on Cambodia's garment industry because of working conditions and child labour. Thus, globalization enables high-income countries to punish poor nations for high levels of child labour.

Evidence on Globalization and Child Labour

A recent study of child labour in Vietnam evaluates how trade policy might affect child labour. Out of a concern for domestic food security, Vietnam restricted its exports of rice starting in 1989. These quotas suppressed the domestic price of rice. Between 1993 and 1997, Vietnam gradually relaxed this export quota so that by 1998, Vietnam was completely exposed to the international price of rice. During this period of liberalization, the price of rice increased by 30% relative to the rise in the consumer price index.

Rice is an important commodity in Vietnam. It is the primary staple in the Vietnamese diet, the largest single component of household expenditure, and 70% of households produce rice. Moreover, in 1993, before the liberalization of rice prices in Vietnam, 26% of children between 6 and 15 worked in rice production in Vietnam, and rice production was far and away the largest employer of adults. Thus, rice price increases should affect both children and adults.

The study finds that rice price increases can account for 45% of the overall decline in child labour that Vietnam experienced in the 1990s. This corresponds to approximately 1 million fewer working children in Vietnam.

The study identifies several ways in which rice price increases affect child labor. Both child and adult wages rise with increases in rice prices. Higher child wages encourage children to work, but the observed rise in adult wages appears to reduce child labour more than higher child wages increase child labour.

The impact on child labour of these wage increases is tiny compared to the decline in child labour attributable to the additional income captured by households owning land for rice production. Rice producing households enjoy higher incomes after rice price increases, and they use this additional income to replace the income previously brought into the household by child labour.

Almost all of the variation in how Vietnamese households respond to rice price increases can be explained by landholdings. Households that do not own any land suitable for rice cultivation suffer with rice price increases. It becomes more expensive for these households to buy food, and the study finds that children have to work more in these landless or non-agricultural households. However, land suitable for rice cultivation is sufficiently evenly distributed in Vietnam that most households with children benefit from increases in rice prices. This equitable land redistribution is why over 1 million children appear to benefit from rice price increases.

These results are startling. Even though rice price increases make child labour more lucrative, parents choose to use increases in household income to reduce the amount that their children work. Moreover, the children who work the most before the price changes are the largest beneficiaries of these improvements in household income. Secondary school age girls experience the largest declines in work. Likewise, their school attendance increases with rice prices by more than any other age and gender group.

Extrapolating from this Evidence

How representative are these findings from Vietnam? The primary contribution of this research is the finding that parents in poor countries use extra income to move children out of work. This effect of additional income occurs even in the face of increased earnings opportunities for children. Thus, the patronizing view held by so many rich country observers, that poor country parents somehow do not care about the well being of their children seems unfounded.

Moreover, these findings suggest that the use of punitive, income reducing sanctions against countries where child labour is prevalent may not have the intended impact. If children work because of poverty, then sanctions and punishments for countries with child labour hardly seem to be policies that have the welfare of children in mind. A more effective way to discourage child labour would be to supplement support for income generating activities with, perhaps, additional incentives for children to stay in school.

The next round of global trade negotiations aims to bring developing countries into the international trading community. Many of these countries are agricultural economies that will experience price movements in agricultural commodities like the rice price changes studied in Vietnam.

Whether children in other countries will benefit like children in Vietnam depends in part on how the gains from trade will be distributed. In Vietnam, over 70% of the population produces rice and hence benefits from the liberalization of rice markets. Children in countries with less equitable distributions of the gains from trade may not benefit from globalization as much as Vietnam.

Thus, the challenge for the rich country observer concerned about child labour is not to fight globalization and international trade. Rather, it is to make sure that the gains from international market integration reach the poor in developing countries. The available evidence suggests that child labour could virtually disappear if the poor of the world could attain living standards that are even a quarter of that currently enjoyed by wealthy countries like the United States and Switzerland.

Conclusion and Suggestion

The main focus of the paper was to examine the how can globalization affect the child labour. The findings of the study reveal that globalization can enhance employment and earnings opportunity in developing countries because of inflows of foreign investment on increase in the value of a developing country export product this lead to increase in the demand for local labour, which force to increase the new job for local labours and higher wages higher child wages rise with encourage children to work but the observed rise in adult wage appear to reduce child labour more than higher child wages increase child labour. This additional income helps parents reduce the workload of their children and send more of them to school. Thus globalization increases employment and wages in developing countries and also eliminates on reduces the reliance on child wages of their parents.

Our country has the dubious distinction of having a very large concentration of working children. If poverty is degrading and dehumanizing indeed then it is nowhere more manifest than in the sorry plight of there millions of children apathetic environment. Child labour an in escapable fall out of the household forms of production under the dominance of merchant and there capital which is being reproduced and strengthened in a given socio economic system.

References

Understanding Children's Work—a joint project of the ILO, the World Bank, and UNICEF: http://www.ucw-project.org/index.html

The International Labor Office Tracks Child Labor Worldwide: http://www.ilo.org/public/english/standards/ipec/simpoc/index.htm

The author's research on child labour is available from his website:

http://www.dartmouth.edu/~eedmonds/7911.

Blonigen, B.A., 2005. A Review of the Empirical Literature on FDI Determinants. *Atlantic Economics Journal,* 33, 383-403.

Cigno, A., Rosati, F., Guarcello, L., 2002. Does Globalization Increase Child Labour? *World Development,* 30 (9), 1579-1589.

Edmonds, E., Pavcnik, N., 2005. The Effects of Trade Liberalization on Child Labour. *Journal of International Economics,* 65 (2), 401-441.

Edmonds, E., Pavcnik, N., 2006. International Trade and Child Labour: Cross-country Evidence, *Journal of International Economics,* 68 (2), 115-140.

Feenstra, R., Hanson, G., 1997. Foreign Direct Investment and Relative Wages: Evidence from Mexican Maquiladoras, *Journal of International Economics,* 42 (3-4), 371-393.

12 *Chapter*

Globalization: Its Effects on Culture

—Anita Gupta

"Globalization" is nowadays one of the most popular words. It is present everywhere in public discourse We can hear it on TV news, in parliament's debates, we can read it in journals. Amazingly far so widely use of this key-term, there is not appear to be any precise, widely-agreed definition of it. In every single instance the word "globalization" seems to have a different meaning in a different situation. I think that everyone will agree with the claim that globalization is a huge, complex process that changes the world in front of our eyes. It effects every sphere of our life—economical, political and social one. In this article I would like to focus on one of the many dimensions of globalization, that is the globalization of culture. In my opinion it is one of the most important issues, that has influence on how people see themselves in the world around them, which is now in the middle of transformation. By showing various opinions and arguments I will try to find an answer to the question which lately has gained a very important meaning. What effects will the culture globalization cause? Does it lead to cultural diversity as one think or may be to cultural homogenization as others claim? Those questions are not easy. They require looking at the problem from different points of view and perspectives. In addition, what is more important, is finding the answer we have to try to understand the whole process to understand its consequences.

What is the "globalization" that everyone talks about? The term is in common usage since "80". By some, it is enthusiastic considered as an inevitable process—a key to economic development and integration. Others regard it with fear believing that it will increase a gap between "poor" and "rich" countries, poverty and unemployment.

At the top political and economic level globalization is a process of denationalization of markets, politics and legal systems. It is a result of technological progress and innovation. But we can not forget that it not only refers to increasing integration of economies around the world, especially through trade and financial flows but also to movement of people (laboru), capital technology, norms, values and ideas. The consequences are visible in local economies, human welfare and in everyday life of anyone of us. Brought changes have a great meaning and it is almost impossible to conceive a significant group in society that will remain untouched by them. We can understand the globalization as a new condition of a modern world, as a complex connectivity. According to John Tomlinson, by this we mean rapidly developing network of interconnections and interdependence that characterize modern social life. "The notion of connectivity is found in one form or another in most contemporary accounts of globalization". To shortly elaborate this idea we need to look at two ways in which it shades into other themes. The first one can be called the proximity. It involves a sense of the shrinking of distances through the dramatic reduction in the time taken with the consequence in the "stretching" of social relations across distance. A world in common conscious appears more intimate and compressed. Being connected means being close in very specific ways, "the connections that effect our lives (...) are made sense of as though they really bring us into closer contact" (J.Tomlinson, 1999). Social relations across large tracts of time—space cause distant events and powers to penetrate our local experience. Globalization changes local order and imply proximity as a general sociocultural condition.

There is also another significant elaboration of the idea of connectivity which is called a global unicity. In the core of it lies a believe that the world is becoming a single social setting. It does not only mean a simplistic uniformity. It is rather considered as a "global-human condition". It requires thinking that local experience has to be raised to the horizon of a "single world". What is more, local practices and lifestyles need to be examined and evaluated in terms of their global consequences.

What is culture? According to Webster's Third International Dictionary we can defined it as : "the total pattern of human behaviour and its products embodied in speech, action, and artifacts and dependent upon man's capacity for learning and transmitting knowledge to succeeding generations." It can also be understood as the order of life in which people construct meaning through practices of symbolic representation. Language, religion, political and legal system, social customs are the most important components of cultural identity. They are considered as the rudiments of people's identity. Even casual examination of the history of conflicts shows that very often conflicts erupt precisely where the cultural faults lines are. Cultural differences are sanctified by their links to mystical and historical roots. Consequently, a threat of one's culture becomes a threat to one's core of identity.

How we should think of culture in relation to globalization. In my opinion the best answer is to see it as a one of the dimension of this multi-dimensional process. Culture matters for globalization in the obvious way—it is the core of whole idea of complex connectivity. The argument, justifying the priority to culture, that symbolic exchanges are now not limited because of the stretching relations and the world unicity, is only scarcely convincing . The real problem lies in the way we conceive of culture as having consequences. People do not produce meaning by themselves. It is the cultural signification and interpretation that constantly orientates them, as well in the individual as in the collective aspect. Because of the connectivity local lifestyles have become global consequential. Moreover, local individual actions are connected with the "global social world". And why globalization matters for culture? First of all, it promotes physical mobility stronger than ever before. In addition, brought changes, a deterritorialization, increase in very significant way the horizon and possibility for spreading cultural values cultural exchange and for emerging the "global culture".

Societies do not passively give into foreign and global influences. Various strategies of dealing with them have been identified. The most important one are resistance and appropriation. The example for the first one is that the states often try to prohibit foreign influences to enter their territory. France attempts to protect in different ways French language from being anglicized. Extreme case is, for instance Iran, which does not allow its citizens to own satellite-dishes.

But more often than resistance we can observe the process of appropriation with the consequences in incorporating foreign influence into peoples' lives. It can be demonstrated in various spheres from media technology to human rights, norms and values. This shows that the society is affected in very deep ways by imports.

As a result of increasing cultural contact a number of traditional practices disappear. But at the same time the globalization of culture leads to emergence of new cultural forms. Pointing this out, everywhere the cultural diffusion creates new practices, worldviews, expressions. In the shadow of this, new transnational communities come into being. "They are more bound together by common interest, social and cultural similarities than by geographical closeness" (J. Breidenbach/Zakrigl). Both processes confirm conceiving of the culture as not static unit but rather as a "flow" which allowed to acknowledge cultural similarities and differences irrespective of origin and geographical place.

The emerging global culture mainly consists of universal categories and standards. On the one hand societies all over the world become more similar to one another. On the other hand, get more and more different. Global structure organizes cultural diversity worldwide. Cultures continue to be distinct and varied but they are different in very uniform ways. What is more important is that very many people develop a comparative consciousness because of availability of certain ideas, information, institutions and goods to an increasing number of people.

The impact of globalization on culture and the impact of culture on globalization merit discussion. The homogenizing influences of globalization that are most often condemned by the new nationalists and by cultural romanticists are actually positive; globalization promotes integration and the removal not only of cultural barriers but of many of the negative dimensions of culture. Globalization is a vital step toward both a more stable world and better lives for the people in it.

Culture is used by the organizers of society—politicians, theologians, academics, and families—to impose and ensure order, the rudiments of which change over time as need dictates. It is less often acknowledged as the means of justifying inhumanity and warfare. Nonetheless, even a casual examination of the history of conflict explains well why Samuel Huntington, in his *The Clash of Civilizations*, expects conflict along cultural fault lines, which is precisely where conflict so often erupts. Even worse is that cultural differences are often sanctified by their links to the mystical roots of culture, be they spiritual or historical. Consequently, a threat to one's culture becomes a threat to one's God or one's ancestors and, therefore, to one's core identity. This inflammatory formula has been used to justify many of humanity's worst acts.

Cultural conflicts can be placed into three broad categories: religious warfare, ethnic conflict, and conflict between "cultural cousins", which amounts to historical animosity between cultures that may be similar in some respects but still have significant differences that have been used to justify conflict over issues of proximity, such as resource demands or simple greed.

Religion-based conflicts occur between Christians and Muslims, Christians and Jews, Muslims and Jews, Hindus and Muslims, Sufis and Sunis, Protestants and Catholics, and so forth. Cultural conflicts that spring from ethnic (and in some cases religious) differences include those between Chinese and Vietnamese, Chinese and Japanese, Chinese and Malays, Normans and Saxons, Slavs and Turks, Armenians and Azerbaijanis, Armenians and Turks, Turks and Greeks, Russians and Chechens, Serbs and Bosnians, Hutus and Tutsis, blacks and Afrikaners, blacks and whites, and Persians and Arabs. Conflicts between "cultural cousins" over resources or territory have occurred between Britain and France, France and Germany, Libya and Egypt, and many others.

That is why by many, globalization, especially in its cultural dimension, is regarded as an Americanzation. "We all become Americans"—it is one of the most popular sentence in mouths of opponents of this process and in the same time it has become one of the most controversial issue connected with it. It is not without a reason that McDonald's and Coca-Cola are a symbols of globalized world. A spread, domination and penetration of the American culture is considered as a great threat to other cultures. McWorld, a culture of fast food, computers, MTV is seen as a "soft imperialism" with a goal in homogenization of global markets and tastes. It presses nation into one global "theme park", tied together by communication, information, entertainment and commerce.

Another category that might be included in our taxonomy is quasi-cultural conflict. This conflict is primarily ideological and is not deeply enough rooted in tradition to fit within standard definitions of culture, yet it still exhibits most if not all of the characteristics of other cultural clashes. The best example here is the Cold War itself, a conflict between political cultures that was portrayed by its combatants in broader cultural terms: "godless communists" versus "corrupt capitalists". During this conflict, differences regarding the role of the individual within the state and over the distribution of income produced a "clash of civilizations" that had a relatively recent origin.

Finally, as a reminder of the toll that such conflicts take, one need only look at the 20th century's genocides. In each one, leaders used culture to fuel the passions of their armies and other millions and to justify their actions among their people. One million Armenians; tens of millions of Russians; 10 million Jews, Gypsies, and homosexuals; 3 million Cambodians; and hundreds of thousands of Bosnians, Rwandans, and Timorese all were the victims of "culture"—whether it was ethnic, religious, ideological, tribal, or nationalistic in its origins. To be sure, they fell victim to other agendas as well. But the provocative elements of culture were to these accompanying agendas as Joseph Goebbels was to Adolf Hitler—an enabler and perhaps the most insidious accomplice. Historians can, of course, find examples from across the ages of "superior" cultures eradicating "inferior" opponents—in the American West, among the native tribes of the Americas and Africa, during the Inquisition, and during the expansion of virtually every empire.

Satellites as Cultural Death Stars

Critics of globalization argue that the process will lead to a stripping away of identity and a blandly uniform, Orwellian world. On a planet of 6 billion people, this is, of course, an impossibility. More importantly, the decline of cultural distinctions may be a measure of the progress of civilization, a tangible sign of enhanced communications and understanding. Successful multicultural societies, be they nations, federations, or other conglomerations of closely interrelated states, discern those aspects of culture that do not threaten union, stability, or prosperity (such as food, holidays, rituals, and music) and allow them to flourish. But they counteract or eradicate the more subversive elements of culture. History shows that bridging cultural gaps successfully and serving as a home to diverse peoples requires certain social structures, laws, and institutions that transcend culture. Furthermore, the history of a number of ongoing experiments in multiculturalism, such as in the European Union, India, South Africa, and the United States, suggests that workable, if not perfected, integrative models exist. Each is built on the idea that tolerance is crucial to social well-being, and each at times has been threatened by both intolerance and a heightened emphasis on cultural distinctions. The greater public good warrants eliminating those cultural characteristics that promote conflict or prevent harmony, even as less-divisive, more personally observed cultural distinctions are celebrated and preserved.

The realization of such integrative models on a global scale is impossible in the near term. It will take centuries. Nor can it be achieved purely through rational decisions geared toward implementing carefully considered policies and programmes. Rather, current trends that fall under the broad definitional umbrella of "globalization" are accelerating a process that has taken place throughout history as discrete groups have become familiar with one another, allied, and commingled—ultimately becoming more alike. Inevitably, the United States has taken the lead in this transformation; it is the "indispensable nation" in the management of global affairs and the leading producer of information products and services in these, the early years of the Information Age.

The drivers of today's rapid globalization are improving methods and systems of international transportation, devising revolutionary and innovative information technologies and services, and dominating the international commerce in services and ideas. Their impact affects lifestyles, religion, language, and every other component of culture. Much has been written about the role of information technologies and services in this process. Today, 15 major US telecommunications companies, including giants like Motorola, Loral Space & Communications, and Teledesic (a joint project of Microsoft's Bill Gates and cellular pioneer Craig McCaw), offer competing plans that will encircle the globe with a constellation of satellites and will enable anyone anywhere to communicate instantly with anyone elsewhere without an established telecommunications infrastructure on the ground near either the sender or the recipient. (Loral puts the cost of such a call at around $ 3 per minute.) Technology is not only transforming the world; it is creating its own metaphors as well. Satellites carrying television signals now enable people on opposite sides of the globe to be exposed regularly to a wide range of cultural stimuli. Russian viewers are hooked on Latin soap operas, and Middle Eastern leaders have cited CNN as a prime source for even local news. The Internet is an increasingly global phenomenon with active development under way on every continent.

The United States dominates this global traffic in information and ideas. American music, American movies, American television, and American software are so dominant, so sought after, and so visible that they are now available literally everywhere on the Earth. They influence the tastes, lives, and aspirations of virtually every nation. In some, they are viewed as corrupting. France and Canada have both passed laws to prohibit the satellite dissemination of foreign - meaning American—content across their borders and into the homes of their citizens. Not surprisingly, in many other countries fundamentalist Iran, communist China, and the closely managed society of Singapore—central governments have aggressively sought to restrict the software and programming that reach their citizens. Their explicit objective is to keep out American and other alien political views, mores, and, as it is called in some parts of the Middle East, "news pollution". In these countries, the control of new media that give previously closed or controlled societies virtually unlimited access to the outside world is a high priority. Singapore has sought to filter out certain things that are available over the Internet—essentially processing all information to eliminate pornography. China has set up a "Central Leading Group" under the State Planning Commission and the direct supervision of a vice premier to establish a similar system that will exclude more than just what might be considered obscene.

These governments are the heirs of King Canute, the infamous monarch who set his throne at the sea's edge and commanded the waves to go backward. The Soviet Union fell in part because a closed society cannot compete in the Information Age. These countries will fare no better. They need look no further than their own elites to know this. In China, while satellite dishes are technically against the law, approximately one in five citizens of Beijing has access to television programming via a dish, and almost half of the people of Guangzhou have access to satellite-delivered programming. Singapore, the leading entrepote of Southeast Asia, is a hub in a global network of business centres in which the lives of the elites are virtually identical. Business leaders in Buenos Aires, Frankfurt, Hong Kong, Johannesburg, Istanbul, Los Angeles, Mexico City, Moscow, New Delhi, New York, Paris, Rome, Santiago, Seoul, Singapore, Tel Aviv, and Tokyo all read the same newspapers, wear the same suits, drive the same cars, eat the same food, fly the same airlines, stay in the same hotels, and listen to the same music. While the people of their countries remain divided by culture, they have realized that to compete in the global marketplace they must conform to the culture of that marketplace.

The global marketplace is being institutionalized through the creation of a series of multilateral entities that establish common rules for international commerce. If capital is to flow freely, disclosure rules must be the same, settlement procedures consistent, and redress transparent. If goods are also to move unimpeded, tariff laws must be consistent, customs standards harmonized, and product safety and labeling standards brought into line. And if people are to move easily from deal to deal, air transport agreements need to be established, immigration controls standardized, and commercial laws harmonized. In many ways, business is the primary engine driving globalization, but it would be a mistake to conclude that the implications of globalization will be limited primarily to the commercial arena.

In politics, for example, as international organizations arise to coordinate policy among many nations on global issues such as trade, the environment, health, development, and crisis management, a community of international bureaucrats is emerging. These players are as comfortable operating in the international environment as they would be at home, and the organizations that they represent in effect establish global standards and expectations—facilitating the progress of globalization. The community of nations increasingly accepts that such supranational entities are demanded by the exigencies of the times; with that acceptance also comes a recognition that the principal symbol of national identity, namely, sovereignty—must be partially ceded to those entities. The United States in particular seems to have problems with this trend. For example, the United States was involved in creating the World Trade Organization and now undermines its effectiveness by arbitrarily withdrawing from its efforts to blunt the effects of the Helms-Burton Act. Still, the recognition that sometimes there are interests greater than national interests is a crucial step on the path to a more peaceful, prosperous world.

A Global Culture

It is in the general interest of the United States to encourage the development of a world in which the fault lines separating nations are bridged by shared interests. And it is in the economic and political interests of the United States to ensure that if the world is moving toward a common language, it be English; that if the world is moving toward common telecommunications, safety, and quality standards, they be American; that if the world is becoming linked by television, radio, and music, the programming be American; and that if common values are being developed, they be values with which Americans are comfortable. These are not simply idle aspirations. *English is linking the world. American information technologies and services are at the cutting edge of those that are enabling globalization.* Access to the largest economy in the world—America's—is the primary carrot leading other nations to open their markets.

Indeed, just as the United States is the world's sole remaining military superpower, so is it the world's only information superpower.

While Japan has become quite competitive in the manufacture of components integral to information systems, it has had a negligible impact as a manufacturer of software or as a force behind the technological revolution. Europe has failed on both fronts. Consequently, the United States holds a position of advantage at the moment and for the foreseeable future. Some find the idea that Americans would systematically seek to promote their culture to be unattractive. They are concerned that it implies a sense of superiority on Americans' part or that it makes an uncomfortable value judegment. But the real truth of the Information Age is that setting technological standards, defining software standards, producing the most popular information products, and leading in the related development of the global trade in services are as essential to the well-being of any would-be leader as once were the resources needed to support empire or industry.

The economic stakes are immense considering the enormous investments that will be made over the next 10 years in the world's information infrastructure. The US Government estimates that telecommunications investment in Latin America alone during this period will top $ 150 billion. China will spend a similar amount, as will the member states of the Association of South East Asian Nations. In fact, the market for telecommunications services is expected to top $ 1 trillion by the turn of the century. During the decade ahead, not only will enormous sums be directed toward the establishment of the global network of networks that the Clinton administration has dubbed the "Global Information Infrastructure", but those sums will pay for the foundations of a system that will dictate decades of future choices about upgrades, systems standards, software purchases, and services. At the same time, new national and international laws will be written, and they will determine how smoothly information products and services may flow from one market to another. Will steps be taken to ensure that Internet commerce remains truly free? What decisions will be made about the encryption of data that will impact not only the security of information markets but the free flow of ideas and the rights of individuals in the Information Age? Will governments allow the democratizing promise of the Internet to enable virtually anyone with a computer to contact anyone else?

The establishment of the Global Information Infrastructure is not just an enormous commercial opportunity for the world's information leader. The development of the rules governing that infrastructure will shape the nature of global politics decisively, either enhancing or undermining freedoms, thereby either speeding or slowing the pace of integration, understanding, and tolerance worldwide. The nature of individual and national relations will be transformed. Those wires and constellations of satellites and invisible beams of electronic signals crisscrossing the globe will literally form the fabric of future civilization.

Consequently, it could not be more strategically crucial that the United States do whatever is in its power to shape the development of that infrastructure, the rules governing it, and the information traversing it. Moreover, even if much of this process of developing what we might call the "infosphere" is left to the marketplace (as it should be), governments will control crucial elements of it. Governments will award many of the biggest infrastructure development contracts offered in the next decade. Some will assist their national companies in trying to win those contracts, and state officials will meet to decide the trade rules that will govern international traffic in the world's telecommunications markets, the global regulatory environment, encryption standards, privacy standards, intellectual property protections, and basic equipment standards. Governments will determine whether these are open or closed markets and what portion of development dollars will be targeted at bringing the benefits of these technologies to the poor to help counteract information inequities. Already some government intercessions into this marketplace have failed. Notably, Japan's efforts to shape the development of high-definition television standards sent that nation down an analog path in what turned out to be a digital race. Yet there are many places where there is an important role for governments and where the United States should have a carefully considered overarching policy and an aggressive stance to match.

Many observers contend that it is distasteful to use the opportunities created by the global information revolution to promote American culture over others, but that kind of relativism is as dangerous as it is wrong. American culture is fundamentally different from indigenous cultures in so many other locales. American culture is an amalgam of influences and approaches from around the world. It is moulded—consciously in many cases—into a social medium that allows individual freedoms and cultures to thrive. Recognizing this, Americans should not shy away from doing that which is so clearly in their economic, political, and security interests—and so clearly in the interests of the world at large. The United States should not hesitate to promote its values. In an effort to be polite or politic, Americans should not deny the fact that of all the nations in the history of the world, theirs is the most just, the most tolerant, the most willing to constantly reassess and improve itself, and the best model for the future. At the same time, Americans should not fall under the spell of those like Singapore's Lee Kuan Yew and Malaysia's Mahathir bin-Mohamad, who argue that there is "an Asian way", one that non-Asians should not judge and that should be allowed to dictate the course of events for all those operating in that comer of the world. This argument amounts to self-interested political rhetoric. Good and evil, better and worse coexist in this world. There are absolutes, and there are political, economic, and moral costs associated with failing to recognize this fact.

Repression is not defensible whether the tradition from which it springs is Confucian, Judeo-Christian, or Zoroastrian. The repressed individual still suffers, as does society, and there are consequences for the global community. Real costs accrue in terms of constrained human creativity, delayed market development, the diversion of assets to enforce repression, the failure of repressive societies to adapt well to the rapidly changing global environment, and the dislocations, struggles, and instability that result from these and other factors. Americans should promote their vision for the world, because failing to do so or taking a "live and let live" stance is ceding the process to the not-always-beneficial actions of others. Using the tools of the Information Age to do so is perhaps the most peaceful and powerful means of advancing American interests.

It is also crucial that the United States recognize its limitations. Americans can have more influence than others, but they cannot assure every outcome. Rather, the concerted effort to shape the development of the Global Information Infrastructure and the ideas that flow within it should be seen merely as a single component of a well-rounded foreign and security policy. (And since it is not likely to be an initiative that is widely liked or admired or enhanced through explicit promotion, it is not an approach that should be part of American public diplomacy efforts.)

Idenity without Culture

Certainly, it is naive to expect broad success in avoiding future conflicts among cultures. But we now have tools at our disposal to diminish the disparities that will fuel some of those conflicts. While we should prepare for conflict, we should also remember that it is not mere idealism that demands that we work for integration and in support of a unifying global culture ensuring individual rights and enhancing international stability: It is also the ultimate realpolitik, the ultimate act of healthy self-interest.

Allowing ourselves to be swept up in the backlash against globalization would undermine America's ability to advance its self-interests. Americans must recognize that those interests and the issues pertaining to them reach across the disciplines of economics, politics, science, and culture. An interdisciplinary approach to international policymaking is thus required. We must also fully understand the new tools at our disposal. We must understand the profound importance and nature of the emerging infosphere—and its potential as a giant organic culture processor, democratic empowerer, universal connector, and ultimate communicator. Moreover, it is not enough to create and implement the right policies using the new tools at our disposal. Policy-makers must better communicate the promise of this new world and make clear America's stake in that promise and the role Americans must play to achieve success. The United States does not face a simple choice between integration or separation, engagement or withdrawal. Rather, the choice is between leading a more peaceful world or being held hostage to events in a more volatile and violent one.

Despite the triumphs of synthetic culture we should always remember about the costs of cross- culture exchange. "Globalized culture illustrates Joseph Schumpeter's metaphor of capitalist production as a gale of 'creative destruction'. Cultural growth, like economic development, rarely as a steady on all fronts at once. While some sectors expand extreme rapidly, others shrink and wither away" (T. Cowen, 2002). Many writers address cross-cultural exchange from the "critical theory" perspective. In contrast, Cowen use a "gain from trade" model. Individuals who engage in the exchange expect those transactions to enrich their cultural lives, increase their menu of choice, will make them better off.

The drivers of today rapid globalization are or sure improving methods and systems of international commerce in services and ideas. Their impact effects lifestyles, religion, language, values and norms and every other component of culture. We cannot disagree with the statement that we live in "information Age". Alvin Toffler made a great description of it in his publication. *Third Wave*. Now the most desired resources are not the capital or earth but knowledge, information and modern technology. They have become a guarantee for a quick and successful development. That is one of the reason why United States is a leader in globalization process. Without the doubt the USA is a information superpower as well as a military superpower. It holds a position of advantage at the moment and this will probably no change in the nearest future. USA dominates the global traffic in information and ideas. The influence of American movie, American television, American lifestyle is visible almost everywhere all over the world. Access to the largest economy in the world—American television, American lifestyle is visible almost everywhere all over the world. Access to the largest economy in the world—America's—is still the primary reason that encourages other nation to open their markets. It is in general interest of the United States to ensure that if the world is becoming linked by television, music, radio and internet, the programming will be American; and if the development of common values will be moving towards those comfortable of American.

What do we call the civilization? It is a cultural identity, the broadest level of people's identification—"villages, regions, ethnic groups, nationalities, religious groups, all have distinct cultures at the different levels of cultural heterogeneity" (S. Huntington, 2002). The civilizations are defined by common objective elements, like language, customs, religion, institutions and the subjective self-identification of people.

In the future the cultural identification is going to be increasingly important. Why? First, the difference (in religion, history, culture, tradition) between the civilizations are basic. They are products of centuries and that is why it is not easy to make them disappear or change. They seem to be more fundamental than ideological and political ones. Of course, the difference does not mean the conflict but in this case the risk of its appearing is bigger. Second, one of the effects of globalization so mentioned earlier the proximity. The world definitely is becoming the smaller place. Thanks to new communications technology, flow of people and information, the interaction between people of different civilizations are increasing. This process intensify a civilization consciousness. We can find many examples: in Europe we are the citizens of different countries but going to Asia or Africa we considered ourselves as European and we see "us" versus them. Third, a social change and the economic modernization are separating people from their local identities. Facing the pressure of emerging "global culture" people trying to find something bigger, with what they can identify with the belong to. Fourth, it is truth that cultural characteristic are less mutable and less easy to compromised than for instance political one. People change the political preferences but it is very hard to "change" the civilizations in which they were brought up, which they know and understand. Finally, we can not forget about the role of the West. "With the end of Cold War international politics moves out its Western phase, and its center-piece become the interaction between the West and non-westernization, as sometimes is called the globalization, which brings new values, lifestyles, norms, very often is making people to feel confused, lost and to look for a way to defense and to find themselves in a new social and cultural environment.

The emerging "global culture" indeed is heavily American in origin and content. But is it really possible that "common" global culture will exist. Very often when people examine this issue they pay to much attention to homogenization of consumer tastes and to the kinds of goods which they buy. But this is the most artificial aspect of culture. A deeper and more important one consists of moral norms and should be understood as the beliefs, values, lifestyles of ordinary people. Consumption of new global products propagated by Coca-cola, McDonald's, Disney, MTV and so on, especially in modern, development states is very often still superficial. There, a hamburger is only a hamburger. However, there is a threat that in low development countries, wearing NIKE T-shirt or eating in McDonald's may be a result of more significant change. Those societies are not prepared for the confrontation with the powerful globalization and they absorb almost everything what it brings. That was a case in Poland, in early 90s, after the collapse of the Soviet Union. Poland opened its markets for international companies. To the first McDonald's all families were coming, first KFC was also very crowded. It was definitely something more than just eating hamburger. It was a willingness of trying something completely new, a joy that we can also participated in consuming "global known goods". Now, after 13 years the situation is different. People got used to it and they are much better prepared for facing the globalization process.

A "cultural earthquake" effects every part of the world. It is very attractive, as well to those who are caught in early stages of the modernization process, as to those who have already experienced the value of individualization. Different people respond in different way, Ones can totally accept it, others totally reject it. What is most logic way of defense? For me, it is coming back to something what we already know, to what we already got used to, what we feel we need to protect. This is the Jihad what Benjamin Barber was talking about. Noteworthy is the relation between it, at one side and McWorld, on the other one. As more dynamic and aggressive the latter one is going to be, the more reaction will cause. Societies has to be prepared for a globalization, especially in such important dimension which is the culture. If not they will see only the "globalization" and the "soft imperialism" against which they have to fight.

In my opinion, it is too early to say that the globalization of culture will bring the homogenization, what think the opponents of this process. Of course, there is no doubt that the culture is going to change. But we do not have to consider that change as a lost but try to make it as best as possible and take as much we can from it in my personal opinion. I agreed with Francis Fukuyana, that the democracy showed that it is the best political system. The most basic values, like human rights, liberalism, the rule of law, equality, constitutionalism, should be common for everyone, no matter in what part of the world we live. The globalization gives people freedom to make their identities in a global world. On one condition, that they will understand it, not afraid of it. We have to learn in a "Disneyworld" as in ironic way is called our world now. I think that although tendencies to homogenization, we are the one who really create that culture. The diversity is possible. The "West" have to understand that it is not the position to use international institutions. Its military and economic power to run the world in way that will maintain the Western domination. The difference have to respect each other.

The Dark Side of Globalization

Critiques of the current wave of economic globalization typically look at both the damage to the planet, in terms of the perceived unsustainable harm done to the biosphere, as well as the perceived human costs, such as increased poverty, inequality, injustice and the erosion of traditional culture which, the critics contend, all occur as a result of the economic transformations related to globalization. They also argue that the process of globalization will lead to a stripping away of identity and the blandly uniform, Orwellian world. They point to a "multitude of interconnected fatal consequences—social disintegration, a breakdown of democracy, more rapid and extensive deterioration of the environment, the spread of new diseases, increasing poverty and alienation" which they claim are the unintended but very real consequences of globalization.

Conclusion

Thus we see that globalization is the convergence of patterns of production and consumption and a resulting homogenization of culture. It has intensified interdependence and competition between economies in the world market. But at the same time, globalization has also thrown up new challenges like exclusive growth patterns, growing inequality across and within nations, volatility in financial market and environmental deteriorations. If we want a truly prosperous world, then plain globalization is not just enough—it should be one which can uplift the world's poor, who are the most deprived and exploited, out of their poverty. Then only can globalization reap rich rewards and fulfil its true intension.

References

http://en.wikipedia.org./wiki/Globalization

www.wikipedia.com

http://sociology.emory.edu/globalization.

"The World is Flat", Thomas Friedmann.

Effects of Globalization on Culture: An Essay on Foreign Policy (June 22, 1997), David Rothkop, Managing Director of Kissinger Associates and an adjunct Professor of International Affairs at Columbia University. He also served as a senior official in the US Department of Commerce during the first term of the Clinton Administration.

Chapter 13

Globalization: Its Impact on the Indian Welfare State

— Jyotsana Shukla

Globalization has been a recent phenomenon that has swept the world. The world has become increasingly interdependent and integrated. It has been the harbinger of radical change. All the Fortune 100 companies have a foothold in the world market and reaping large revenues. The trade barriers have been lowered worldwide, resulting in expansion of trade, foreign direct investment, exchange of technology, greater movement of people across borders.

The world economy is most prosperous today. The roots of this prosperity lie in globalization. Globalization is the growing integration of economies and societies around the world (The World Bank Group, 2004). Internationalization differs from globalization in that globalization also includes non-economic factors.

Globalization is the development of rules by nations to govern international trade for the purpose of increased efficiency in use of resources. These rules are developed and enforced by organizations such as the WTO, with 149 nations under its umbrella.

We talk about globalization almost every day. What does this globalization mean for Indian economy and society and the rest of the world? How can the gains be maximized and the costs be reduced?

The Motivation behind Globalization: The Principle for Comparative Advantage

This principle is attributed to David Ricardo(1772-1823), who proposed that nations can be most productive through specialization in areas where they have ratio advantage, relative to other nations in the production of goods and sciences.

According to Montek Singh Ahluwalia, the finance secretary, perceptions about globalization and its effects vary, and have gone through a definite cycle in the past ten years or so. It is not surprising if the average man or woman in India is plagued by doubts about the nature of globalization, what impact it will have on ordinary people and what it implies for our policies.

Globalization is no more a matter of choice. It is not something with which we can be in favour or stand opposed to. It is not a set of policies but a process that is taking place across the globe, controlled by international forces, which are outside the control of any single nation in this multi-polar world.

The benefits of globalization must be seen against the backdrop of our unique socio-economic, cultural, and political conditions prevailing before India ventured towards globalization.

We as Indians must be ready to accept the fact that globalization has been there for good. It has brought us to a state where we feel proud to be living in a country which the world admires not only for its snake charmers and the Tajmahal but also for its technological and economic prowess. The country now stands as the lady in shining armour beckoning anyone to challenge it in any area where technology or enterprise is required. The world stands in owe of this lady lest she become the controlling hand behind the world's economy.

Twenty years ago we could just dream of such a time in our future but today it's a reality. Let's not be critical, let's look at the harvest of success that we have reaped in the last fifteen years. The hard work put in by a large number of our country men in the areas of trade and commerce, manufacturing, automobiles, primary and higher education, print and electronic media, insurance and banking, science and technology, research and development has brought tremendous results.

While looking at the benefits of globalization, following issues may be considered:

1. Does it protect wages and reduce income inequalities?
2. Is it good for the economy?
3. Does it boost economic growth?
4. Is it bad for workers?
5. Does it increase poverty and inequality?
6. Is it a threat to the environment?
7. Does it improve our society ?

The economic reforms were introduced in 1991 and have been continued by successive governments. In the words of our Prime Minister Mr. Manmohan Singh, the reforms laid the foundations of an economy poised to reap the potential benefits of globalization.

Globalization and the Indian Economy

India's business environment has transformed at a faster pace in the recent past. India has come a long way from the welfare-centred economy it used to be in the 1970s. In 1990s the country was witness to the birth of a new India. The Indian markets were open for foreign companies and investors. More and more privatization began to take place and India turned into a more capitalized form of economy. The liberalization, privatization and globalization policy of 1991 opened up new horizons of opportunities for the Indian business (Source: Indian Business in the Present Scenario in *Indian Business.*)

In the last fifteen years or so, India has done extremely well in the following sunrise sectors:

1. Information Technology Sector.
2. Business Process Outsourcing Sector.
3. Telecommunication Sector.
4. Electronics and Hardware Sector.
5. Pharmaceuticals Sector.
6. Biotechnology Sector.
7. Banking and Insurance Sector.
8. Food Processing Sector.

(Source: Business-MapsofIndia.com)

The Indian business scene has totally changed in the recent past. As a result of inflow of foreign funds, fast paced infrastructure development, use of advanced technology, increasing exports and outsourcing initiatives, the Indian commerce has seen a surge. Thus, the growth of the Indian business has been the driving force behind the rising growth rate of the Indian economy.

Since globalization, India has experienced low rates of inflation, increase in employment as well as rising standards of living for its people, higher GDP growth rates. The recent rise in inflation may be more of a correcting feature than a serious consequence of globalization. The corrective measures have already been taken and according to media reports as of 29th April, 2008, despite the worldwide concerns regarding rising prices Indian need not worry.

Globalization and the Social Sector

According to Dr. Manmohan Singh, the present prime minister, while globalization presents many potential benefits, it also poses special challenges. In a democracy, it is necessary that the process of reform be perceived as equitable and caring. In a world in which information flows are unfettered, growth processes in which some are seen to benefit while others are excluded are not viable. This is particularly sensitive in a democratic polity in which public dissatisfaction can be quickly converted into electoral defeat. This is indeed the message of the recent elections in India. They were not, as some have said, a vote against reforms. They were a vote against a process of reform that was seen to be unbalanced, a process which neglected the needs of our rural areas and the agricultural economy.

As far as the social sectors are concerned, it is believed that as globalization continues, people tend to discard long standing restrictions and prejudices and discriminations based on gender, race, colour and religions. It is perceived that the rigours of globalization are such that it has no place for fundamentalism of any kind to flourish.

Social justice advocates argue that globalization has provided an opportunity to focus global attention on previously neglected issues of corruption and lack of transparency in certain countries, including India, including issues arising from globalization itself, such as the accountability of international organizations and the costs and benefits of globalization to the world's poorest people.

Benefits of globalization in the developing nations can also be observed in the improvement of the socio-economic status of women there. This is because in the competitive world of today the role of women has become more significant and more valuable, hence nations like Saudi Arabia cannot develop themselves with their existing culture that exclude women from participating in the state affairs. The developed nations on the other hand, encourage education for women and this thereby improves the economic prospects of their respective states dramatically. India has seen a rapid rise in the status of women, looking at the presence of women in every field.

The advancement in medicine, new and amended public health policies, and increase in food supplies also count as other benefits of Globalization. India is fast becoming a centre for medical tourism. The advances in the medical services have diminished the infant mortality rate and increased the expectancy of life.

There are many who believe that with the rise in opportunities and economic welfare since globalization, we will ultimately achieve a just society with civil liberties and efficient use of our resources.

Globalization and Indian Manufacturing

In spite of doomsday predictions, pessimists are finding themselves bewildered by the fact the economic reforms initiated by the Congress government in 1991 and supported by the subsequent Bharatiya Janata Party administration have at last begun to bear fruit. The reforms involves putting an end to the License Raj, reduction of high industrial tarrifs, the privatization of aluminium, car manufacturing, telecoms and information technology companies, the liberalization of the exchange rate regime and the cautious relaxation of rules governing foreign direct investment. Their cumulative effect has triggered a consumption-led boom that, in turn, has for the first time created a genuine mass market for Indian manufacturers.

Mergers, takeovers, global alliances, joint ventures, and collaborations are taking place, almost every day, in all the industry and manufacturing sectors . The latest in the series have been the Tatas, who having made history by taking over Anglo-Dutch steelmaker Corus and Britain's premium auto brands Jaguar and Land Rover, is now considering a partnership with Brazilian aircraft maker Embraer, for production of aircraft.

According to Jo Johnsons of *Financial Times* (2005), "Made in India" is coming of age. With its call-centres and software houses, India leads the world in off shored back-office services. It has so far failed, however, to fulfil its potential as a global manufacturing hub. But its share of the pie could quadruple in a decade, according to McKinsey, the consultancy.

After making history, the Tatas by taking over Anglo-Dutch steelmaker Corus and Britain's premium auto brands Jaguar and Land Rover, it is now considering a partnership with Brazilian aircraft maker Embraer, for production of aircraft.

Jim Walker, chief economist at Credit Lyonnais Securities Asia, says that "People have been rapidly disabusing themselves of the idea that India was going to leave manufacturing to China".

According to *Yale Global*, an American publication, manufacturing has become a rapidly growing sector of the economy, writing the Indian Success story alongside the services sector. Throughout India, new factories provide alternatives to farming, and the jobs do not require an expensive education. Foreign automobile makers in particular look to set up shop in India, due to the abundant, young and cheap labour force. While many provinces still erect massive barriers of red tape preventing foreign investment, others, such as Tamil Nadu, have been trying to eliminate the bureaucratic measures that stifled India's productivity for decades. Such manufacturing hubs have emerged in Chennai hinterland, which now calls itself "the Detroit of India".

If India is able to match this growing market with a labour force well suited to high-tech work and factory labour, foreign investment should continue to grow by leaps and bounds. Perhaps China should start looking over its shoulder.

According to McKinsey, we can hope that manufacturing will end the "jobless growth" of the last few years, when the India's service sector globalized. It will help bring out a large number of employable youth out of poverty, and help make India an economic superpower. In order to achieve that, India has to enact more free market policies, and open its markets for Foreign Direct Investments.

There is no denying the fact that infrastructure remains the main bottleneck to "Made in India" emerging as a world force. With the exception of telecommunications, the cost of most infrastructure services is 50–100 per cent higher than in China, with Indian manufacturers paying twice as much for electricity and three times as much for rail freight. The gap is widening, too. China spent seven times as much as India on infrastructure in 2003, the latest year for which figures are available, and three times as much relative to the size of its economy—$150bn (10.6 per cent of gross domestic product) compared with $21bn in India (3.5 per cent of GDP), according to Morgan Stanley.

For Kamal Nath, India's Commerce and Industry Minister, the game is just starting. "India has already shown its prowess in the service sector and now we want to become a global techno-manufacturing hub", he says in an interview.

In no sector is India's emergence as a force in global manufacturing more evident than in mobile telecommunications equipment. It is not difficult to see why. With its operators adding 2m subscribers a month—and the figure is rising—India is the world's fastest-growing big mobile telecoms market, with 52m subscribers today and probably more than 300m in 2009, analysts say.

"India's telecom sector is exploding and all the big handset makers are talking about setting up manufacturing facilities here so that they can cater to this strong domestic demand", says Shirish Sankhe, a partner at McKinsey in India. "They will then use India as a global manufacturing hub to source markets around the world, which is exactly what happened in China 10–15 years ago."

This shows that even in a sector where imports were cheaper because of zero duties, "Made in India" is being preferred. Manufacturing capacities are being expanded the country is emerging as a global source.

According to Nath (2000), global alliances are a means of expanding internationally more rapidly which makes it possible to enter new markets using the distribution networks and the specific knowledge of the local partners.

Globalization, Wages and the Income Inequalities

Research indicates that FDI tends to increase wage levels and reduce poverty in both developed countries. For developing ones, it increases income inequalities in the short term but decrease then with greater investment over time. For developed countries FDI tends to decrease income inequalities. Income inequalities among the richest and poorest nations seem to be decreasimg.

According to the liberals, globalization is an effective tool for eliminating want and for permitting the poor people to get hold of a steady grip of the global economy. For instance, as per World Bank reports, within the two decades from 1980s to 2001, those people living on US$1 or less per day, reduced from 1.5 billion to 1.1 billion. Alongside there is a rise in the total population of the world. So, it is an obvious conclusion that in the developing countries, the percentage of those people got reduced from 40% to 20%.

Whether analyzed in terms of import prices or of import volumes nearly all research finds only modest effect of international trade on wages and income inequality. Moreover, the belief that globalization threatens wages and jobs is contradicted by the historical evidence that free trade and mobility of labor and capital improves global welfare and to improve national welfare for all countries involved (Slaughter and Swagel, 1997).

As a result of globalization, it is expected that with the increase in the income level of the country, there is a decline in the use of child labour. Although inequalities within and between nations still persist, a global middle class has emerged from the 1980 onwards.

Despite the overall benefits of globalization, for national welfare, it entails challenges for particular groups within a nation, it produces its winners and losers. The displacement of some group of workers due to import competition, lack of information about new opportunities, relocation and the loss of firm or industry-specific knowledge. Policy-makers must keep in mind potential dislocation and ensure that those who are displaced do not become marginalized.

A more positive view of globalization would be that it has the potential to boost productivity and living standards everywhere because a globally integrated economy can lead to a better division of labour and the right conditions for companies to exploit greater economies of scale. It is also claimed that, with globalization, capital can be shifted to whatever country offers the most productive investment opportunities, creating economic growth.

Globalization and Education

India has become a hub of information technology outsourcing, after the government decided to privatize education ten years ago. The most dramatic impact of the 21st century "foreign Hand" is in the opening of the higher education sector to foreign institutions. Most recently, the Ministry of HRD (Human Resource Development) is reported to have withdrawn the requirement for prior approval before Indian institutions enter into MOUs with foreign institutions. This is undoubtedly a pragmatic step, which reinforces the autonomy of universities and institutions (Balaram, 2004). (*Current Science*, Vol. I 87, No. 6, 25 Sep. 2004).

Globalization and Environment

There is no denying the fact that pollution is a reality associated with increased manufacturing shift to developing countries. In an empirical study, Dande (2006), applying panel data technique, found that globalization increase CO_2 emmission is the main culprit of global warming.

Many economists have, however, argued that trade is not the root cause of environment damage(Birdsall and Wheeler, 1993; Lee and Roland Holst, 1997; Jones *et al.*, 1995).

Antweiler *et. al.*, (2001) and Liddle (2001) argue that trade may be good for environment through *Technological effect* – the pollution reducing innovation brought by higher environmental regulation and technology transfer to underdeveloped countries.

Globalization by increasing competition for investment, may trigger the environmental race to bottom (Wheeler, 2000), which means that poor economies may be able to improve their environmental quality as investment raises their income levels, and they are able to purchase environmental friendly technology or else pollution preventing technologies, and thus sustain their progress.

Tisdell (2001) points out that globalization can be a driving force for global economic growth. Still the conflict persists between the supporters of economic reforms on the one hand and those of environment protection on the other.

However, since a polluting activity in a high income country entails high regulatory costs than in a developing country (Mani and Wheeler, 1998), hence the pollutiobn intensive country tends to migrate to countries with weaker environmental regulations (Copeland

and Taylor,1995). Globalization by increasing competition for investment, may trigger the environmental race to bottom(Wheeler, 2000). As a result of increasing investments and rising income levels poor economies may be able to improve their environmental quality by investment in environmental friendly technology.

Stephen Roach, chief economist of Morgan Stanley, argued in a report in March, for example, that by reverting to "an economic model of yesteryear" and by regarding services as "elitist" in terms of their employment potential, India's growth miracle would be jeopardized.

Due to the immense advancements in the fields of technology, medical facilities, media and entertainment industry, spread of democracy and financial integration, the rich and poor nations are becoming integrated. Globalization is perceived by all as a progressive and emancipate force and it is here to stay.

A more positive view of globalization would be that it has the potential to enhance productivity and raise the living standards everywhere, since a globally integrated economy makes for a better division of labour and an environment which can be exploited by the large companies to achieve economies of scale. It is also claimed that, with globalization, capital can be shifted to whatever country offers the most productive investment opportunities, creating economic growth.

According to Kofi Annan, the UN Secretary General, the major challenge for all of us continues to be making globalization work for all the world's people. The benefits of globalization are obvious: faster and more sustained growth, higher living standards, more employment, and new opportunities. Yet, he says, a backlash has begun, because these benefits are very unequally distributed; because the global system of rules seems to be tougher in protecting intellectual property rights than in protecting human rights; because market forces by themselves are not sufficient to address a range of social objectives. According to him, far too many people in the world today, greater openness looms as a threat. Moreover, government need to listen more to the business community, and work to create the enabling environment in which business can do its part in meeting the pressing needs of our societies.

The concept of corporate social responsibility needs to become a globally accepted fact alongside the globalization of markets, since it will ultimately benefit the business. One must not only look at the potentials and opportunities that globalization brings but also at the responsibilities and obligations that come with it.

References

Ahluwalia, Montek Singh, *Policies for Development in a Globalizing World*, Thirty First Foundation Day Lecture of Indian Institute of Management, Bangalore delivered on 28th October 2004.

Antweiler, W. & Copeland, B.R. & Taylor, M.S., "Is Free Trade Good for the Environment?," *American Economic Review*, American Economic Association, Vol. 91(4), pp. 877-908, September, 2001.

Balaram, P., *Current Science*, Vol. I87, No. 6, 25 Sep. 2004.

Birdsall, N and D. Wheeler (1993), Trade Policy and Pollution in Latin America. Where are the Pollution Havens? "*Journal of Environment and Development*", Vol. 2 No. 1 (Winter), pp. 137-49.

Brian, R. Copeland & M. Scott Taylor (1995), "Trade, Spatial Separation, and the Environment," NBER Working Papers 5242, National Bureau of Economic Research, Inc. Published as: *Business Today*, 2001, Vol. 10, No. 6.

Copeland, B.R. and Taylor, M.S. (1995), "Trade and Environment – A Partial Synthesis", *American Journal of Agricultural Eonomics*, 77, 765-771.

Dinda, S., Globalization and Environmnent: Can Pollution Haven Hypothesis Alone Explain the Impact of Globalization on Environment? First Preliminary Draft, 15th October,2006 (S. R. Fatehpuria College, Beldaya, Murshidabad, WB, India, Economic Research Unit, Indian Statistical Institute, Kolkata, India.

Globalization, Trade, and Health, WHO.

India Development Report, 1999-2000 (ed.), Kirit S. Parikh, Indira Gandhi Institute of Development Research.

Jo, Johnson, India Gains Credibility as an Emergent Export Titan, *The Financial Times*, 1st December 2005.

Annan, Kofi, Special Address by H.E. Mr. Kofi Annan, Secretary-General, UNO March 15th, 2001.

Lee, H. & Roland Holst, "The Environment and Welfare Implications of Trade and Tax Policy", *Journal of Development Economies* 52(1997), 65-82.

Liddle, B., 2001, Free Trade & the Environment Development, *Ecological Economics*, 39, 21-36

Muthukumara, M. and Wheeler, D. In search of Pollution Havens? Dirty Industry in the World Economy, 1960 to 1995, *The Journal of Environment & Development*, Vol. 7, No. 3, 215-247 (1998), Sage Publications.

Nath, A., Globalization, Strategic Alliances and Insurance Sector: Some Issues for the Indian Firms.

Slaughter and Swagel, 1997 of IMF.

Stiglitz, Joseph E., Globalization and Its Discontents, New York: W. W. Norton & Company, 2002.

The World Bank Group, "Globalization", April-May 2004.

Tisdell, C. (2001), Globalization and Sustainability: Environmental Kuznets Curve and the WTO, *Ecological Economics* 39(2): 185-196.

Wheeler, D., Beyond Pollution Havens in Global Environment Politics,Vol.2. No.2, pp. 1-10, On-line Mar. 13, 2006.

World Development Report. 1999/2000, Entering The 21st Century, World Bank.

14 *Chapter*

Globalization and Indian Education

— Sonika Singh

Introduction

The principal objective of education has been the development of the whole individual. The minimum level of education that was necessary to achieve this goal in the agrarian society was basic or primary and in the industrial age, secondary. In the present borderless information society, education needs to be able to respond to additional demands of a rapidly globalizing world by raising awareness of environment, peace, cultural and social diversity, increased competitiveness, and the concept of a global village. Such education is to a knowledge or information society what secondary education was to an industrial economy. Education prepares the individual to connect—and live in harmony—with the environment around him. Globalization has changed the size, nature and quality of that environment. The challenge for higher education, therefore, is to reform, create and develop systems that prepare the individual to work in a borderless economy and live in a global society. In other words, our educational institutions need to produce global citizens.

The collapse of the Soviet Union in 1991 allowed liberal

democracies to claim victory for the capitalist system and contributed to increasing the pace of globalization that was already under way. As globalization gained momentum, market substituted political ideology as the dominant force guiding national and global policies. What followed next, therefore, does not seem so illogical. National governments everywhere—partly in deference to the ascendancy of the market and partly in response to pressure from the private sector to expand their sphere of activities—began to relinquish control over the delivery of social goods. Everything began to be viewed as a commodity that could be produced and delivered by the private sector in line with market forces and according to the principles of supply and demand. One by one—water, electricity, postal services, health, and now education, have been turned into a commodity.

The withdrawal of state from higher education has also been helped by economists, who have had an overly simple way of assessing the return on investments in higher education. The basic problem is that they have measured the return on education exclusively through wage differentials. With reference to someone who has no education, someone who has been to primary school, someone who has completed secondary school, and someone with a university degree, one can ask how much more each earns than the previous. These differences are then compared to the incremental amounts invested in their education to find the return. The results generally suggest that higher education yields a lower return than primary or secondary education—and they have been used to justify the skewing of government budgets and development funds away from higher education institutions.

The rate of return calculations are flawed because they do not take account of the full range of benefits to those who receive higher education. For example, higher education can enhance health, openness, peace, and social development, and at the same time reduce disease, bigotry and blind nationalism—so the private benefits to the individual and to society are not just the direct labour productivity benefits, as the rate of return analysis suggests.

Higher education confers benefits above and beyond enhancing the incomes of those who receive it. And many of these benefits take the form of public goods, such as the contribution of higher education to enterprise, leadership, governance, culture, and participatory democracy, and its potential for lifting the disadvantaged out of poverty. These are all vital building blocks for stronger economies and societies and all routes by which the benefit of investment in higher education multiplies throughout society.

Liberal democracies have traditionally operated on the principle of separation of activities in the social sphere just as they have on the principle of separation of powers in the political sphere. The private sector had been given a relatively free hand in the production and delivery of economic goods while the state concentrated on the provision of health care, education and other infrastructure goods, also known as public goods. Globalization has changed all that. The rapid expansion of the influence of the private sector at the global level necessitated a corresponding expansion in their sphere of activities by diversifying into the production and delivery of public goods that had always been within the purview of the state. The takeover was swift and remarkable in the sense that the effort did not meet much resistance.

One of the major consequences of the globalization of education has been commodification and the corporatization of institutions of higher learning. It is said that the for-profit education market in the United States is worth more than US $500 billion in revenue for the involved corporates. More than one thousand state schools have been handed over to corporations to be run as businesses. But there is a fundamental problem with the way business models have been applied to the delivery of education and other public goods. Unthinking adoption of the private sector model prevents the development of a meaningful approach to management in the public services in general or to the social services in particular based on their distinctive purposes, conditions and objectives.

There is another, more serious, problem with corporatization of education. Corporations operate on the principles of cost reduction and profit maximization. These require introducing standardization and the packaging of product in compact, measurable, byte-like, configuration. Applied to education, these approaches would possibly negate its basic fabric and purpose. Education has always encouraged and represents openness, inquiry, diversity, research and limitless learning. Corporatization of education would make it elitist—the one provided by corporations for the masses and the poor who cannot afford going to the traditional institutions of learning, and the other for the rich and the affluent.

The delivery of public goods and services is and should remain the primary responsibility of the state. Representative government may not be the ideal or perfect arrangement for governance but it represents the best that is available, and certainly more desirable than the private sector management of public services such as education. If the state relinquishes its control over education and education policy, we run the risk of diminishing it to the status of a packaged for-profit product which it is not. Openness, diversity, scholarship, research and disinterested learning will be its biggest victims.

Globalization is a "*qualitatively new phenomenon*"[1] of multi-dimensional nature posing a variety of "*complex trends*"[2] in the economic, social and cultural fabrics of all societies. The above phenomenon and trends stemming from it have placed formidable challenges and changing demands of lasting consequences everywhere; humanity is at crossroads now; almost all people feel powerless to check the proliferating effects; there is a bewildering mixture of uncertainty, risk, insecurity, division and yet opportunity; millions of people move across borders in search of a better life, or any life at all. Globalization impacts on all conceivable facets of life, including education. Rapid developments in technology and communication are forcing changes within educational systems across the world as ideas, values and knowledge, vital to education, cross nation states and boundaries. There would be a new "*social universe*" (phrase used by Postone, 1996) in the days to come.

The World Trade Organization's (WTO) "education agenda" is in the nature of facilitating penetration of education services by corporate capital. The key WTO agreement for this purpose, the General Agreement on Trade in Services (GATS) incorporates the aim of "*unleashing progressive liberalization of trade in services including public services like education.*"[3] No area of social life would be exempt from the imminent "*businessification*" due to the vortex of corporate capital penetration; the "*value- form of labour*" (phrases used by Glenn, 2002) would certainly be different than now. In the changed context of GLP (*Globalization, Liberalization and Privatization*), "*human labour becomes a commodity like all other commodities and is exchanged for wages*"[4]. Consequently, education services would naturally be commercialized, privatized and capitalized (CPC); education would soon be wearing a new face—"modernized" for a "knowledge economy" based on information technologies; its values, preferences and tastes would certainly be different. "*Old traditional modes of working, professional values, notions of public service, putting community needs before the drive for profit*"[5] would become obsolete in the context of market, competition and profit making trends.

It is certain that the dawn of the new age in India and elsewhere "will be characterized by unimaginable advances in knowledge and synthesis of knowledge, triggering major changes in the objectives, contents, and methods of higher education"[6]. The future of countries would be largely determined by their abilities to compete in a global market where industrial based economies are giving way to knowledge based industries. "The educational need in the post-industrial society of the present is preparation for and involvement in life"[7], not mere graduation. The needed preparation can be achieved by enabling our learners to acquire appropriate "knowledge, skills and the intellectual capacity to meet the challenges of accelerated change and uncertainty". The demand of the emerging global society from the enterprise of education is quicker, cost-effective production of "global citizens"—"intelligent people with a broad range of skills and knowledge" excellently equipped for employment in competitive, information based"[8] techno-driven environment.

The Indian Scene

The National Policy on Education (NPE), 1986 lamented on the poor equipments of education in our country, lambasted the defect of the existing system and charged the system pointing out that "little consideration was given to the employability of university graduates and or the absorptive capacity of the job market". The apex body in charge of higher education in India, the University Grants Commission (UGC) took note of emerging demands for "a whole range of new skills... from the graduates of humanities, social sciences, natural sciences and commerce, as well as from the various professional disciplines". At the whipping of the NPE and acting on the understanding of realities, the UGC established Curriculum Development Cells (CDC) for 27 subjects[9] mandating them for "modernizing the courses and restructuring them into unit courses and to develop alternate models with emphasis on learning".[10] The UGC has also identified 35 vocational subjects with an "emphasis on providing knowledge and skills required for entry into gainful employment, particularly self-employment."[11] These are not enough.

Educational institutions are still playing an ambivalent role in man power production; they should understand that the organized sector has only limited absorptive capacity and hence the need to concentrate on diversification to a very great extent; development of capabilities for not only self-employment but also for venturing into informal sectors, up gradation of productivity of household occupations. Ours is the age of a techno-scientific revolution, the pace of change taking place in the work place "requires people to re-equip themselves, as new knowledge and new skills are needed... to compete, survive and prosper".[12] The forecast from futurists is that a lifelong career in one organization is soon bound to become rare. People will require new knowledge and skills to control and manage their own working lives. If the present traditional pattern of education is continued "sooner or later . . . countries will have to contend with one of the most explosive problems of discontent and frustration . . . of graduate unemployment."[13] The warning statement is: "More of the same—will not suffice as a strategy for meeting today's challenges."[14]

It is happy augury that the Govt. of India is aware of the emerging trends. The presentation of the Country Paper by Union Minister for Human Resource Development, at the UNESCO Conference (1998) evidences such awareness. The Minister has acknowledged India's recognition of the new global scenario posing unprecedented challenges on the higher education systems of nations. Indicating the major objective for future education in India, the minister has underscored the need for Lifelong Education (LLE) and has declared that "great emphasis will fall upon lifelong education and the realization of a learning society" in the country. We learn that UNESCO is also greatly inspired by the paradigm of "Lifelong Education" (LLE), which holds "the key that allows us to cross the threshold of the twenty-first century".

Lifelong Education

The very phrase "Lifelong Education" (LLE) appears to be puzzling and sounds rather vague. It is true that the expression has not yet really fired the imagination of the people at large, especially those not engaged in learning beyond educational institutions—at work, in the community, in their homes and families and in their leisure and recreational lives. To some people, the notion of "LLE" may even sound like a penal sentence or endurance test than an invitation to pleasure, achievement and progress.[15]

LLE is a very vast field defying any precise definition.[16] The vastness of LLE is both its attraction and weakness. The essence of LLE could be inferred from its salient characteristics: LLE aims to (1) constitute a continuous process of forming whole human beings—their knowledge and aptitudes, as well as the critical faculty and ability to act, (2) enable people to develop awareness of themselves and their environment and encourage them to play their social role at work and in the community.[17] LLE ranges from the most highly formal and structured educational activities to the most informal and tentative explorations of understanding; LLE encompasses many different levels, purposes, contents, outcomes and motives for learning; LLE anticipates a great variety of learning styles and approaches and it celebrates diversity. Due to these features, LLE may even appear to be "so all-inclusive" that it inhibits sharpness of focus and so strategies to promote LLE may become multi-stranded wherein the development of a clear sense of priority may get prevented. Still, as UNESCO sees it "LLE holds the key!" as people's needs of lifelong learning are constantly expanding.

LLE cannot be the one imposed by any agency; it should happen as part of a learning culture, depending and thriving on a great variety of initiatives taken by many actors in many different spheres. The government's role shall be to monitor and steer developments and redistribute resources so that opportunities are equitable, systematic, flexible and efficient. The very diverse, pluralistic and lifetime duration of LLE requires coordination among many policy sectors, involving both macroeconomic and structural policies.

Countries need to develop a new learning culture, a culture of lifelong learning for all. The culture of LLE is essential to help the country and all the people meet the challenges they now face in the wake of GLP. We have noted that the challenges crop from many different spheres of life, the economy and labour market competition and so on. They are evident in the demand for new products and services and in the radical and far-reaching transformations in technology, information and communications now in train. There are also wide-ranging changes to be addressed in families, communities, and relationships and in people's aspirations and very identities.[18]

Recommendations for Designing Curricula for Lifelong Education

The output of the university education process, as of now at the first level, is a graduate with a degree qualification and certain abilities, which should qualify him or her for activities in the industry sector. It has been emphasized earlier that the level and skills profile should be relevant to the labour market requirements. Therefore the learner/graduate qualification should be described as a set of abilities required to exercise the profession, rather than just listing the knowledge acquired in the education process. To identify the set of abilities required for each programme and to define learner outcomes from the programmes, the main stakeholders here—the College/University professors, representatives from the profession (e.g., industry), industrial and professional associations, accreditation bodies, government, and also the students should have regular channels of communication. A valuable input for defining the outcomes of curricula would be the core *Generic Skills Profiles*[19] (GSP), for each programme, that have to be formulated and established by the stakeholders.

For designing useful curriculum and undertaking it as a continuous process, active Working Groups (WG) or Curriculum Development Cells (CDC) in each IHE should be constituted. The WG/CDC should aim at providing scope for vast flexibility, reflecting needs in curriculum for change, broad basing of skills, business knowledge, behavioural skills, more mobility, etc. There should be a clear perception in the minds of curriculum makers of what competencies do learners need for successful performance in industry/user-systems? (Technical, professional and personal competencies) and what knowledge should be taught?

The planners should study existing curricula by involving user representatives (industry) to identify gaps (skill requirement) and formulate content outlines. It is a fact that there is no one single way to design the best curriculum. One can find one's own best solution; nevertheless, a framework based on experience and best practices can lead to a set of useful guidelines.

The Curriculum

The curriculum defines the Education Process (the sequence of adjusted lectures and exercises which deliver knowledge), the Examination Process (which evaluates the students' achievements), and the Training Process (which helps practice these skills and develop abilities).[20] The college/ university curriculum should aim to bridge the gap between the input and output requirements. An ideal curriculum is strictly focused on outcomes, lifting the students' qualification from entry to a clearly defined exit/output (graduate) level. The qualification process has to be defined without any ambiguity.

Knowledge Cycle

The cycle of knowledge creation, distribution, learning and utilization is becoming shorter. This in turn leads to a need for continuous qualification of the workforce and an update of the learning content. As a result, new curricula reflecting novel content, learning objectives, teaching methodology, certification and relevant learning process need to be designed. These curricula should meet the needs of traditional full-time learners as well as non-traditional learners such as part-timers and mature students. In order to meet all these requirements the new curricula need a highly flexible structure on a modular basis so that they can be easily adapted to different target groups, different skills profile needs and the rapid pace of change.

Quality Control

IHEs should set up a quality control process; the findings/results shall be documented and the information gleaned should be applied to the further improvement of the programme. Such a process should take feedback from the student in terms of how well the course matched outcome objectives and whether the student felt he or she got the right knowledge and skills for the job from the course. The quality control process should also get feedback from industry in assessing the former students' competencies in both technical and behavioral areas. This requires following of learners' recruitments in user-systems. [For example, a feedback request could be sent to all students after they graduate/undergo specific training and to their employer sometime between one and three years later.]

Coordination

The quality of the educational process depends hugely on co-ordination between the sub-processes as well as between the protagonists (internal and external) involved and the feedback loops put in place at all levels. The internal protagonists in all these processes are students, professors and other academic and administrative staff. Externally, industry representatives are involved whenever students spend the placement period, work on theses or work in industry during holiday periods. Co-ordination between all the players is to be ensured with out any breakdowns.

Curriculum Structure

In general, no curriculum can prepare students for activities at expert level in all skill profiles. However, every LLE curriculum should provide a common platform at basic level, enabling the learners to work in teams on common projects and to communicate in common LLE language even if they have specialized in different sectors.

The curriculum for LLE programmes shall consist of hierarchically organized modules: sets of core modules; sets of area-specific core modules; sets of optional (elective) modules.

1. **The Core Modules:** represent the Scientific and Technology Base giving the fundamentals and basis for all LLE skills profiles. They represent also the slow changing knowledge.

A selection from these modules is recommended to be scheduled during the first year/phase of study.

2. **The Area Specific Core Modules:** represent the Technological base which are specific for the technological area of the group of core skill profiles targeted and they represent the faster changing knowledge. It is suggested that they be scheduled in the second or later years of study.
3. **The Elective Modules:** reflect the fastest changing knowledge with a period of ageing of this knowledge of 3-5 years. They reflect the novel technological and other specific knowledge. These modules are used to provide a specialized and in-depth approach and to equalize the differences, thus giving a flexibility and possibility to specialize in certain areas.

Along with all the above listed skills, Personal and Business Skills shall also be developed during the entire study, starting in the first semester. Primarily they should be integrated into the teaching of technical/applied subjects. Where additional modules are necessary, they should follow the same structure as the technical knowledge area. This structure can be applied for curricula leading to both first (UG) and second (PG) degree taking into account that all the modules in a second-degree programme should be designed at an advanced level.

Distribution

A basic knowledge of chosen subject field is essential for a broad understanding of further processes and their utilization in technical applications; however, it also serves as a foundation for attaining a breadth and depth of knowledge in a specialist field of application. A broad foundation is also an important prerequisite to enable graduates to communicate effectively with colleagues from other areas using a common "technical language". So, the core of qualifications to be attained during education should comprise a scientific base and a technology base, i.e., a broad spectrum of mathematical, scientific and technical knowledge; application base/systems thinking and personal and business skills.

This core should extend to all subjects under consideration, thus laying the foundation for subsequent professional mobility. The teaching of this core need not be at a deeper level but should give students a balanced overview. The following distribution between STAP (Scientific, Technological bases and Application and Personal business skills) has been suggested:[21]

1. **The Scientific Base:** This aims to cover the fundamental principles relevant to the concepts used in the industry/ establishment. In addition to a foundation in science and mathematics, the scientific base should foster an understanding of scientific methods for analysis and design. The percentage suggested for this segment is 30%.
2. **The Technology Base:** This is more concerned with giving a broad overview of the various technologies available, the functions they can perform and their advantages and constraints. In addition to studying the current capability of a technology, students should be given some insight into how that technology might develop in the future. For this segment also a 30% distribution is suggested.
3. **Application Skills:** A command of the basics is not in itself sufficient for assuring professional competence in industry. In order to meet the demands of the job, graduates also need an in-depth fundamental knowledge of their specialized fields, general knowledge of problem solving methods, and *finally particular application knowledge* in accordance with workplace demands for the particular job profile. The key requirements here are knowledge of system functions in the field in question, and understanding of the technological possibilities ("hardware and software") to realize or implement those functions with the help of procedural methods. Given the growing complexity of modern devices, equipment and

systems, the ability to see things as a whole, to think in terms of systems and to communicate at a systems level with all those working on the project and with the customers is increasingly important. It is suggested that this segment can have a distribution at 25%.

4. **Personal and Business Skills:** These skills have to be developed through team projects, commercial simulations, negotiation, presentations, etc., throughout the course. Coupling this implicit learning with feedback and coaching from lecturers not only on the academic aspects, but on how well these skills are acquired and deployed should provide the on-going learning stimulus needed to develop these skills which are vital for a career. Particular attention should also be paid to embedding the teaching of these essential personal and business skills, into the more technical subjects areas. The suggested percentage for this segment is 15%

Apart from the above, the curriculum should have provision for Practical/Work experience and Project Work.

Practical/Work Experience in LLE Programmes

A minimum of three months (or longer, for longer programmes) is necessary to emphasize the connections between different aspects, to encourage a broad systems view and to illustrate the practical, technological and human constraints of solving real-world problems.

Project Work

Project work is vital to develop the skills listed above and it is recommended that at least three months be allocated for the project and the dissertation. It is recognized that there are difficulties in assessing the performance of individual students when team projects are being undertaken. Nevertheless, some experience of team working on a significant real project is an essential element of a good education. The challenge of assessing and crediting teamwork by students needs to be addressed by academia. The industry has developed means of assessing and improving group works of its workforce. Academia might benefit from this industry experience of assessment of these skills.

Recommendations for Implementing LLE

No country like India could afford to continue the model of general education as it has been persisting in for the large bulk of the student population. A major change and investment is required to make human resource productive by coupling the older general disciplines of humanities, social sciences, natural sciences and commerce to their applications in the new economy. Our efforts shall be directed to provide for adequate field based experience to enhance knowledge with skills and develop appropriate attitudes. While preparing for this tremendous task, it may be helpful to take guidance from Aurobindo: "*The past is our foundation, the present our material, the future our aim and summit. Each must have its due and natural place in a national system of education.*"

1. Higher education itself is a complex process. The challenges posed by the present time are bound to increase the complexity of the system that performs the sacred function of preparing the next generation. The system has to reconcile with the new awakening that all knowledge is interdisciplinary and no more compartmentalized, department/ teacher-centred, fossil courses could be justified and sustained. Multi / Cross-disciplinary programmes in frontier developments in subjects and work areas with constantly renewed, updated curriculum have to be planned and implemented.
2. It would not be enough if the Institutions of Higher Education (IHE)—colleges and universities—continue the age-old long term (2 yrs/3 yrs) degree programmes and attempt tinkering with them by introducing some vocational components here

and there at the first degree level or elsewhere. Even after leaving the college, the learner could be provided with opportunities to come back for renewal and updating of knowledge and sharpen his skills for new work situations. IHEs should turn to become vibrant centres to provide opportunities for their alumni and other members of the society unending opportunities "to renew, update and widen their knowledge and skills throughout life". Suitable curriculum for such further educational opportunities needs to be evolved in close collaboration with user-systems.

3. In the new situation of GLP and CPC environment, the conventional modes of delivery may not be of much use; there should be more of evening, part-time, flexi-time programmes (including week end/ holiday courses) for a vast array of varying requirements of different segments of the society; for people who wish to learn new job skills; for people seeking advanced knowledge/skills/degrees in their own specialties; for people simply wanting to improve their minds/developing new interests or just to know more; for people in transition/migration from jobs; for people rendered jobless due to technological changes from obsolete jobs and skills and so on. It would even be worthwhile to think of certain programmes under a combination of distance and direct modes of delivery providing more flexibility for the learners.
4. Ready access and flexibility shall be the hallmarks of LLE initiatives. At the same time, flexibility shall never be at the cost of quality. All short duration, flexi-time programmes would be designed to ensure highest quality and relevance for specific, current and projected needs of user-systems.
5. The programmes shall be designed under interactive modular patterns/framing. The learner should be free to choose any module and get appropriate training therein and earn due credits for each module he/she completes. She/He should

also have the freedom to complete requirements for any degree/diploma etc suiting his/her own pace of study and or convenience. Accumulation of earned credits from different modules of learners' choice and transfer of credits to fulfil degree/diploma requirements should be permitted. It would not be out of place to think of allowing credit transfer from other institutions, universities and also from distance education modes. The cafeteria approach that permits such flexible credit transfers shall be implemented in our IHEs.

6. The quality of the outcome of higher education is generally measured based on the learners' success in profession/life situations. The success of the learners depends on different stakeholders inside and outside the IHEs. In order to become successful, IHEs have to necessarily involve all the key players from the beginning in the design, control and operation of this process. Such a need has been stated earlier and repeated here to point out the imperative that educational institutions should forge excellent linkages with industries and major user-organizations and embark upon joint efforts in curriculum planning, providing hands-on/shop-floor experience, testing of laboratory findings/products, funding chairs, projects, research, infrastructure, etc.
7. Generally entrants to the higher education (i.e., at the UG level) have qualification profile and level acquired through the higher secondary education up to the age of 17-18 years. Second level (PG) courses will normally build on a first level degree. The key players in the scene—college/university professors, high and higher secondary school teachers, and departments for education, learners and their parents—should organize permanent functioning communication links amongst them for improving performance of the higher secondary education process (that precedes the university education process) and increasing

the ability of first year students to respond well to the objectives of the curriculum of the College/ University/LLE.

8. The days of Open University system—allowing persons to sit for university degree examinations without insisting upon earlier qualifications except age requirements—have come to stay in our educational framework. The open system should be extended further to cover all course/degree/ programme insisting only on specific knowledge, skills and abilities, instead of any formal earlier qualification. The required knowledge/skill level should be specified and should be such that could be tested easily at the entry level. The entry requirements or expectations should reflect the institutional policy and the goals of the programmes.

To make any programme a success, there should be, amongst other things like resources, infrastructure, etc., adequate planning, necessary preparedness and commitment on the part of institutions and key players, a conducive environment for innovation and experiment and above all a determination to go ahead and reach goals for common good. The stakes are high in education in the new situation (GLP) and climate (CPC). Hope now lies with education, the chief enterprise through which we can prepare the present for the future. Awake, Arise and Act.

References

1. . . . caused by the coincidence in time of three interdependent processes—"The Decline and Fall of Real Socialism, the Fast-paced Information and Communication Technologies (Information Era), and Neoliberalism," Francisco López Segrera, 2001.
2. Jay Drydyk, Globalization and Multi-cultural Knowledge of Human Rights (www.bu.edu/wcp/Papers/Huma/HumaDryd.htm).
3. Glenn Rikwoski, "Globalization and Education" (Paper prepared for the House of Lords Select Committee on Economic Affairs Inquiry into Global Economy, 22nd Jan. 2002)
4. Peter McLaren and Ramin Farahmandpur, "The Globalization of Capitalism and the New Imperialism: Notes towards a Revolutionary

Pedagogy", *The Review of Education, Pedagogy and Cultural Studies*, Vol. 23, No. 3 (2001).

5. Glenn cited above.
6. Mr. Murli Manohar Joshi, Min. for HRD, GOI, "Higher Education in India: Vision and Action", Country Paper, UNESCO World Conference on Higher Education in the Twenty-first Century, Paris, 5-9 October 1998.
7. Raja Mutthirulandi, "*Curriculum and Instruction for the Twenty-first Century*" (pp. 114-121), Higher Education: Vision and Mission for Twenty-first Century, Lady Doak College, Madurai, 1998.
8. Kate Francis, Kate Fitzgerald, Rebecca Lacey, Kate Hancock& David Ockendon, "*The Effects Of Globalisation On Education*" (www.ssn.flinders.edu.au/global)
9. 27 CDCs in 1986:10 for Science and 17 for Humanities indicate where the need is more. As in 2001, there are CDCs for 32 subjects.
10. Inderjit Khanna and M.V. Krishnaswamy, Priority Programme of UGC, *Journal of Hr. Education*, Vol. 17, No 3, Monsoon 1994.
11. Claimed as "a recent innovation", the vocational education scheme, at the undergraduate level with 35 vocational subjects and recently some more vocational subjects related to agriculture and rural areas added is in operation; nearly 1,500 colleges have been given facilities for vocational education, Country Report,1998.
12. American Association of University Professors (AAUP), Statement on Government of Colleges and Universities, 1966 (modified in 1990).
13. Mjint, H., The Economics of Developing Countries (4th Edn.), Hutchinson Co. Ltd., London, 1974.
14. Jean-Claude Paye, Sec.-Genl. of the OECD (1995), "Making Life-Long Learning a Reality for All".
15. Adopted with modifications from: "Creating Learning Cultures" (www.lifelonglearning.co.uk/)
16. For a deeper discussion on LLE and for the definition advanced by Jacques Delors, on behalf of UNESCO, which is based upon four "pillars": learning to live together, learning to know, learning to do and learning to be, ref: Jacques Delors *et al.*, 1996, Learning: The Treasure Within, Report to UNESCO of the International Commission on Education for the Twenty-first Century.
17. Jacques Delors, cited above.
18. Adopted with modification from: Lifelong learning for the Next Five Years, Part 1, (www.lifelonglearning.co.uk). This section is adopted

with modifications from Career- Space-Curriculum Guidelines, "New ICT Curricula for the 21st Century" (www.career-space.com/cdguide/serv5.htm)

19. Career- Space-Curriculum Guidelines, cited above.
20. Cited above.
21. Career-Space cited above.

15 Chapter

The Cultural Impact of Globalization

— Mohd. Rais Khan

(Economic Activities and Social Changes)

India's Dilemmas: A Comment on Policy-making in a Globalized World

In this paper I tried to discuss the cultural impacts of globalization in reference of economic activities and social changes by trade and commercial way. Globalization is the process of bringing the world economics closer to one another, the information and technological revaluation has changed the world. Globalization involves removal of trade barriers and restrictions and encouragtes liberalization, privatization and free market economics. It encourages healthy competition for mutual benefit and promotes trade. The success of any economy will depend on the sharing of food and services and healthy competitive trade with other countries. The days of "isolation" are over. The path to progress and prosperity now lies in globalization.

In recent years, unfortunately, the terms "globalization" has been in so many contexts that it has lost the precise meaning it once might have had and, as a result, discussions regarding globalization can become confusing. Allen Greenspan in the symposium of global economic integration defined globalization as "the increasing interaction of national economic system". In order to overcome this imprecision, we will examine various theories regarding globalization. In doing so, the concepts of homogenization, and hybridization are discussed. I also tried to discuss about India's dilemmas in policy-making in a globalized world in a positive way.

In a variety of ways, economic activities exert a powerful catalytic force, often called "globalization" in order to refer to Western culture impacting the rest of the earth in ways that lead to greater worldwide cultural homogeneity. In reality, of course, the East has the rich history, which influences the West, just as the West transforms the East; thus, it is commonplace to buy cheap Chinese food, served up in a Styrofoam container, instead of eating a Big Mac. Nonetheless, the monolith of McDonalds proliferating internationally, not an array of small Chinese restaurants scattered throughout the United States, has emerged as the darling of marketing and management though.

According to those who embrace the paradigm of cultural distinctiveness, each culture has its own sense of beauty that has been developed through history and is composed of attitudes, values, and related behaviours (Ball and McCulloch, 1996). Cultures and nations largely function through basic structures such as the family, local groups, circumscribed traditions, etc. As a result, organizational structures (and their functioning) are impacted by distinctive cultural traditions (e.g., Hofstede, 1980). The cultural emphasis upon individualism that is so prevalent in America, for example, is often not effective in the more collectively oriented East (as any number of "insider studies" of Japan emphasize). The local culture and its ethos can significantly impact the effectiveness of managerial practices and how they should be employed.

Researchers have long pondered the premise that the specifics of the cultural tradition dictates what motivates employees and that people typically do not act in a universal kind of way that responds to some sort of generalized and rational cost-benefit analysis (i.e.,

Bigoness and Blakely, 1996). To whatever extent this is true, management strategies need to be linked to subtle cultural understanding.

In addition, various thinkers have come to emphasize that a person's culture is a very powerful phenomenon that has the ability to help people in times of stress. Thus, applied anthropologist G.N. Appell forcefully acknowledges: "A society undergoing change... [such as that wrought by international business] has a right to its cultural traditions, its language, and its social history." A main benefit of cultural traditions, Appell continues, is that they help people cope with the trauma of change and they can provide a degree of stability that facilitated adaptation.

In recent years, unfortunately, the term "globalization" has been used in so many contexts that it has lost the precise meaning it once might have had and, as a result, discussions regarding globalization can become confusing. Allen Greenspan in the symposium of global economic integration defined globalization as "the increasing interaction of national economic system". In order to overcome this imprecision, we will examine various theories regarding globalization. In doing so, the concepts of homogenization, and hybridization are discused.

As far back as the early 1980s, marketing guru Theodore Levitt used the term globalization to depict an emerging cultural homogeneity caused by increased communication, technological convergence, and their impact upon marketing.

Today, this "cultural homogeneity version" of global theory has often been dubbed "McDonaldization", a term that implies that the popular consumer culture of the economically dominant West is relentlessly and inevitably transforming other, regions, cultures, nations, and societies (be they part of the developed or developing worlds). Such perspectives imply that technological change, the mass media, and consumer-oriented marketing campaigns work in tandem to remake whatever they touch in their own image. Besides consumption patterns, some observers suggest that even attitudes and ideas about society, religion, and technology are transformed by culture diffusion brought by globalization.

At least four major contributing factors to homogenization can be identified; they include the global transformation of local culture, the emergence of a consumer mentality, the impact of elite culture and the influence of the internet.

As a result of mass marketing and the tendency for global firms to standardize their product, organizations such as Coca-Cola, McDonalds, Nike, MTV, and Calvin Klein have emerged as global icons. According to the strategies anticipated by Theodore Levitt , mass marketing, on an international level, displaces strategies that revolve around national, regional, and cultural differences, Distinctiveness fades to the point where young japanese tourists in America have marvelled, upon visiting a McDonalds, "that America also has Japanese food".

While in America, McDonalds represents fast, cheap and convenient food while this is not true worldwide. Going to McDonalds in Argentina and China, as in Russia, involves a cultural experience, and, as in Russia, people pay high prices for the American ambience of the visit. Therefore, as a cultural force (or at least as a popular cultural force), the United States exerts a powerful impact upon many other countries and societies.

A consumer mentality is often regarded as a by-product of homogenization. Shopping and spending have, in many circumstances, become ends in themselves. The consumer is bombarded with an array of well-orchestrated message and products that encourage the consumption of products that often make a fashion statement or convey a message in the process. The resulting consumer mentality exerts a profound international impact upon marketing and economic activity. The global media can profoundly influence how people choose to spend their spare time.

Homogenization and globalization tend to be the realm of the elite because in many parts of the world they are the only people who are affluent enough to buy many of the products available in the global marketplace. Highly educated, well traveled, and wealthy individuals from different backgrounds typically interact within a Westernized millieu and they do so by choice. In addition, since the trappings of Western culture are symbols of affluence and power, the elite often embraces Western styles of products and pattern of behaviour in order to impress others and/or to maintain their image. Today, Western patterns of behaviour and the English language are staples of international business. These conventions have become universal and they are expected and demanded by the elite international traveler and the international executives class (Tomlinson, 7). Profound impacts result from this trend.

The theory of hybridisation argues that globalization has not created a world that it accurately depicted by either homogeneity or polarisation. Specific aspect of the homogenization/polarization dilemma lies in the fact that many religions and cultures fiercely oppose being swallowed up by the Western world; as a result, the tendency towards homogeneity is resisted and countered. While many global theorists asserts that cultural homogeneity is the inevitable wave of the future, the loyal opposition of many cultures, societies, and religions debate that premise and actively work to oppose such trends.

As applied to religious movements, the term "fundamental" had its origins in North America in the early twentieth century, when it was used to depict specific protestant groups who reacted against the "liberal Christianity" of the year. These conservatives believed that worldly and scientifically oriented liberal Protestant theology was diluting and undercutting their faith in hurtful and unacceptable ways (see Mardsen, 1991 for a discussion of this movement). Since that time, the notion of fundamentalism has been applied to many traditional religions that attempt to get back to their basic, fundamental essences (Hallencreutz and Westerlund, 1966). These movements typically oppose the influences of the secular, scientific and (in some cases) the Western world. In such a context, the term "fundamentalism" has been applied to a wide range of conservative religious movements. This type of response is often embraced by the traditional cultures of the non-Western, developing work.

It is worthwhile to note that the empirical pattern of observable behaviour can make it appear as if these traditions are dying off and/or are vestigial remains; after all, the young tend to act globally while the old are primarily the ones who embrace the norms of their heritage. Making this observation, it is easy to falsely conclude that these traditions are exclusively the province of old people and speculate that when the current generation goes to its grave, their traditions will die with it. It reality, this is often not the case; 20 years later, these traditions, are likely to continue to be alive and well, being carried on by the current senior citizens, who, in an earlier era of their lives, while covert carriers of traditions were embracing global and mainstream responses.

The theory of hybridization argues that globalization has not created a world that a accurately depicted by either homogeneity or polarization.

Good example is the fact that in Europe the majority of teenagers want to wear American jeans, listen to English and Latino music, eat American, Arabic and French food while maintaining a nationalistic viewpoint. Such examples document the value of the theory of hybridization that deals with relevant aspects of both polarization and homogenization. While certain traditions from foreign cultures such as Calypso music (a style of music created in the Caribbean regions) were welcomed and Sweden, other alien traditions/products, such as Coca-Cola were despised and rejected. Such disparity demonstrates how Sweden, while preoccupied with maintaining its distinctive cultural traditions, is also will the *status quo*. Acceptance seems to be particularly forthcoming in the case of weaker traditions, such as Calypso music, that are not viewed as a threat to the Swedish way of life.

The dialectical method of Frederick Hegel's provides a useful way of modelling this process. Using the theses/antithesis/ synthesis paradigm, Hegel depicted the initial *status quo* situation as the "thesis". For our purposes, this can be envisioned in terms of the culture before contact with the outside world (or an outside gel calls the "antithesis": some alternative or disruption that conflicts with the *status quo*. For our purposes, this is represented by disruptive outside contact (such as products being sold or cultural traditions being introduced). Ultimately, "synthesis" which represents a reconciliation of the two. This synthesis, in turn, emerges as a new thesis and the process begins all over again in an ongoing cycle. This process of thesis, antithesis, and synthesis, of course, closely parallels the process of hybridization that we have been describing.

A benefit of the dialectical approach is that it provides a theory and a testable hypothesis that can easily be applied to a wide range of situations involving international business. In general, this hypothesis suggests that the status quo is impacted by outside forces and that both are transformed in the process. The model also provides a means of envisioning the new situation that arises as well as conceptualizing it as part of a continual and ongoing process. This is exactly the kind of models that are needed by both scholars and practitioners involved in international business.

Now we start talk about India's dilemma in policy-making. The world of foreign policy is murky in the best of times. For India this is a time of the growth of the Indian economy is important to the us and other industrialsed nations for the demands that this creates for goods and services and, in particular, for the exporters of weaponry and defence-related material ("defence" in these situations, in case the reader needs to be reminded, is a euphemism for "defence and offence"), the ideal situation in Asia is a build-up towards war but no war. A war is too destabilising for the whole world; so not desirable. But a build-up towards war means more profits for the defence industries.

Indian takeover of western firms and corporations have not met with as much political opposition as China's attempted takeovers. China National Offshore Oil Corporation's (CNOOC) move to by some

American firms and the attempt by China's major producer of household appliances, Haier, to take over Maytag in the us resulted in a kind of concern that goes beyond the purely commercial and reflects this general worry about China's rise and potential political dominance. The worry is accentuated by the fact these mega Chnese companies are largely state-owned. 70 per cent of CNOOC'S shares are owned by the government of China. Haier is technically called a collective effect, it is controlled by the state. Hence, the entry of these corporations in the us is often viewed as conduits for the entry of the Chinese government.

These essentially political matters have had spillovers for the Indian economy. About half of all H1-B visas that the us gives out (these are visas for engineers, scientists and other professionals) go to Indians; about 70 per cent of India's software exports end up in the us (Murthy, 2007). There is big market for India's pharmaceutical industries is North America (Chaudhuri, 2005).

These are not matters on which the us takes an unambiguous stand since China is a major trading partner of the US, much more important than India. Hence America's business and political communities often have differences of opinion on what constitutes "American interest". But, with their focus on the long-run, the recent influential neoconservative writings in the US have made frequent reference to the need for the "containment of China". And it is now widely recongnized that, since 2002, the us has been viewing India as an important pole in a future multi-polar world and, as such, a safeguard against the risk of the world becoming bipolar, with the us witnessing a safeguard against the risk of the world becoming bipolar, with the us witnessing a face-off with China in a playback of the cold war days.

These changes are viewed in India as presenting the nation with a serious dilemma—whether to retain its commitment to the policy of non-alignment, which India has adhered to with considerable diligence through the years, or to collaborate with the us on vital matter such as nuclear energy, defence, trade and investment. The fear, often expressed, is that to enter into these kinds of collaborations will amount to India giving up its independent foreign policy positions and falling totally into the ambit of Western nations. In an elegant and skilfully-argued essay Chenoy and Chenoy (2007) have analyzed the recent shift in Indo-American relations, its implications for our economy and the risky foreign policy options that India is faced with today as a consequence of it.

Greater interaction with the us on matters of nuclear energy and trade is unlikely to damage India's relation with China. Our relation with China has been improving in recent times, with bilateral trade now being at an all time high and growing in leaps and bounds, and with several Indian firms directly investing in China. If India continues to grow economically, India will be a vital trading partner of China and a stable political relation will then be in our mutual interest. Both nations would be more inclined to solve cooperatively the relatively small irritants that exist between them, such as border disputes. It is likely that in common Asian currency area and a more united market across multiple Asian nations—these are natural concomitants of globalization. Provided that India remains on the high growth path that it is currently on, India and China will clearly be the main constituents of such a multi-country Asian initiative.

With the US, India has a relation where there is a lot to be gained from trade, investment and engagement in general. In fact, it India can utilize the strategic advantage of the moment and further its economic prowess, this will be a better guarantor of both India's ideological independence and good relations with China and other Asian nations, which will then have an even greater stake in trade and investment with India. And if India is to initiate a globally-coordinated effort to control the scourge of extreme inequality-global coordination being, as was discussed in the previous section, essential for making a serious dent on inequality—then it is essential for it to be major player in the world economy, and for it to have strong multi-country engagement.

Conclusion

Today, international business is growing and global strategies are being employed as never before in modern times. Unfortunately, even though global themes have become ubiquitous, speaking about them in precise terms can be difficult. This article has addressed that issue by discussing three implications of globalization: the tendencies towards homogeneity, polarization, and hybridization. As businesses expand worldwide and the search for new markets intensifies, hitherto isolated cultures and nations are increasingly drawn into the Western sphere of economic and cultural influence. Certainly, these societies will borrow heavily from those with whom they come into contact. But this does not inevitably imply that they will be completely transformed.

There was a time when humanists tended to assume (as today's homogenizes do) that older, circumscribed cultural traditions would inevitable fade and be supplanted by the modern world. In earlier generations, for example, folklorists visited hinterland enclaves in order to "salvage" cultural traditions because they believed the cultural heritage they were studying was rapidly and inevitably dying off as the modern world established itself within the hinterland.

Today, in contrast, humanists typically emphasize that traditions often survive by adapting to new conditions. Many individuals, for example, are both members of their traditional culture and citizens of their nation or the world. The issue is not one of the survival vs. the demise of local traditions, but how people embrace life in a way that is typified by cultural hybridization.

We live in a world in which converging technologies, distinctive ways of life, and diverse belief systems creator a complex "global stew". This is a complicated and fluid situation for which no "pat" and standardized answers exist. We are well advised to remember that fact. By modelling this process of hybridization in terms of the dialectical method, a well respected and directly relevant means of dealing with such phenomena can be embraced.

References

Atkinson, A.B.: "Is Rising Inequality Inevitable? A Critique of the Transatlantic Consensus", WIDER Annual Lecture 3, Helsinki (1999).

Nader Asgary, Walle Alf. H. Cross-cultural Management Fairbanks, Alaska, USA, (2002).

Basu, Kaushik: Prelude to Political Economy: A Study of the Social and Political Foundations of Economics, Oxford University Press, Oxford and New York (2000).

Gilpin, R.S.: The Political Economy of International Relations (1987), Princeton University.

Malcolm Waters: Globalization, Routledge, London, *International Society*, Vol. 15th, June 2005.

Rosenau, J.: The Study of Global Interdependence, Princeton University 1990.

Virmaini, Arvind: *Propelling India from Socialist Stagnation to Global Power*, Volume 1: *Growth Processes*, Volume 2: *Policy Reforms*, Academic Foundation, New Delhi.

Economic and Political Weekly.

Index